P9-CBV-557

LB   Raths.
1033   Values and teaching
.R37   : working with
1978   values in the
          classroom.

DATE DUE

APR 19 '81			
SEP 29			
DEC 0 6 1983			
MAY 2 6 1986			
NOV 6 '91			
MAY 2 7 1994			
DEC 6 1994			
MAR 1 0 1995			

DEMCO 38-297

3 1215 00005 7767

MISSION COLLEGE
LEARNING RESOURCE SERVICES

Values and Teaching
Working with Values in the Classroom

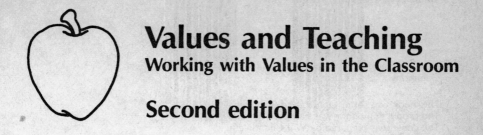

Values and Teaching
Working with Values in the Classroom

Second edition

LOUIS E. RATHS
Adjunct Professor
State University College, Fredonia

MERRILL HARMIN
Southern Illinois University

SIDNEY B. SIMON
University of Massachusetts

CHARLES E. MERRILL PUBLISHING COMPANY
A Bell & Howell Company
Columbus   Toronto   London   Sydney

Merrill's International Education Series
Kimball Wiles, Founding Editor

Published by
CHARLES E. MERRILL PUBLISHING COMPANY
A Bell & Howell Company
Columbus, Ohio 43216

This book was set in Optima and Souvenir.
The production editor was Frances Margolin.
The cover was prepared by Will Chenoweth.
Cover photograph courtesy of Bruce Charlton.

Copyright © 1978, 1966 by Louis E. Raths, Merrill Harmin, and Sidney B. Simon.
All rights reserved. No part of this book may be reproduced in any form, electronic or
mechanical, including photocopy, recording, or any information storage and retrieval
system, without permission in writing from the publisher.

Library of Congress Catalog Card Number: **78-51145**

International Standard Book Number: **0-675-08514-4**

Printed in the United States of America
1 2 3 4 5 6 7 8 9 10 11 12
78 79 80 81 82 83 84 85 86 87

Preface

Seventy-two years ago, when I was a little boy in Dunkirk, New York, I was six years old and in the second grade of Public School No. 5. I had what was perhaps a bad habit of sucking the sleeve of my shirt near the elbow. My older brother laughed at me and teased me and ridiculed me for doing this, and my aunts and uncles did too. A year before, the first grade teacher had commanded me on several occasions to stop doing it.

Now I was in the second grade and had a new teacher, Miss Carothers. Whenever I was free for a few minutes I started in on my shirt. My mother was aware that I especially liked to do it when the shirt was just freshly laundered. And so when I went home for lunch she would see to it that I had a clean, freshly laundered shirt to wear to school for the afternoon. Miss Carothers probably noticed this, and she used to walk up and down the aisles once in a while talking with individual children. She came to my desk one day and, leaning over close to me, she said, "This is your favorite position, isn't it, Louis?" Some time during the next week or two I stopped doing it, and my mother announced to the family that I no longer sucked my sleeve. I very clearly remember Miss Carothers saying that to me, and I believe that I can remember thinking about it afterwards. I probably thought about it after school and at home and in school, too. I probably thought that I had not chosen it from many positions, and perhaps I could not understand why she called it my *favorite* position. Miss Carothers' nonjudgmental comment stimulated me, I believe, to examine my practice. And I myself rejected it. I had overcome a habit that teasing and ridiculing and authoritarianism had not conquered.

The point I am making is very important; it is one that I believe teachers overlook all too frequently. A great deal of learning takes place when we silently think about our lives and what we did and what we are doing. A question asked in school may be thought about most seriously after school or at night. A value-type question asked in school may be discussed with friends, or talked over with brothers and sisters, or raised as a question at mealtime for the whole family to pitch in, or saved for those precious few minutes when a child is alone with a parent just before falling asleep.

It is more than eleven years now since the first edition of this book was published. We had been in the longest war that our country ever had in Viet Nam—a war characterized by *misinformation* communicated to the people by the highest military and government officers. The war divided the nation: there were violent demonstrations; there was much corruption. TV and radio, newspapers, and magazines brought a great deal of this conflict into our living rooms. All of those experiences are a part of us and are going to be passed on to those who come after us.

At the same time, the country went through many demonstrations dealing with the problems of minority groups, especially blacks. Here again there was violence, marching, demonstrations, speeches, and divisiveness. That has become a part of our background.

In those eleven years, we have had if not directly then indirectly before us the terrible prospects of nuclear war. At times we seem stunned by the terrible consequences that might ensue, and yet we don't talk much about it. Have we repressed it or have we more or less absorbed it into ourselves, as we have absorbed the whole Viet Nam experience and the whole racial conflict?

As a country, we have been experiencing increased unemployment and, at the same time, increased inflation. Most of us are very confused about these changes, and our leaders do not seem able to clarify the issues for us.

We are very much concerned about the use of drugs, including alcohol by our young people and by some older people, too. We are not doing too well in helping young people reconstruct their attitudes towards drug use, and here again we are somewhat bewildered.

To mention only one more of these troublesome problems, there is the question of violence in our lives. Many people seem to want to have whatever they want almost immediately after they feel a need. If they don't get it, they seem to be willing to be destructive in their efforts to obtain it.

How can our wonderful channels of communication be used to help people see the alternatives that lie before us and see them clearly? How can we be helped to see the consequences that may flow from each alternative available? How may we see more clearly the resources we have for attacking these most serious problems of our society? And, finally, how may we be helped to choose priorities?

We thought in 1965 that there was a most serious need for methods to help clarify the purposes and aspirations, the interests and attitudes, the beliefs and activities of young people in the schools of America. Our book was widely acclaimed and has been used in hundreds upon hundreds of schools and school districts. Now, in 1978, we are only able to say that the need is even greater than it was a decade ago. The rapid pace of technological change, the rapid changes taking place in our industrial relationships with other countries, the newer sciences of war and destruction, the serious problem of survival—all need more and more attention. We need to listen to young people as we have never listened before. We need to ask them about their ideas, about their purposes, about their beliefs, and we need to begin a dialogue with each of them that will help to shape the way of the next fifty years. We hope that this revision of our book will make some contribution toward that end.

In this revision we have received much help from our readers. In the first edition we, the authors, made many value judgments. We tried to make clear what we believed to be the best kind of value education. One belief of ours, strongly emphasized, was that children should be free to state their own interests, their own purposes and aspirations, their own beliefs and attitudes, and many other possible indicators of values. Some readers thought *we* were claiming to be value-free, and that *our book* was value-free. But we wanted *children* to be free, within broad limits, to reflect *their* reactions to their own life experiences. This point of view is stated often throughout the book.

We also expressed the idea that different groups of people might have different values and that, where these were within the laws of the country, all views should be open for discussion, examination, possible affirmation, rejection, or doubt. In other words, people should be free to differ in their value indicators, and their positions should be respected. For this we were labeled ethical relativists. In one interpretation, the label is correct: we do believe that in the world today there is not *one* true religion, *one* true morality, *one* true political constitution. But a second interpretation does not describe our point of view: we do not believe that any one belief, or purpose, or attitude, is as good as another. We too have preferences; we too have made choices; and while we do not believe that our views are eternal, or that they should be made universal, with some small modicum of doubt we do believe they are to be preferred. Besides choosing them, we cherish them, and try to act on them. Our values are involved in what we say, and feel and do, and we hope to continue living in that fashion.

We are also under deep obligation to our production editor, Ms. Frances Margolin. It has been no easy job to coordinate the ideas and the writings of three writers often more than a thousand miles distant from each other. We acknowledge with deep appreciation the patience, the persistence, and the intelligence of Ms. Margolin in the production of this revised edition of our book.

L.E.R.

Contents

With grateful acknowledgment for the support,
devotion, and concern shown by our wives . . .

Values and Teaching
Working with Values in the Classroom

one

INTRODUCTION

Values Clarification:
Nature and Goals

The approach to values and teaching used in this book is based on a theory we call *values clarification*. The theory recognizes that many people today have difficulty "pulling themselves together." Decisions seem too complicated, pressures seem too varied, changes seem too unsettling. As a consequence, some people flounder in confusion, apathy, or inconsistency. They cannot get clear on their values. They cannot find life patterns for themselves that are purposeful and satisfying.

The theory of values clarification promises that we can assist such people by helping them to clarify their values. If we succeed in clarifying them, the theory asserts that results will show up as changes in behavior. As a result of our efforts, for example, the people described above would show less confusion, apathy, or inconsistency.

What kind of assistance are we to offer? In general, the theory tells us to encourage people to give more time and energy to value-related thought. We should encourage them to reflect more deliberately and comprehensively about their own values and about the value questions of society as a whole.

This methodology has four key elements:

1.   A focus on life. Often the first step is to focus people's attention on aspects of their own lives that may indicate things they value. One might, for example, focus their attention on some of their behaviors. Or attitudes. Or goals, interests, aspirations, feelings, beliefs, or worries. Thus, we might one day ask a student "Have you any plans for the weekend?" Our assumption here is that a weekend plan may indicate something about the values of that student.

In another situation, we might start by focusing on a general life issue, especially one that often complicates life or muddies values: What is to be done about friendships, fears, cooperation, money, love, law and order, poverty, loyalty, violence, tenderness, and so on. These might be either personal or societal issues.

2.   An acceptance of what is. Secondly, when our intention is to clarify values, we need to accept others' positions nonjudgmentally. We do not necessarily communicate approval of whatever someone may say or do. Rather, value clarifying requires that we communicate acceptance of a person's total being as it is. This acceptance is meant to assist others in accepting themselves and in being honest with themselves and each other, no matter how confused or negative their thoughts or feelings might be. Thus, we might say to a student "Sounds as if you expect to have a problem this weekend," trying to communicate understanding without judgment.

3.   An invitation to reflect further. We must do more than accept, however. We should invite further reflection on values especially more comprehensive reflection. The general thrust in this approach is toward encouraging (1) more informed choices, (2) more awareness of what it is a person prizes and cherishes, and (3) better integration of choices and prizings into day-to-day behavior.

So, we might say to our student "How about identifying three different things you could do this weekend in case that problem comes up?" Our intent here would be to encourage the student to prepare for a more informed choice.

4. A nourishment of personal powers. The overall message communicated by the methodology of values clarification is that people *can* look reflectively at values issues, that they *can* better integrate their choices, prizings, and actions, and that they can *continue* to do that for themselves in the years ahead. Thus, values clarification not only encourages the exercise of clarifying skills, but also nourishes a sense of the possibility for thoughtful self-direction.

The message of values clarification is not meant to be insistent, however. We do not wish to imply that *everyone should* be more thoughful about values issues or lead a more integrated life. Rather, we recognize that there are many people who are not up to it, or who prefer not to, or whose circumstances make it too painful. We do not want to communicate that a person is defective because his or her life remains confused, inconsistent, or fractured. We simply wish to offer space, time, encouragement, support, and guidance to those who are ready to change, to those who are ready to work at organizing their lives around a set of values.

This, then, in oversimplified terms, is what values clarification is about. To get a more concrete picture of how it looks in practice, you might want to read some of the field reports in chapter 15.

APPLICATION OF VALUES CLARIFICATION

Values clarification can be helpful to groups as well as to individuals. Some groups tend to get stuck in confusion, indecision, or apathy. The theory suggests that we could assist such groups by calling their attention to relevant values issues, by modeling an accepting attitude, by encouraging comprehensive reflection, and generally by communicating that group value-direction is possible. The test of the theory for those groups, then, would rest on the groups' exhibiting less confused, indecisive, or apathetic behavior.

Values clarification does not claim to be the only factor that contributes to this kind of value-directed living. A healthy environment helps. We also need to have our basic physical and emotional needs cared for. Further, it helps to be around others who model thoughtful, value-directed behavior. And basic understanding often comes with access to the accumulated knowledge and art of the culture and opportunities for varied experiences.

Values clarification does seem, however, to add another ingredient, and according to the theory, it is an ingredient that will make a difference. It will be especially likely to make a difference for those who suffer extreme value confusion. Thus, we often recommend focusing values clarification on those who are particularly apathetic, uncertain, or flighty, on those who seem not to know their own minds and continually conform, dissent, or play artificial roles; or on those who behave very inconsistently or who drift aimlessly.

But whether values clarification makes a difference in such lives or does not help at all is, we think, a question to be tested empirically and personally by those who are interested in it. It is less important to us to wonder if the theory can be made true for all people and all times than to wonder if it can serve particular people in these times.

We like to think that we are presenting a helpful *teaching* theory, a guide for those who work with today's young people and who wish to promote intelligent, self-directing behavior. To them we say: Try the theory and see if it works for you. We have attempted to write the book so as to facilitate such trials.

And we hope many adults will try the theory. We believe that people today cry for help with values. Years ago young people did not so much seem to need value-clarification experiences. But now, with so much change and instability in the air, with so many people struggling to find a center and meaning for their lives, we believe the methods provided by values clarification can make a significant contribution both to personal and social fulfillment.

But this description is only a skeleton of the message of this book. Read ahead to get more of its substance and many hints about how you might even experience values clarification for yourself.

BEHAVIORS THAT SIGNAL
VALUE DIFFICULTIES

We have found it useful to identify what a value-directed life is *not,* for that helps us to focus the methodology on those who need it most. This approach is analogous to that of the physician who identifies and treats not health but symptoms of a lack of health. What types of behaviors signal a lack in this area of values? We have identified eight types of people who to us seem *not* to be living integrated, value-directed lives.

1. *Apathetic,* listless, uninterested people. We have in mind people who are energized by nothing, who remain passive and uninvolved regardless of what happens in the world around them. In the absence of other causes, such as physical or emotional reasons, people who exhibit pervasive apathy might well profit from values clarification.

2. Then there are the *flighty* people, those who are interested in many things, but only for fleeting moments. Such people often become involved in projects with high spirits, but with equally high spirits and in short order they abandon these activities and move on to other favorite interests. If there is no other explanation for this flightiness, we would suspect a lack of ability in making value decisions.

3. *Extreme uncertainty,* when it is a pattern, also suggests to us of a lack of valuing ability. We have in mind here people who seem to hardly ever make up their minds, who seem only bewildered by the choices the world offers them.

4. Then there are *very inconsistent* people, those involved in many things that are mutually inconsistent, if not mutually destructive. Unlike their flighty compatriots, they may have patterns in their lives, but if they exist, the patterns tend to be incompatible. An example might be the student who is alternately generous and selfish, or who is hard working this week and totally without energy the next week.

5. Others might aptly be called *drifters.* These people exhibit a pattern of behavior characterized by planless and unenthusiastic drifting from this to that, moving without power or rudder in the sea of life.

6. A large number are *overconformers.* Not having a clear idea of what they want to do with their lives, many choose to conform, accommodating themselves as best they can to what they perceive to be the dominant viewpoint of the moment. These are the people who are other-directed with a passion.

7. Some are *overdissenters*—not occasional and reasoned dissenters, but chronic, nagging, complaining, irrational dissenters. It is as if these people, not feeling able to clarify their own values, try to obtain an identity by opposing others. Overdissent is, of course, no more independent of others than is overconformity.

8. Finally, we note a group of *poseurs* or *role players,* people who cover their lack of clarity about the meaning of their lives by posturing in some role that is no more real for them than a cardboard image. Examples include the class clown or the bully on the block. Each poseur adopts a counterfeit existence to conceal the lack of a real one.

Although these eight categories may seem a dissimilar group in many ways, all eight behavior types are alike in the difficulties they represent in leading thoughtful, self-directing lives. A group like this contains prime candidates for the value-clarifying methodology. The theory would predict that people in the group whose behavior was not caused by other factors— such as physical or emotional causes—would be able to change their behaviors away from patterns of apathy and so forth as a consequence of that methodology.

These eight behavior patterns are, of course, not the only ones that signal a high probability of value confusion. As one example of other types, some researchers (see chapter 12) have found that some young people who abuse drugs are also likely to be value-confused. The eight patterns we have presented are, nevertheless, a good place to start when thinking about who value clarification can most assist and what behaviors it is most likely to change.

VALUING AS A PROCESS

The meaning of the term *value* is by no means clear in the social sciences or in philosophy (Macmillan & Kneller, 1964; Superka, Ahrens, & Hedstrom, 1976). There is no consensus for definition. About the only agreement that emerges is that a value represents something important in human existence. Perhaps because it is such a pivotal term, each school of thought invests the word with its own definition. For the same reason, a particular definition is not often acceptable elsewhere. This book's definition, developed more fully in chapter 3, is closest to those which emphasize the *process* of valuing, rather than any identifiable institutional sense of the term. We believe that it is more useful to consider the posture of a person facing his world, how he uses his muscle and spirit to relate to his surroundings, than to consider what he might find valuable at any one time or in any one particular circumstance or in a series of similar times or circumstances, for that matter. "How did she get her ideas?" is a more fundamental question for us than "What did she get?"

We believe that each person has to wrest personal values from the available array. As is elaborated later, values that actually penetrate living in intelligent and consistent ways are not likely to be produced in any other way. Thus it is the process of making such decisions that concerns us. "Instead of giving young people the impression that their task is to stand a dreary watch over the ancient values," says John Gardner (1964), "we should be telling them the grim but bracing truth that it is their task to recreate those values continuously in their own time." Giving students a process of valuing is giving them something that should serve them well and long.

Our emphasis on *valuing* rather than on *values* is not universally shared. Many researchers aim to measure what values people have and not the processes they used to get them. For us, the concern is less whether or not a person says she values thrift than it is where did she get her ideas of thrift. For example, did they come unthinkingly from her father? Is she thrifty only because thrifty persons surround her? Did she come to it freely and thought-fully? We would, of course, also be interested in knowing if our mythical Ms. So-and-so is, in fact, thrifty, a dimension of values that has all but been ignored in the research on values to date, and for good reason: actual personal behavior is virtually impossible to measure for large numbers of people.

There is an assumption in our value theory and the teaching strategies that grow from it that humans can arrive at values by an intelligent process of choosing, prizing, and behaving. At least we assume that humans can arrive at *something* via that process, and with some support in the literature, we prefer to call that something "values."

That assumption (which may seem essentially semantic) need not unduly bother the practical-minded classroom teacher, however; in operation the assumption is transformed into a hypothesis of a different order. If children are helped to use the valuing process of this book, we assert that they will behave in ways that are less apathetic, confused, and irrational and in ways that are more positive, purposeful, and enthusiastic. This hypothesis is readily testable by anyone who wishes to do so.

VALUES AS A
SOURCE OF PROBLEMS

A major theme of this century has been the study of children, and a major outcome of this study has been awareness of the role that emotions play in the life of a growing child. In fact, as the emotional aspects of childhood began to gain prominence in research findings, a trend developed which implied that almost all problems of children arose from emotional distur-bances. This reaction is understandable; emotions explain so much that it is easy to assume they explain everything. One other major theme of this century, the measurement of intelligence, had a similar influence. The result has been that all too often a child's behavior problem—especially a school problem—is attributed to either an emotional disturbance or something called a low I.Q.

There is a parallel with these reactions in work done in medicine during the last century. When it was discovered that some illnesses were "caused" by germs, it became a common practice to assume that practically all manifestations of bad health were caused by germs. As a result, it became very difficult, for example, to convince certain segments of the medical profession that pellagra had its origin in dietary deficiency. The idea of germ causation was so strongly entrenched that it was difficult for some to accept any alternative explanation.

With children it was never quite as simple as that. Emotions and I.Q. were and are often prime suspects for explaining behavior problems, but there has been some understanding as well of the way physical conditions influence behavior and—especially in recent years—the influence of group pressures and social conditions. However, there has been little more than a vague understanding of the influence that values might be having on behavior. Many of us have spoken of values as if they were important, perhaps crucial. Could it be that a number of children's problems currently attributed to emotions, for example, are more usefully seen as resulting form value disturbances? The study upon which this book is based answers that question affirmatively. We have found that several kinds of problems children often exhibit in school and at home are profitably seen as being caused by values, or more precisely, by a *lack* of values. In other words, we have found that when children with certain behavior problems are given value experiences of a particular kind, those problems often ease in intensity and/or frequency.

It seems to us that the pace and complexity of modern life has so exacerbated the problem of deciding what is good and what is right and what is desirable that large numbers of children are finding it increasingly bewildering, even overwhelming, to decide what is worth valuing, what is worth their time and energy. Life is certainly less neat and simple than it was even a few generations ago. "A perfection of means and a confusion of goals" is the way Einstein characterized this age. Could this be a cause for much of the apathy, confusion, and irrational behavior that seems to make life so difficult for some students? We suspect so.

VALUES EDUCATION— NOT A CURE-ALL

It may be reassuring or disappointing, depending on how you look at it, to know that this value theory is not a cure-all for what ails children and education. It provides unique and powerful tools for some problems of many children, but it does not pretend to help solve behavior difficulties whose causes lie outside of value issues.

In this modest mood, it is worth noting that the approaches of this book will not be radically new for all teachers. Many sensitive teachers have been working along these lines—even if they have been calling it something else—for many years. This book may only help them organize and conceptualize those practices, perhaps permitting them to use them more systematically and pointedly.

It is likely that new teaching ideas will be suggested to even the most experienced and sensitive teacher, however. Our experience in presenting this theory to hundreds of teachers has shown that the ideas in this book include ones that teachers find most useful. The theory has helped the larger number of them to multiply their effectiveness in important ways. This alone is enough to justify a book for teachers.

Many readers will note the similarity between the value theory and certain approaches to critical thinking. It is also reasonable to say that the value theory provides that amalgam of subject matter, personal concerns, and attitude development that has been such an elusive educational problem for so many years. In this regard, subject-matter specialists, such as most college and secondary-school teachers, may be especially interested in chapter 10.

There is much similarity between the basic orientation of this value theory and the work of a number of authors. Those who desire to see some writings in a related view or to examine different implications of this general approach might consider Dewey's work—especially his 1939 essay *Theory of Valuation* and his *Moral Principles in Education*—Gordon Allport, *Becoming: Basic Considerations for a Psychology of Personality;* Gardner Murphy, *Human Potentialities;* Asch, *Social Psychology;* Edgar Friedenberg, *The Vanishing Adolescent;* and Carl Rogers, *On Becoming a Person.*

For alternate approaches to values and moral education, look in the bibliography for works by Kohlberg (for example, 1975), Metcalf (1971), Rokeach (1975), and Fraenkel (1976).

AN INTRODUCTORY
SUMMARY

As society enters the stage in which our physical needs are increasingly easily satisfied by an increasingly productive and efficient economy, other problems come into focus. One of these, already evident to many in the Western world, is the question of what to do with the extra time and energy left over after work is done. The problems older and younger people in our society have in confronting this question can be seen most dramatically. How unfortunate is the older person left with time and energy who sees nothing to do with either. In a similar situation are those young people, perhaps the majority of them, for whom schoolwork and family life are not adequately fulfilling. Is the situation any different for the increasing numbers of middle-class spouses who stay home, finding little to do with their time? Devoting one's life to picking up the children after Cub Scouts only to deliver them to dancing class does not seem very satisfying to many. And what about the worker who finds increasing leisure as much a burden as a blessing?

The problem is simply stated: What is to be done with one's life and force? Once a question mainly for philosophers, in these times of increasing complexity, change, and abundance, it is a question that challenges almost all of us, although often we move through our lives unaware of it. This is its terrible power: it is a question that cripples us as long as it remains unanswered. A growing tragedy is that it is not usually even asked. Witness the teenager who does little other than escape to temporary, sometimes desperate, excitements. Witness the job-hopper who seems unable to find any work satisfying. Witness the student who daydreams, unmoved by the combined exhortation of teachers and parents with an occasional threat from the principal thrown in. Witness, too, the successful adult who achieves what he or she was supposed to achieve only to wonder what it was all for: "If this is success, why did I want it?"

We would say that these people—and they are legion in our increasingly affluent society—may well suffer from unclear sets of values. Such people do not seem to have clear purposes, to know what they are for and against, to know where they are going and why. With unclear values, they lack direction for their lives, lack criteria for choosing what to do with their time, their energy, their very being. It seems unlikely that animals other than humans can have values. It is one of our most precious potential gifts. Yet it seems increasingly apparent that all too few humans do, indeed, have clear values.

This, then, is our reason for writing this book. It outlines a theory of values and a methodology for clarification of values. It shows how to work with others so as to help them clarify their value statements and behavior. It should be useful to persons of all ages and walks of life, but is directed most specifically to those who work professionally with children, such as teachers. It is an eminently practical book in that it shows how the theory of values operates and how procedures grow from the theory. Furthermore, the theory is set up in such a way that you can give it your own tests.

The reported procedures in this book have already helped many students change patterns of behavior that were characterized by apathy, drift, and conformity. In different words, many students have been helped to become more purposeful, more enthusiastic, more positive, and more aware of what is worth striving for. This, of course, is the kind of behavior teachers and parents have wanted to promote for some time, but until recently, clear procedures based on adequate theory have not been available.

In a different perspective, this book may assist us in advancing personal wisdom—not wisdom as mere book learning, but wisdom as insight into the wholeness of life or as the capacity for integration of rationality, emotionality, and actual behavior.

two

A THEORY OF VALUES

2

The Difficulty of
Developing Values

Modern life in the United States is rich with change, choices, and opportunities, but as a result it is also very confusing for a child. Although few of us would willingly return to the simple and more austere life of earlier days, we must recognize the penalty we pay for the complexities of the present. One of those penalties is the diffuseness of modern values. It has become quite difficult for a child to develop clear values.

CHANGES IN
FAMILY LIFE

Look at the family, for example. Many people believe that values develop in and around the family. But the changes in the family from more stable days are dramatic if not frightening.

According to recent figures, two out of every five mothers are working outside the home. Recent estimates suggest that two out of every five families represent a broken home. (In this context, the word *broken* means that one of the parents is dead, the parents are divorced or separated, or one of them is institutionalized.) Quite often the result of a broken home or two working parents is a decrease in the amount of contact the child might have with either parent. It should also be added that one out of every six families with children is a one-parent home, and that the average yearly income for these families in 1976 was $3900. In this fluid, often stressful, environment, it is all the more difficult for an individual child to develop clear values.

The character of the parents' jobs and their relation to family life has changed considerably. It is almost universally true today that the children really do not know very much about what their parents do outside the home to earn a living. Children do not often see parents at their work and may not be informed enough about it to enter into meaningful discussions about the nature of a particular career—its problems and its successes. In other words, a major part of working parents' lives is almost beyond the possibilities of communication with their children.

It is said that one out of every five American families moves every year. Think of what this means for the stability of the children's lives. Friendship patterns are often destroyed. There are new children and new teachers to meet. There is the requirement of becoming oriented to new communities, new neighbors, new congregations, and perhaps new and different patterns of living. This very high geographical mobility is something quite unique in our history. Even so, it is becoming an expected part of family life. It is another demand on the developing child and the family, draining time and energy that might otherwise be spent on values questions.

There is some truth in the saying that the family has become a refuge from the world. Father, mother, and children go there to hide from the pressures of life outside. Very often parents commute several hours daily. They leave the house too early in the morning to have intelligent conversations with children. They come home late at night, fatigued, not only from their work, but also from the travel. They would like the home to be a quiet haven and they wish that the children would be still. Before long, the children go to bed, and another opportunity is lost for discussing the meanings of the day's activities, whatever they may have been.

CHANGES IN COMMUNICATIONS

In recent years tremendously potent new means of communication have been introduced into family life rituals. In the early days of the century the telephone was brought into families. Then, in the second decade, radio came into being. Those in charge of programming began to develop programs which they thought would be interesting to children. Not much attention was paid to the question. What programs would be *good* for children? The motion picture also began to have a great impact upon life in the United States. And then, after World War II, television arrived.

If values represent a way of life, if values give direction to life, if values are those things which make a difference in living, one might expect that, in our concern for developing values among children, there might be a focus in potent new communication media upon one or two ways of life which might give stability to the child. Yet the rapid incursion of these new media meant the presentation to children of many, many different ways of life. The output was vast on radio, in the movies, and on the television screen. Children could see many things and hear many views which in the ordinary run of life would never have been present as a part of family living. Inanity, crime, violence were hour-by-hour occurrences. Acts that can truly be called depraved were committed by people who were seemingly well-educated, while people watched, listened, and took it in. Surely children must have imbibed some ideas from all of this.

There is another possible inference: being exposed to so many different alternatives, perhaps the child was left with *no* ideas, but instead absorbed just the confusion. It is possible that the biggest contribution these media made was to baffle the child's budding understanding of what is right and what is wrong, what is true and what is false, what is good and what is bad, what is just and what is unjust, what is beautiful and what is ugly.

Radio, movies, and television were not the only forces at work. As these media were developing, new and cheaper ways of distributing printed materials were discovered. The comic book came into being, and there were publishers who saw great riches in the children's market. Comic books became another purveyor of crime stories, horror stories, and all sorts of strange ways of life. They found a market, for children bought these books and bought them in large quantities.

At about the same time, the family newspapers changed greatly. More crime stories, more sex stories, more corruption were reported; more suggestive pictures were printed. And our children read them all, along with the newspaper comic strips.

We are not suggesting here that the alternatives which life offers should be blacked out. Nor are we suggesting that the children cannot learn something from all of this exposure. We are suggesting, however, that by themselves children cannot profit greatly from exposure to this myriad of choices. If the family as a *unit* had been exposed to all these choices, if the family as a unit could have discussed the reasonableness or unreasonableness of what had been presented, every child might have learned something of the meaning of these new ways of living. But, as has been suggested, with both parents working and one or both away all day and, with more broken homes, there was even less family sharing. The consequence, we submit, has been a growing confusion in the life of children as to what is good and what is bad, what is right and what is wrong, what is just and what is unjust.

In addition to all of these other technological innovations, one must not lose sight of the impact of the automobile. At the beginning of the century it was probably quite unusual for a family or children to travel very much. In general, families stayed home except for short excursions on trolley cars—if they were lucky enough to live near trolleys—or on trains. With the advent of the automobile, it became the usual custom to travel quite a bit. The family car moved from luxury to necessity. Under these circumstances, children met new people more often. They were in more frequent contact with the customs of another town or another region. They saw other children doing things which perhaps were unthought of in their own community.

Out of this welter of traveling and communications, there came not only confusion and uncertainty but also the idea that perhaps anything was all right, nothing really mattered, that while many people were different, there was nothing particularly significant in the differences. One way of life was as good as another. Nobody really was an example of what was the right way to be.

INTERNATIONALISM

World events also had an incalculable effect upon family life. In the first forty years of this century, there were two terrible world wars; and in the past thirty years, the newspapers have shouted almost continual news of cold wars and hot wars. Under these circumstances it must be very difficult for children to believe in nonviolence and in peace as a reality. The atomic bomb, which has already been used by educated men on human populations, has given way to the neutron bomb, whose specified purpose is to devastate a human population while protecting property. The threat of annihilation is as ever-present as the arms race.

During these same years, there have been disastrous famines at a time when, in other places, large amounts of excess food overflowed storage bins. In the last world war, millions of human beings were exterminated by a country which had been regarded as one of the most civilized and educated in the world. Children are sometimes told that the Communists are "ahead" in education—whatever that means—and are also told that these educated Communists want to capture the world, to crush liberty everywhere, and to make human beings the slaves of the party or the state. Under these circumstances, isn't it natural for children to come to believe that education has very little to do with what is good and what is bad?

CHANGE INTO CONFUSION

During this time of uncertainty and confusion, schools began to be criticized for representing a single set of religious values. There had been a time when the schools celebrated the Christian holidays, Christmas and Easter. Other religious and nonreligious groups called this practice into question and suggested that the school should not represent one religion any more than another. As a result, school practices concerning the celebration of religious holidays changed. The schools had in the past emphasized a daily prayer, but the rulings of the Supreme Court decided that a common prayer should not be demanded of all children in the schools. As it was with religious matters, so it became with other matters of deep concern. If someone was for something, someone else was against it. To avoid controversy, some schools began to stand for nothing.

In response to this turmoil, teachers turned toward "teaching the facts." If controversy was to be troublesome, a teacher should stay away from it. Administrators tended to prefer teachers who did not raise "issues." In communities of strangers living together, people who did not know one another well, people with many different backgrounds, it became easier to have schools which themselves represented an absence of consensus. Moral, ethical, aesthetic values were quietly abandoned as integral parts of the curriculum. Thus, the gap widened between what we *said* the schools were to foster and what was actually taught.

Children see this gap between reality and something perhaps more promising. They see many other gaps too. A child who asks his parents to buy a gadget advertised on television and who quotes its supposed good qualities is often told that he should not believe what the television says. When he repeats to his mother what the clerk in the store has said about a product, his mother lets him know that he should not believe what clerks say. As he attempts to accept some of the things that appear in newspapers and magazines, he is again told to be suspicious. What can he believe? Is it true that most people in the adult world regularly lie, and in general, lie for money? Why isn't something done about this?

Children see much the same thing when it comes to most matters on a larger scale. They are surrounded by repetitive statements pledging a dedication to peace, and all around them are signs of war. They are told that we must be militarily strong; might is at least as important as right. In school and out of school, our country is held up to them as a model of equal rights before the law. They also hear reports over and over again that minority groups and women in our culture do not receive equal rights. But they are so accustomed to duplicity that they very often do not wonder how this can be so.

In school and out, they are told that to cooperate is not only excellent but is practically a necessity in our world. At the same time, they are told that people should look out for themselves, that "if you don't look out for yourself nobody else will." "You are to get yours and everyone else is to get his." They are told that women are the equal of men, and as they grow up they see that in many situations women are not treated as equals. In school they learn a romanticized version of the vigilantes in California history. They come to believe that these were fine people. And at the same time they are supposed to pledge loyalty to a society that is ruled by law. They learn about some of the great patriots who initiated our revolution, people who stood up and spoke their minds. And while they are learning these things, people close to them advise them to be careful of what they say, not to get into any trouble, go along with the authorities, and make the best of whatever the situation is.

They learn a lot of verbalisms about religion; and as they grow up, they also learn that one should not let religion interfere with making money. They are told again and again that education is a fine thing and that it helps to enrich life; but they are apt to learn that it is the certificate, the diploma, or the degree which is really significant. It is not education itself which is so important, but the accepted symbols of education that open up the door to success. While they are told that knowledge is power and that skill is to be respected, they are also told that it is not what you know but who you know that really counts.

Many more such conflicts could be added to our list, but enough are represented to suggest that the child's world is indeed a confused one. It must not be easy to grow in a society characterized by these conflicts.

Does this suggest that human beings are more inconsistent now than ever before in the history of mankind? Probably not. What it does suggest is that with the development of all the new means of mass communication, with increased travel, with increased mobility of people, more children are exposed to more of these inconsistencies. This means that it is probably increasingly difficult for growing children to develop clear values of their own. There is so much confusion surrounding them and so little attention paid to their dilemma, so few persons with the time and patience to listen to them and to help untangle some of the confusion, that they simply do not clarify their beliefs or purpose.

FROM THE CHILD'S EYE

One way of summing up what has been said is to indicate that children of today confront many more choices than children of yesterday. They have so many more alternatives. In one sense, this makes them less provincial and more sophisticated. In another sense, the complex array of choices makes the act of choosing more difficult. How can they size up all of the available alternatives? How can they examine the grounds on which each rests, and how can they anticipate the consequences toward which each one points? In short, how do they know what to believe? The job seems so staggering that even adults are tempted to throw up their hands in despair at the outset.

Just take this matter of choosing: Think of the alternatives which confront a child in the world of products. There are all these different automobiles with their presumed uniqueness. Think of the toothpastes, the soaps, the toys, and the clothes which are offered. How do you choose? Is it true that one thing is as good as another and that discrimination is fairly useless? Is it not possible that in situations like this a kind of apathy about choice develops, and a person begins to think that almost nothing makes a difference?

On the international scene, television, radio, newspapers, and magazines bring to children news of violence and conflicts and disaster from all over the world. These things assail the eyes and ears of our children; and in some vague, unknown way, the idea is communicated that we should all be concerned about these happenings. Concerned in what way? Will someone help us to relate these particular happenings to some general notions of value, of what is good and just?

THE USUAL
ADULT RESPONSE

If a young person were to reveal some of her or his value confusion in front of an adult, we could confidently predict the adult's response. Directly or indirectly, through statements or clever questions, the adult would probably attempt to show the youngster which way was the wise, correct, or best way.

Somehow or another, adults hold the idea that their chief function in relation to children is to *tell* them things: to tell them what to do, when to do it, where to do it, how to do it, how often to do it, and when to stop doing it. If the child resists, she is apt to be characterized as disobedient, impertinent, unstable, or rebellious. In other words, typically, the adult only adds to the array of directives already urged upon the child by television, radio, movies, newspapers, magazines, textbooks, teachers, and other children.

The real problem is that almost no one sees the necessity for helping children make some order out of the confusion which has already been created inside their heads. Almost no one sees the necessity for helping children sort out and examine all those confusing ideas.

In one sense, adults are led to believe that children are not people. Children are to follow the proposals of adults. They are to follow the aspirations which adults have for them. Children are to have the same feelings as adults *without*, by the way, having had the same experiences as those adults. Children should have the "right" attitudes, and the "right" attitudes are those which correspond to those held by the adults who have control over the children at the moment. Notwithstanding the tremendous amount of new knowledge which has accumulated in recent decades and assuming that beliefs are related to knowledge, there is nevertheless a tendency on the part of grownups to assume that adult beliefs should persevere unmodified, that children should have the beliefs of their elders.

And when, as is frequently the case, children do not have the same beliefs as adults say they should have, grownups become frustrated and sometimes angry. They begin again to tell the child what to believe. They push more ideas into the child's already confused mind. They pressure him, bribe him, sometimes frighten him. This manipulation only further confuses many children. One person will tell a child one thing. Her father insists something different. The child's friends are certain of something else. Successful people all around demonstrate yet other notions. What is the child to believe? How is she to know? Who is to help the child unravel this bewildering array of ideas? Would it help for a teacher to sit the confused child down and add another lecture or reasoned argument to the turmoil? No, we believe this is likely only to add to the problem.

SUMMARY

This distressing and familiar survey of what problems and dilemmas confront a young person growing up in this culture need not go on any longer. We do not wish to return to a simpler and less rich life. But we do wish to develop methods for helping children deal with the complexities of modern living. We recognize that it is indeed a confusing and complex world into which we welcome our youth. We must now ask, how does all of this affect the behavior of children? In what ways does it show up in how they think, how they react, how they plan, and how they dream? What does it mean for teachers and others who would help young people make more sense of their lives?

Distinguishing Values and Valuing

People grow and learn through experiences. Out of experiences may come certain general guides to behavior. These guides tend to give direction to life and may be called *values*. Our values show what we are likely to do with our limited time and energy.

Since we see values as growing from a person's experiences, we would expect that different experiences would give rise to different values and that any one person's values would be modified as those experiences accumulate and change. A person in the Antarctic would not be expected to have the same values as a person in Chicago. And a person who has an important change in awareness or in patterns of experience might be expected to modify his or her values. Values may not be static if a person's relationships to the world are not static. As guides to behavior, values evolve and mature as experiences evolve and mature.

Moreover, because values are a part of everyday living, they operate in very complex circumstances and usually involve more than simple extremes of right and wrong, good or bad, true or false. The conditions under which behavior is guided, in which values work, typically involve conflicting demands, a weighing and a balancing, and finally an action that reflects a multitude of forces. Thus, values seldom function in a pure and abstract form. Complicated judgments are involved and true values are ultimately reflected in the outcome of life as it is finally lived.

We therefore see values as being constantly related to the experiences that shape them and test them. For any one person, they are not so much hard and fast verities as they are the results of hammering out a style of life in a certain set of surroundings. After a sufficient amount of hammering, certain patterns of evaluating and behaving tend to develop. Certain things are treated as right, desirable, or worthy. These become our values.

In this book, we shall be less concerned with the particular value outcomes of any one person's experiences than we will with the process that is used to obtain those values. Because life is different through time and space, we cannot be certain what experiences any one person will have. We therefore cannot be certain what values, what style of life, would be most suitable for any person. We do, however, have some ideas about what *processes* might be most effective for obtaining values. These ideas grow from the assumption that whatever values a person obtains should work as effectively as possible to relate that person to his or her inner and outer worlds in a satisfying and intelligent way.

From this assumption comes what we call the *process of valuing*. A look at this process may make clear how we define a value. Unless something satisfies *all* seven of the criteria noted below, we do not call it a value, but rather a "belief" or "attitude" or something other than a value. In other words, for a value to result, all of the following seven requirements must apply. Collectively, they describe the process of valuing.

1. Choosing freely. If something is in fact to guide our lives, whether or not authority is watching, it will probably have to be freely chosen. If there has been coercion, the results are not likely to stay with us too long, especially when we are out of the range of the source of that coercion. It seems that values must be freely selected if they are to be fully valued. Put another way, the more a person feels that a value has been actively and freely selected, the more she is likely to feel that that value is central to herself.

2. Choosing from alternatives. This definition of values is based on choices made by individuals, and obviously, there can be no choice if there are no alternatives from which to choose. Thus, we say that it makes little sense to include something in the value category when the person involved was aware of no options. Likewise, we would say that the more alternatives open to us in a choice situation, the more likely we are to find something we fully value. When we approach an issue by brainstorming possible options, for example, we increase the likelihood that a value will emerge.

3. Choosing after thoughtful consideration of the consequences of each alternative. The selection of an alternative impulsively or thoughtlessly does not lead to values of the type we are defining. For a value to guide a person's life intelligently and meaningfully, we believe it must emerge in a context of understanding. Only when the consequences of each of the alternatives are understood and considered is a choice not impulsive or thoughtless. There is an important cognitive factor here. The more we understand about the consequences that flow from each alternative, the more we can make an informed choice, a choice that flows from our full intelligence. Thus, we prefer to exclude from the term *values* those choices not making a full use of intelligence.

4. Prizings and cherishing. The values we are defining have positive tones. We prize a value, cherish it, esteem it, respect it, hold it dear. We are happy with our values. A choice, even when we have made it freely and thoughtfully, may be a choice we are not happy to make. We may choose to fight in a war, but be sorry that circumstances make that choice reasonable. In our definition, values flow from choices that we are glad to make. We prize and cherish the guides to life that we call values. We judge them positively.

5.   Affirming. When we have chosen something freely, after informed consideration of the alternatives, and when we are proud of our choice, glad to be associated with it, we are likely to want to affirm that choice when asked about it. We are willing that others know of our values. We may even be willing to champion them. If on the other hand we are ashamed of our choice, if we would prefer that no one ever knew about it, we would be dealing with something not as positive as a value, but with something else. We prefer, then, to exclude from the term "values" those choices that we are ashamed to affirm to others.

6.   Acting upon choices. Where we have a value, we believe it should show up in aspects of our living, in our behavior. We may do some reading about things we value. We may form friendships or join organizations that nourish our values. We may spend money on values. We very likely budget time or energy for them. In short, for a value to be present, life itself must be affected. Nothing can be a value that does not, in fact, give direction to actual living. The person who talks about something but never does anything about it is acting from something other than a value, in our definition.

7.   Repeating. Where something reaches the level of a value, it is very likely to influence behavior on a number of occasions in the life of the person who holds it. It will show up in several different situations, at several different times. We would not think of a behavior that appeared only once in a life as representing a value. Values tend to be persistent. They tend to show up as a pattern in a life.

To review this definition, we see values as based on three processes: choosing, prizing, and acting.

- **Choosing:**   (1) freely
-              (2) from alternatives
-              (3) after thoughtful consideration of the consequences of each alternative
- **Prizing:**   (4) cherishing, being happy with the choice
-              (5) enough to be willing to affirm the choice to others
- **Acting:**   (6) or doing something with the choice
-              (7) repeatedly, in some pattern of life

Those processes collectively define valuing. Results of this valuing process are called values.

You may want to pause for a moment and apply the seven criteria for a value to one of your hobbies, be it sewing, skiing or hi-fi. Is it prized, freely and thoughtfully chosen from alternatives, acted upon, repeated, and publicly known? If so, it may be said that you *value* that hobby.

VALUE
INDICATORS

Obviously not everything is a value, nor need it be. We also have purposes, aspirations, and beliefs that may not meet all seven of those criteria. However, values often do grow from our purposes, aspirations, and beliefs. Let us briefly discuss some things that could indicate the presence of a value but that are different from values. We call these expressions which approach values, but which may not meet all of the criteria, *value indicators*.

1. Goals or purposes. Purposes give direction to life. If the purpose is important to us, we cherish it and we organize our life to achieve the purpose. This does not mean that every stated purpose is a value. Instead, we should think of a stated purpose as a potential value or a value indicator. If, in our presence, a child states a purpose, we must assume it is merely a stated purpose, until we inquire further and we have an opportunity to pursue with the child whether or not he prizes it, has freely chosen it, has wanted it for some time, and is willing to do what is necessary to achieve it. Some stated purposes are dropped when these processes are applied. The child finds out that what he said is not what he really wants. He might have had what amounts to a passing interest in the idea, but even brief examination often results in depreciation of the stated purpose. Thus a purpose *may* be a value, but, on the other hand, it may not be.

2. Aspirations. We sometimes indicate a purpose that is remote in terms of accomplishment. It is not something that we wish or expect to accomplish today or tomorrow, or within a week or sometimes even in a month. The statement of such an aspiration frequently points to the possibility of something that is valued. We do not know if it is truly a value until we have asked questions which relate to the seven criteria which have been mentioned. When the responses are consistent with those criteria, we can say that we have touched a value.

3. Attitudes. Sometimes we give indications that we have a certain value by expressing an attitude. We say that we are *for* something or *against* something. It is not always a sound practice to infer that such a statement represents a value. Is it really cherished? Has some consideration been given to alternatives? Does it come up again and again? Is it related to the life activities of the person who expresses it? Unless these criteria are met, it may be just so many words. That is, it may be an attitude and not a value.

4.   Interests. Very often you hear people say that they are interested in something. Care should be taken, however, in concluding that this means that a value is present. Very often when we say we are interested, we mean little more than that we would like to talk about it or to listen to someone talk about it, or that we might like to read a little more in that area. It is not a combination of the criteria which have been proposed. It may be a bit more than a passing fancy, but very frequently it does not work out to be a value.

5.   Feelings. Our personalities are also expressed through our feelings and through statements about how we feel. Sometimes we feel hurt. Sometimes we feel outraged. On other occasions we are glad, sad, depressed, excited; and we experience dozens of other feelings. We cannot always say that a value is present related to these feelings. Our feelings may be responses which are dissipated by very brief reflection. We should have to ask a number of questions in order to find out if the feeling reflects an underlying value.

6.   Beliefs and convictions. When we hear someone state what she believes, it is all too easy to accept the statement as a value. A woman may believe that there should be discrimination with respect to race, but also may be ashamed of that belief. She may not prize holding it. Moreover, upon examination, she may have doubts about the truth or goodness of that belief. It is the examined belief, the cherished belief, the freely chosen belief, and the belief that pervades life that rises to the stature of a value. The verbal statement provides a pointer, but it is only through careful examination that we get to know whether it represents a value.

7.   Activities. We sometimes say about a figure in public life "That's what he says, but what does he do?" We seem to be saying that not until a person does something do we have some idea of what he or she values. With values, as with other things, actions speak louder than words. Of course, it is not true that everything we do represents our values. For example, we are pretty sure that going to church does not necessarily mean a commitment to religion. A person may go to church for many reasons. Another person may go often and regularly to bridge parties, all the while wishing that he did not have to go. He may do a certain kind of work every day without having chosen that work or prizing it very much. In other words, just by observing what people do, we are unable to determine whether values are present. We have to know if the individual prizes what he is doing, if he has chosen to do what he is doing, and if it constitutes a pattern in his life. All by themselves, activities do not tell us enough, but they may indicate a value.

8.   Worries, problems, obstacles. We hear individuals talk about worries or problems, and we sometimes infer from the context that we know the values that are involved. Here again we may be giving undue importance to verbal statements. If we were to ask questions bearing upon the seven criteria which have been proposed, we might find out that nothing of great importance is involved; that the statement is made only to further conversation. Many of us talk a good deal, and we may mention problems or worries only as ways of entering into a conversation. Examining the worry or the problem may reveal that something *is* deeply prized, that a belief *is* being blocked, that one's life *is* being disturbed. Under such circumstances, we can be more confident with the judgment that a value is involved.

We have discussed briefly eight categories of behavior which have a significant relationship to valuing. There is no implication that other categories of behavior may not be just as important. However, these eight categories—goals and purposes, aspirations, feelings, interests, beliefs and convictions, attitudes, activities, and worries—are often revealed in the classroom. We believe it is important that opportunities for revealing these become a vital part of teaching, for the next step—as will be discussed in later chapters—is for the teacher to help those children who choose to do so to raise these value indicators to the level of values—that is, to the level on which all seven of the valuing processes operate.

We now want to turn our attention to one of the value processes that seems to have particular importance for work with children growing up in this confused and complex world, the process of choosing.

THE CRUCIAL
CRITERION OF CHOICE

Because we see choosing as crucial to the process of valuing, it may be useful at this point to expand on the conditions that must exist if a choice is really to be made.

The act of choosing requires alternatives. We choose something from a group of things. If there is only one possibility, we cannot make a choice, and according to our definition, no value is indicated in that area. Yet so often we eliminate all but one alternative for children or we restrict alternatives available to them. For example, we say to a child that she must either sit silently in her chair or stay after school. Or we ask, "Wouldn't you like to learn your multiplication table, Iris?" If we restrict alternatives, so that the child's preferred choice is not among them, we cannot say that the subsequent choice represents a value. It is common practice to give children either-or choices, both of which may be undesirable from their standpoint, then wonder why they do not value their own behavior.

Unless we open up decisions and include alternatives that a child might really prefer, we may only give the illusion of choice, at least in terms of this value theory. Values must grow from thoughtful, prized choices made from sufficient alternatives.

Thus, when we take the lead in presenting alternatives to children, we should also take some care in seeing to it that the *alternatives have meaning* for them. A student may be familiar with only one of the possible choices and may not be aware of what the others involve. We can discover this by asking questions; and if the student does not know what other choices could mean, we can help the child to understand them better. It is useless, therefore, to ask a young child to make choices from among alternatives he does not understand. It is also misleading to think a choice has been made when, for example, a child selects democracy over autocracy without much understanding of either.

We should also help children to see the probable *consequences of a choice* and find out if they are willing to accept the consequences which may follow. Once a child is on record as being willing to take the consequences, the situation has to that extent been clarified, and the choice has some meaning. Without such an understanding of and acceptance of the consequences, we can hardly call the choice meaningful.

We must further recognize that the child needs to be really *free to choose.* If for many reasons we do not want a child to choose a particular alternative, like setting fire to the house, we should let her or him know that this is not within the realm of choice. We should not try to fool her into thinking that she is a free agent and then disappoint her when we refuse to honor her choice. Rather, we should be clear and forceful when we deny choices. Otherwise, we subvert the faith of the child in the very process of deciding and choosing. When we are concerned with values, we must be willing to give the child freedom to choose.

In short, we are saying that a coerced choice is no choice at all. It is not likely that values will evolve from a choice imbued with threat or bribery, for example. One important implication of this condition of value theory for teachers is a reduction of the punishment and reward systems so widely used in schools. Choices cannot be considered sufficiently free if each one is first to be weighed, approved, disapproved, or graded by someone in charge.

Does this mean that the whole world should be open for choice and that we should respect a child's choice no matter what it is? Most teachers, in the light of policies suggested by a school board or school administrators or out of their own basic needs for order, make quite clear to students that there are areas where choice is not possible. One of these relates to life itself: We do not allow children to engage in activities which might result in serious danger.

We say to children about areas where serious injury is a strong possibility that they cannot choose, that their behavior is restricted. The reason we give is that the consequences of an unwise choice are not tolerable or that the alternatives may not be well enough understood to allow a meaningful choice.

Many of us are also against vulgarity in many forms. Profane language, obscene behavior, filth, and dirtiness are matters on which many of us take a stand. We may indicate to children that they may not engage in behavior of this kind; that the policies for which we stand do not allow such things to go on; that deviations from our standards bother us too much to be tolerated. When an individual reveals this kind of behavior, we may intervene directly and perhaps talk privately with the student.

In almost every culture and in many communities there are areas which are sometimes called "hot" or "very delicate." In some communities, it may be matters pertaining to religious issues; in other communities it may be matters relating to political issues. Sex is frequently such an issue. Where these hot issues are matters of civil rights, rights which belong to all individuals, teachers may wish to challenge restrictions or taboos. It is good policy, however, to do this on a professional level, working among colleagues first, and not to take up issues with children in a public way which may be against public policy. It is usually wiser to make attempts to clarify public policy and to modify it before involving the children in affairs that might be extremely embarrassing and extremely provoking. Whether children should be encouraged to reflect and choose in a controversial area is not the point. They *must* reflect and choose if values are to emerge. The question is what teachers should do first in communities which frown upon opening certain issues.

In summary, if children—or adults, for that matter—are to develop values, they must develop them out of personal choices. These choices, if they are possibly to lead to values, must involve alternatives which (1) include ones that are prized by the chooser; (2) have meaning to the chooser, as when the consequences of each are clearly understood; and (3) are freely available for selection.

THE PERSONAL NATURE OF VALUES

We have said that values are a product of personal experiences. They are not just a matter of true or false. We do not go to an encyclopedia or to a textbook for values. Our definition of valuing shows why this is. People have to prize for themselves, choose for themselves, integrate choices into the pattern of their own lives. Information as such does not convey this quality of values. Values emerge from the flux of life itself.

Consequently, we are dealing with an area that is not a matter of proof or consensus, but a matter of experience. If a child says that he likes something, it does not seem appropriate for an older person to say, "You shouldn't like that." Or, if another child should say "I am interested in that," it does not seem quite right for an older person to say to her, "You shouldn't be interested in things like that." If these interests have grown out of a child's experience, they are consistent with his or her life. When we ask children to deny their own lives, we are in effect asking them to be hypocrites. We seem to be saying in an indirect way, "Yes, this is what your life has taught you, but you shouldn't say so. You should pretend that you had a different life." What are we doing to children when we put them into positions like this? Are we helping them to develop values or are we in effect saying that life is a fraud and that a person should learn to live a lie very early in life.

We have an alternative approach to values which will be presented in the following chapters. For now, it is important to note that our definition of values and valuing leads to a conception of these words that is highly personal. It follows that if we are to respect a person's life, we must respect his experience and his right to examine it for values.

It should be expected that in a society like ours, governed by our Constitution, teachers might well see themselves as obliged to support the idea that all people are entitled to the views that they have and to the values that they hold, especially where these have been examined and affirmed. Is this not the cornerstone of a free society? As teachers, then, we need to be clear that we cannot dictate to children what their values should be since we cannot also dictate what their environments will be and what experiences they will have. We may be authoritative in those areas that deal with truth and falsity: Do flowers consume oxygen? Where does the state get its income? But where the question involves a personal activity (Do you ever take care of flowers?), an attitude (Are you happy with the way the state spends its money?) or a worry, interest, feeling, purpose, aspiration, or belief, our view is that it is unreasonable for a teacher to assume he or she has the correct answer. By our definition, and as we see it, by social right, values are personal things.

As a matter of cold fact, in the great majority of instances we really do not know what values a child has. We are apt to make inferences which go beyond the available data and to attribute values to children which they do not hold. We probably are better off assuming only that we really do not know. If we are interested in knowing, we might well initiate a process of investigation and inquiry. More attention will be given to this notion later.

Life As a Process

One final analogy will reemphasize our focus. Some people, when they travel, seem to be much more interested in the motels or hotels at which they stop than in the experiences which they have along the way. Other people are much more interested in the road than in the inn. Our approach to values could be likened to the latter group's interest. We are interested in the processes that go on in valuing. We are not much interested in identifying the values which children ultimately hold as a result of these processes. We are more interested in the process because we believe that in a world that changes as rapidly as ours, children must develop habits of examining personal aspirations, purposes, attitudes, feelings, activities, interests, beliefs, and worries if they are to find satisfying ways of integrating their own thoughts, emotions, and behaviors within themselves and in relation to the world.

The development of values is a personal and life-long process. It is not something that is completed by early adulthood. As the world changes, as we change, and as we strive to change the world again, we have many decisions to make and we should be learning how to make these decisions. We should be learning how to value. It is this process that we believe needs to be carried on in the classrooms; it is at least partly through this process that we think children will learn about themselves and about how to make some sense out of the buzzing confusion of the society around them.

Values Clarification:
Process and Content

Earlier we noted some of the uncertain and confusing aspects of society and speculated upon the difficulties children have making sense of it all. We also said that we use the term *value* to denote those beliefs, purposes, attitudes, and so on that are chosen freely and thoughtfully, prized, and acted upon. We suggested further that, since the development of society and the people in it is best seen as dynamic, it is perhaps wiser to focus upon the process of *valuing* than upon any particular values themselves.

Now let us be a bit more explicit about that process. What, according to the theory that we propose, do we *do* if we want to take on the task of helping children develop values? Briefly, we assist children in using the process of valuing. This process flows naturally from the definition of values presented earlier. That is, an adult who would help children develop values would be advised to:

1. Encourage children to make more choices, and to make them freely.

2. Help them discover alternatives when faced with choices.

3. Help children weigh alternatives thoughtfully, reflecting on the consequences of each.

4. Encourage children to consider what it is that they prize and cherish.

5. Give them opportunities to affirm their choices.

6. Encourage them to act, behave, live in accordance with their choices.

7. Help them be aware of repeated behaviors or patterns in their life.

In this way, the adult encourages the process of valuing. The intent of this process is to help children (although it is equally applicable to adults) clarify for themselves what they value. This is very different from trying to persuade children to accept some predetermined set of values. It is based on a conception of democracy that says people can learn to make their own decisions. It is also based on a conception of humanity that says human beings are capable of being thoughtful and wise and that the most appropriate values will emerge when people use those capacities in defining their relationships with each other and with an ever-changing world. Furthermore, it is based on the idea that values are personal things, that they cannot be very personal until they are freely accepted, and that they cannot be of much significance if they do not penetrate the life of the person who holds them.

APPLYING THE
PROCESS TO CONTENT

Three sources of content are especially suited for clarifying thought. First are those aspects of a person's life that we earlier called "value indicators": goals, aspirations, attitudes, interests, feelings, beliefs, activities, and worries. Thus, a teacher in a value-clarifying posture might focus the attention of students on their worries by asking the group to mention two or three things they sometimes worry about or several things which are problems in their lives or obstacles to getting what they want. The assumption behind this approach is that any of these value indicators, touching as they do on aspects of our current aliveness, is ripe for clarifying thought.

Another source of content for values clarification are those personal issues that we all face and that so frequently complicate living. For younger children, such issues include questions about what to do with fears or desires, how to be accepted by adults and peers, and how to corral ornery impulses. For adolescents, they include questions about love and friendship, about sexuality, and about the role of work in a life. For adults, they include questions about marriage, loyalty, and money. Developmental psychologists can guide us to the life issues people in general face at different ages. Sensitive questioning, with careful listening, can probably do better at pinpointing the issues relevant to a particular person or group.

Third are those issues that are somewhat more social than personal. Some such issues deal with the relationship between the individual and society at large: what an individual should do about rules, about changing things in the family or neighborhood or school, about cooperating with others, and about handling the tension between self-interest and social interest. Other issues deal with what we want for society itself. There are questions about poverty in our communities, in our nation and in the world, about racism and sexism, about law and order, about bureaucracy and freedom, about democracy and change, and about war and peace.

We could, of course, wait for such social issues to become live concerns for the individuals we deal with, but we prefer to reach out and initiate reflections on key social issues in ways appropriate to the interests and maturity of our students. We take this approach partly because students can often reflect and clarify values related to those issues better *before* they get too far entangled in emotions about those issues and partly because students too often, after they leave our schools, have insufficient time or support to give deliberate, clarifying thought to the issues.

What, then, do we ask people to think about, to reflect on, to process through those seven lenses of the clarifying process? We ask about their goals, attitudes, and other value indicators. We ask about personal issues that complicate their lives. And we ask about social issues that tend to complicate the lives of all of us.

ESTABLISHING A MOOD OF ACCEPTANCE

It is clear that if we want students to reflect on issues as delicate and rich as those above we must avoid taking any stance that will make open reflection difficult. What, after all, makes it difficult for any of us to think openly and honestly about our values? Fear of censure. Fear of appearing stupid or foolishly rattled. Fear of rejection. Suspicion that others do not really care about us and are just talking rather mechanically for their own benefit. Fear of revealing too much of ourselves. Make the list vivid by recalling experiences from your own life. When have you been tempted to replace honest reflection and sharing with pretense or withdrawal?

It is vital, we believe, for a teacher to establish a mood that is accepting. The effective value-clarifying teacher communicates that he or she does not judge where students happen to be at any point in their lives; she assumes that, wherever they are, they can move on. This is a stance of respect for students. The teacher cares for students and shows it. She listens carefully and patiently. She smiles with their joys and suffers with their troubles. The teacher invites but does not require self-disclosure and clarifying thought. She is gentle and, when naturally moved to do so, speaks openly about personal continued searchings for clearer values. In so doing, the teacher creates a mood that encourages students to take an accepting posture with each other when engaging in clarifying thought.

Part three of this book describes this approach in much more detail and gives many examples of how the clarifying process might be used by teachers at many grade levels and in many subject areas. At this point it might be useful to contrast the value-clarifying approach with more traditional approaches to values.

TRADITIONAL APPROACHES TO VALUES

Here are some ways that have often been advocated for helping children develop values.

1.   Setting an example either directly, by the way adults behave, or indirectly, by pointing to good models in the past or present, such as Washington's honesty or the patience of Ulysses' wife.

2.   Persuading and convincing by presenting arguments and reasons for this or that set of values and by pointing to the fallacies and pitfalls of other sets of values.

3.   Limiting choices by giving children choices only among values "we" accept, such as asking children to choose between helping wash the dishes or helping clean the floor, or by giving children choices between a value we accept and one no one is likely to accept, such as asking children to choose between telling the truth and never speaking to us again.

4.   Inspiring by dramatic or emotional pleas for certain values often accompanied by models of behavior associated with the value.

5.   Rules and regulations intended to contain and mold behavior until it is unthinkingly accepted as right, as through the use of rewards and punishments to reinforce certain behavior.

6.   Using the arts and literature, not solely to expand awareness, but to model and promote what "always has been" and what "should be."

7.   Cultural or religious dogma presented as unquestioned wisdom or principle, such as saying that something should be believed because "our people have always done it this way."

8.   Appeals to conscience, appeals to the "still, small voice" that we assume is within the heart of everyone; often used with the arousing of feelings of guilt if a person's conscience fails to suggest the "right" way, such as telling a child that he should know better or that he shamed his parents.

We have no doubt that such methods as those listed—and there are others that could be listed—have in the past controlled behavior and even formed beliefs and attitudes. We assert, however, that they have not led and cannot lead to values in the sense that we are concerned with them, values that represent the free and thoughtful choice of intelligent humans interacting with complex and changing environments.

In fact, those methods do not seem to have resulted in deep commitments of any sort. The values that are supposedly being promoted by those methods in our society—honor, courage, devotion, self-control, craftsmanship, thrift, love, and so on—seem less than ever to be the values that guide the behavior of citizens. On the pragmatic test of effectiveness alone, the approaches listed above must receive a low grade. They just do not seem to work very well. This alone suggests that we should try a new approach.

We emphasize that these methods are not without some useful effect. It is certainly useful, for example, for adults to set examples for the kinds of behaviors that they say they support. Also, most of us have had our lives stirred and enriched by inspiring words and deeds. And many have found that religion is able to nourish virtue and hope, even in an otherwise desperate and dark life. Our main point, then, is not that the above approaches to values have been without use, but that they have not worked as well as we might have hoped and that we now have some understanding of why this might have been.

Each of the listed approaches involves persuasion. The "right" values are predetermined and taught by one method or another of selling, pushing, urging those values upon others. All the methods have the air of indoctrination, which some merely more subtle than others. The idea of free inquiry, thoughtfulness, reason seems to be lost. The general approach seems not to be how to help the child develop a valuing process, but rather how to persuade the child to adopt the "right" values.

When we ask people why such persuasive approaches are employed, why there is little effort to have the child think through issues and freely choose what *the child* prizes, we most often receive certain answers.

1.   "Children are not old enough or experienced enough or wise enough to choose values for themselves. We are responsible for starting them off on the right track. We have to drill values into children now; later they will learn to value for themselves."

The assumption here is that one does not have to practice valuing for oneself at an early age and that after twenty years or so of indoctrination one can readily break the habit of conforming to the values of others.

2.   "It takes too much time to help children figure out their own values. It's faster and simpler merely to show them the best way."

There are probably assumptions here about what it is most important to produce with a limited amount of time and energy, implying that something other than values is most important. Also implied is the assumption that everyone can get values from being shown "the best way," even though any child is exposed to many varied models of "best ways." Note also the implication that the best ways are already defined in such a form as to be generally applicable.

3.   "You can't really trust children to choose the values that would serve them best. Both their inexperience and some tendency to obstinacy may lead them to poor choices. We may have disastrous results, and most certainly we will have many regrettable results."

This view assumes that we would have children choose in all areas, whether they understood the alternatives or not and whether the choice could lead to disaster or not. It also reflects some limited faith in the intelligence and goodwill of children.

4. "Think of the problems that will develop from wrong choices! Time wasted, unnecessary hurt and pain, and perhaps even irreparable human damage. Besides, how can adults contain themselves when they see children going astray? What, after all, are adults for if they do not point the way to wisdom and righteousness?"

There are two separate sets of assumptions here. One set has to do with the problem of "poor" choices, which assumes that children cannot learn from such choices, that the consequences of such choices are not educational, and in fact, that children can learn about values *without* making some poor choices. There is the idea that a person is helping if she prevents a child from making a mistake.

The second set of assumptions, more an implication, seems to say that adults will feel some loss of function, perhaps of power, if they do not intervene in the decisions of children. One almost imagines an adult looking back at a long childhood of being manipulated at the whim of surrounding adults and hoping that his turn to assert himself will not be denied.

5. "Look, what can I do? Everyone else tries to give values to children. My children will think I'm crazy if I do otherwise, and certainly other adults will look at me and wonder at my laxness."

This says quite plainly that many adults feel pressure from others to conform in some way. It would be unwise to underestimate the strength behind that pressure, but the statement does assume that adults under pressure do not have the strength of purpose to assert whatever values they hold. For some, this may be true. But such hesitance may also be the result of an adult's own lack of values. One might assume that if a person did not have a clear set of values in a certain area, that person would be likely to look around and see what others are doing. Thus, some conformity is not the result of a desire to conform, but represents a desire to do what is best in circumstances which are unclear. Perhaps, then, clarity here as elsewhere is what is needed.

6. "I really do not want to get too deeply into examinations of values. It is too confusing and I do not understand it well enough myself. Maybe professionals can do it, but it is much easier to let things be and direct my attention to other things."

The assumption that is clearest here is that adults should not work with children in areas in which they are not experts, that it would be too threatening to do so. There may also be an implication that some adults do not want to recognize how ineffective their own valuing process has been.

7. "It is a matter of will power. If people want to do something, all they need is the will to do it."

This assumes, of course, that people do want to do something, that purposes are clear, that nothing is blocking the achievement of personal goals. It does not seem to take in the possibility that purposes are not clear and that ambivalence is not in control.

8. "Frankly, children are more difficult to handle if they are deciding too many things for themselves. If children expect to learn what they should believe and value from us, it is easier all around. There will be fewer discipline problems."

The assumption here is that children who are tractable are more valuable than children who have values. There is the additional assumption that the indoctrination of values does lead to more obedient children and fewer behavior problems.

9. "Children appreciate being told what to do and what to believe. It gives them security. Freedom is frightening to many of them."

The assumptions here focus on the cause of insecurity that arises when duties cease to direct children. Are children insecure only because they now would have free time and free choice, or are they insecure because they have had no help in acquiring real values to direct their use of that freedom? Is the answer to keep children under pressure, keep them busy, keep them under control? Or is the answer to help them to develop values so that they can be responsibly self-directing in an ever-changing world?

Now these reasons for wanting to persuade children to take on certain values seem to us to be based on questionable assumptions, although some of the assumptions seem more temptingly tenable than others and some are probably reasonable for some situations and not for others. There is at least one additional reason for adults trying to impose their values on children, and it is perhaps the overriding reason: no other alternative that is clear and testable has been provided. Since they are not aware of another choice, who can blame adults for doing what they think best? The observation that many children and adults do not, in fact, seem to have many clear values may have raised questions about the efficiency of trying to sell adult beliefs to children, but what alternative choice is there? We believe this book offers one.

REASONS FOR A
NEW APPROACH

There is widespread concern that youth, and adults in some cases, do not seem to live by any consistent set of values. They act impetuously, erratically, and sometimes destructively. Many children find nothing enjoyable to do with their free time. Even in school many seem purposeless and listless, motivated only—but not always consistently—by outside pressures. Our population is becoming other-directed, it is asserted. We guide our lives not by what we believe is right and proper, but by what others do or say. Does this not suggest that many people have unclear values?

We note the wide discrepancy between what people do and what they say. Many political leaders, business executives, military leaders, workers of all sorts, and even professional people are known to *do* things that are inconsistent with what they *say* are their values. Charges of corruption are not unusual. So many people can be "bought." Does this not suggest that the approaches to values that have been so widely used in the past have been less than effective?

Adults have been trying to set examples for years. They have tried often with ingenious manipulation to persuade children to accept certain values. They have carefully limited choices given to children. They have attempted to inspire identification with particular values. They have made rules and insisted on certain patterns of behavior. They have relied upon religion and cultural truisms. They have appealed to the consciences of young people. But even a casual look at the results of these approaches is discouraging. They simply do not seem to have worked.

In the past we have *told* children, children who have been exposed to many different and confusing stimuli, that they *should* believe in one thing or another. We have *said* this in many ways: by our example, our rules, our arguments, and so on. But as we spoke, the children were surrounded by other examples and arguments which stood for different values. When a child indicated confusion by a lack of purpose or a disregard of purpose, we insisted, punished, pleaded, and otherwise campaigned even harder for one of the many values that we were convinced the child must adopt. More than likely this only further confused many children and made them less able to decide in what to believe.

Thus many children grow up to become adults who know only how to pretend to believe. We pretend we believe in democracy and we pretend we have religion. But for so many of us such beliefs are indeed thin. We have never been taught how to internalize beliefs that have the body and life of values.

Why must teachers see their role only as putting things *into* the mind of the child? Why can't a role be defined that would help a child take out some of the confusion that already exists in his mind, remove it, look at it, examine it, turn it around, and make some order out of it? Why can't teachers learn to spend some of their time helping children sort through the bewildering array of beliefs and attitudes that saturate our modern life? Is this not the road to values, to *clear* and *personal* values?

We believe it is. We believe that as children are helped to use what we call the valuing process, they will move toward value clarity in a more sensible and dramatic way than ever before. Peck and Havighurst (1960, p. 191) put it succinctly:

> It is temptingly easy and insidiously gratifying to "mold" children, or "whip them into line" by exercising one's superior status and authority as an adult. It is often personally inconvenient to allow children time to debate alternatives, and it may be personally frustrating if their choice contradicts one's own preferences. If there is any selfish, sensitive "pride" at stake, it is very hard for most adults to refrain from controlling children in an autocratic manner. Then, too, like any dictatorship, it looks "more efficient"—to the dictator, at least. However, the effect on character is to arrest the development of rational judgment and to create such resentments as prevent the growth of genuine altruistic impulses. For thousands of years, the long-term effects have been ignored and sacrificed to short-term adult advantages, most of the time. Probably it is no accident tht there are relatively few people who are, or ever will become, psychologically and ethically mature.

OTHER NEW
APPROACHES TO VALUES

In general recognition of the weakness of traditional approaches to values, several schools of thought have recently developed, many with procedures and styles that overlap with those of values clarification (Superka, et al., 1976). One might, for example, look at the works of Rokeach (1975), Metcalf (1971), and Kohlberg (1975). Each of those approaches seems to us compatible with aspects of our work. Yet none of the approaches seems as comprehensive or as flexible when put to use by teachers or others in the helping professions. Be that as it may, it is noteworthy that these newer approaches, as does values clarification, emphasize that people must learn to think through value issues for themselves. We will have more to say about this after we have looked more closely at how values clarification appears in practice. (See chapter 14.)

A SUMMARY OF THE THEORY

So far we have presented a view of the concept of value that is based on a particular notion of human potential, one which emphasizes the human capacity for intelligent, self-directed behavior.

We have reserved the term *value* for those individual beliefs, attitudes, activities, or feelings that satisfy the criteria of (1) having been freely chosen, (2) having been chosen from among alternatives, (3) having been chosen after due reflection, (4) having been prized and cherished, (5) having been affirmed to others, (6) having been incorporated into actual behavior, and (7) having been repeated in one's life.

In different words, we might say that something will not qualify as a value if *any* of the following conditions apply.

1. It has not been *freely* chosen. (There is no room in this theory for values that are imposed by outside pressures.)

2. It is without one or more available alternatives. (A real choice must exist, not a spurious choice.)

3. It has been chosen without thoughtful consideration. (This excludes impulse or highly emotional choices from the category of values.)

4. It is not prized or cherished. (We exclude from the level of values those things which we have or do which we are not proud of and would rather not have or do—as when one chooses the least objectionable of several undesirable alternatives.)

5. It is denied to all others. (To be ashamed to affirm something is to indicate that one does not value it fully.)

6. It is not in some way reflected in one's actual behavior. (A person who chooses democracy and never does anything to put that choice into practice may be said to have an attitude or belief about democracy but not a value.)

7. It is a passing fancy and lacks any persistence over time. (A one-shot effort at pottery making, for example, would not qualify as a value.)

The meaning here for schools and, more particularly, for the busy classroom teacher is implicit in the definition. If a person wishes to help children develop clearer values, he or she must help children use the process of valuing. That is, we must help children: (1) make free choices whenever possible, (2) search for alternatives in choice-making situations, (3) weigh the consequences of each available alternative, (4) consider what they prize and cherish, (5) affirm the things they might value, (6) do something about their choices, and (7) consider and strengthen patterns in their lives. It is as simple and as complex as that. As the teacher helps students use these processes, she or he helps them find values.

The basic sequence of the value-clarifying process is often as follows:

1. Attention is focused on an issue in life. The teacher may call to attention one of the student's attitudes, feelings, activities, beliefs, goals, aspirations, interests, or worries—what we call "value indicators." Or the teacher may raise a more general life issue, such as children's allowances or the sharing of school materials or, for older students, questions related to abortion or methods of social change.

2. Acceptance of students is communicated. The teacher communicates an acceptance of students' expressions of values, although not necessarily agreement with what is expressed. The teacher may emphasize this acceptance in value discussions by nonjudgmental messages saying that a student has been heard, understood, and respected: "I hear what you say, Billy, and I appreciate how you feel."

3. An invitation is offered to reflect further on choices, prizings, and actions. A follow-up message built on one of the seven valuing processes is communicated to invite students to do additional thinking on what they have said or done. This not only invites growth toward a more integrated set of thoughts, feelings, and behaviors but also teaches skills that students can use by themselves outside of school for the rest of their lives.'

It should be increasingly clear that the adult does not force personal values upon children. What the adult does do is create conditions that aid children in finding values *if* they choose to do so. When operating within this value theory, it is entirely possible that children will choose not to develop values. It is the teacher's responsibility to support this choice also, while at the same time realizing that value development is likely to be one of the school's goals and that it should be encouraged by providing regular experiences that will help raise to the value level the beliefs, feelings, interests, and activities children bring with them along with values work on the issues that are central to our times.

Part three details procedures that teachers can use to do this. Procedures are presented that teachers can use without taking time away from ongoing programs or activities. Also outlined are techniques for relating value lessons to the familiar subject matter.

The teacher who activates the value theory in some of the ways suggested in this book can expect that children will have more values, be more aware of the values that they have, have values that are more consistent with one another, and especially, be ready to use the valuing process as they continue to grow and learn.

But there are also purposes that are more concrete, more relevant to the typical school task, and more readily measurable that seem to be promoted by the valuing process. For example, research (discussed more fully in Chapter 12) shows that when the valuing process was promoted with children who were very apathetic, overconforming, flighty, and likely to act in a variety of poses or "phony" roles, this type of behavior became noticeably less acute and less frequent. There is also evidence that these techniques help children who are very indecisive, who are very inconsistent, or who are chronic dissenters. Other research showed the valuing process to help underachievers improve in the following:

- Attitudes toward learning
- Raising questions and alternatives
- Initiation and self-direction of classroom activity
- Perseverance
- Active participation

In general, the research shows that students become more vital and purposeful when given opportunities to clarify their values. How this may be done specifically is the subject of the chapters which follow.

three

METHODOLOGY

A Dialogue Strategy

THE CLARIFYING RESPONSE

The most flexible of the value-clarifying strategies is called the clarifying response. It is a response a teacher makes to something a student has said or done when the purpose is to encourage that student to do some extra thinking. As you will see, a clarifying response is sometimes made orally, in an informal dialogue with one student or in the midst of a whole-class discussion. And the clarifying response is sometimes used when writing comments on student papers.

Imagine a student on the way out of class who says, "Ms. Jones, I'm going to Washington, D.C., this weekend with my family." How might a teacher respond? Perhaps, "That's nice," or "Have a good time!" Neither of those responses is likely to stimulate clarifying thought on the part of the student. Consider a different kind of response, for example: "Going to Washington, are you, Sally? Are you glad you're going?"

To sense the clarifying power in that response, imagine the student saying, "No, come to think of it, I'm not glad I'm going. I'd rather play in the Little League game." If the teacher were to say nothing other than "Well, we'll see you Monday," or some noncommittal equivalent, we still might say that the student would have become a little more aware of her life. In this case, she would have recognized that she is capable of doing things that she is not happy about doing. This is not a very big step, and it might be no step at all, but it might contribute to her considering a bit more seriously how much of her life she wants involved in activities that she does not prize or cherish. We say this is a step toward value clarity.

Consider this example. A student says that he is planning to go to college after high school. A teacher who replies, "Good for you," or "Which college?" or "Well, I hope you make it," is probably going to serve purposes other than value clarity. But were the teacher to respond, "Have you considered any alternatives?" the goal of value clarity may well be advanced.

That "alternatives" response is likely to stimulate thinking about the issue, and if the student decides to go to college, that decision is likely to be closer to representing a value than it was before. It may contribute a little toward moving a potential college student from the position of going because "it's the thing to do" to going because he wants to get something out of it.

Here are two other samples of exchanges using clarifying responses.

Student: I believe that all men are created equal.

Teacher: What do you mean by that?

Student: I guess I mean that all people are equally good and none should have advantages over others.

Teacher: Does this idea suggest that some changes need to be made in our world, even in this school and this town?

Student: Oh, lots of them. Want me to name some?

Teacher: No, we have to get back to our spelling lesson, but I was just wondering if you were working on any of those changes, actually trying to bring them about.

Student: Not yet, but I may soon.

Teacher: I see. Now, back to the spelling list.

Teacher: Bruce, don't you want to go outside and play on the playground?

Student: I dunno. I suppose so.

Teacher: Is there something that you would rather do?

Student: I dunno. Nothing much.

Teacher: You don't seem much to care, Bruce. Is that right?

Student: I suppose so.

Teacher: And mostly anything we do will be all right with you?

Student: I suppose so. Well, not anything, I guess.

Teacher: Well, Bruce, we had better go out to the playground now with the others. You let me know sometime if you think of something you would like to do.

THE EFFECTIVE
CLARIFYING RESPONSE

You may already sense some criteria of an effective clarifying response, that is, a response that encourages someone to look at his or her life and ideas and to think about them. The following are among the essential elements of this response.

1. The clarifying response avoids moralizing, criticizing, giving values, or evaluating. The adult excludes all hints of "good" or "right" or "acceptability," or their opposites in such responses.

2. It puts the responsibility on the students to look at their behavior or ideas and to think and decide for themselves what it is *they* want.

3. A clarifying response also entertains the possibility that the student will *not* look or decide or think. It is permissive and stimulating, but not insistent. The student will often be expected to decline to answer when asked clarifying questions.

4. It does not try to do big things with its small comments. It works more at stimulating thought related to what a person does or says. It aims at setting a mood. Each clarifying response is only one of many; the effect is cumulative.

5. Clarifying responses are not used for interview purposes. The goal is not to obtain data, but to help students clarify their own ideas and lives if they want to do so.

6. Usually an extended discussion does not result. The purpose is for the student to think, and this is usually done best alone, without the temptation to justify thoughts to an adult. Therefore, a teacher would be wise to carry on only two or three rounds of dialogue and then offer to break off the conversation with some noncommittal but honest phrase, such as "Nice talking to you" or "I see what you mean better now" or "Let's talk about this another time, shall we?" or "Very interesting. Thanks." (Of course, there is no reason why a student who desires to talk more should be turned aside, the teacher's time permitting.)

7. Clarifying responses are often for individuals. A topic in which Clem might need clarification may be of no immediate interest to Priscilla. An issue that is of general concern, of course, may warrant a general clarifying response—say to the whole class—but even here the *individual* must ultimately do the reflecting. Values are personal things. The teacher often responds to one individual, although others may be listening.

8. The teacher does not respond to everything everyone says or does in a classroom. There are other responsibilities. (In chapter 8, we discuss how clarifying responses can be used with those students who need them most.)

9. Clarifying responses operate in situations where there are no "right" answers—as in situations involving feelings, attitudes, beliefs, or purposes. They are *not* appropriate for drawing a student toward a predetermined answer. They are *not* questions for which the teacher has an answer already in mind.

10. Clarifying responses are not mechanical things that carefully follow a formula. They must be used creatively and with insight, but with their purpose in mind. When a response helps a student to clarify thinking or behavior, it is considered effective.

The ten conditions listed above are very difficult to fulfill for the teacher who has not practiced them. A tendency to use responses to students for the purpose of molding students' thinking is very well established in most teachers' minds. That a function of the teacher is to help the child clarify some of the existing confusion and ambiguity is an unfamiliar idea for many of us. After all, most of us became teachers because we wanted to *teach* somebody something. Most of us are all too ready to sell our intellectual wares. The clarifying strategy requires a different orientation—not that of adding to the child's ideas but rather one of stimulating the child to clarify the ideas he or she already has.

Here is another classroom incident illustrating a teacher using clarifying responses, in this case to help a student see that free, thoughtful choices can be made. The situation is a classroom discussion in which a boy has just made it clear that he is a liberal in his political viewpoints.

Teacher: You say, Glenn, that you are a liberal in political matters?

Glenn: Yes, I am.

Teacher: Where did your ideas come from?

Glenn: Well, my parents I guess, mostly.

Teacher: Are you familiar with other positions?

Glenn: Well, sort of.

Teacher: I see, Glenn. Now, class, getting back to the homework for today . . . (returning to the general lesson).

Here is another actual situation. In this incident, the clarifying response prods the student to clarify her thinking and to examine her behavior to see if it is consistent with her ideas. It is between lessons and a student has just told a teacher that science is her favorite subject.

Teacher: What exactly do you like about science?

Student: Specifically? Let me see. Gosh, I'm not sure. I guess I just like it in general.

Teacher: Do you do anything outside of school to have fun with science?

Student: No, not really.

Teacher: Thank you, Lise. I must get back to work now.

Notice the brevity of the exchanges. Sometimes we call these exchanges "one-legged conferences," because they often take place while a teacher is on one leg, pausing briefly on the way elsewhere. An extended series of probes might give the student the feeling of being cross-examined and might make the child defensive. Besides extended discussion would give the student too much to think about. The idea is, to raise a few questions, without moralizing, leave them hanging in the air, and then move on. The student to whom the questions are addressed and other students who might overhear may well ponder the questions later, in a lull in the day or in the quiet moments before falling asleep at night. These are gentle prods, but the effect is to stimulate a student who is ready for it to choose, prize, and act in ways outlined by our theory. And, as the research reported in chapter 12 demonstrates, these one-legged conferences add up to large differences in some students' lives.

THIRTY
CLARIFYING RESPONSES

There are several responses that teachers who have worked with the clarifying approach have found very useful. A list of some of these is presented below. As you go through the list, you might make note of some you would like to try—that is, make your own list. There are too many clarifying questions noted here to keep in mind at one time. It is probably best, then, to gather a dozen or so together—ones which sound as if they could be used comfortably—and try them out, perhaps expanding or revising the list as experience dictates.

You should remember, however, that the responses listed here are recommended as useful clarifying responses only when they are used in accordance with the ten conditions listed earlier. Ultimately, the acid test for any response is whether or not it results in a person reflecting on what he has said or done, clarifying, getting to know himself better, examining his choices, considering what he prizes, looking at patterns in his life and so on. If the response makes the student defensive, gets her to say what the adult wants her to say, or gives her the feeling that the adult is nagging, it is being used improperly or with poor timing. An accepting, noncommittal attitude on the part of the person making responses is crucial.

Some of the responses listed below are geared directly to one or another of the seven valuing components: prizing, searching for alternatives, thinking critically, choosing freely, incorporating choices into behavior, examining patterns of living, and affirming choices. Other responses stimulate reflection in a more general sense. In *all* cases, responses are open-ended—that is, they lead the student to no specific value. No one must deliver a "right" answer to a clarifying response. Each student must be permitted to react in a personal and individual way.

1. Is this something that you prize? To respond in a way that gets students to consider whether they prize or cherish something they have said or done helps them to clarify their values. The response could, of course, be in a different form and have the same intent—for example, "Are you proud of that?" "Is that something that is very important to you?" "Is that idea very dear to you; do you really cherish it?" The particular situation in which the response is made, as well as the age of the child to whom it is directed, will help determine the precise wording.

2. Are you glad about that? This question encourages students to see whether things they feel, say, or do are things that they are happy about and make them feel good. A teacher could also ask if the students are unhappy about something. Such questions stimulate children to evaluate their lives and to consider changing if *they* are not satisfied. Note how different the effect of this response is from the scolding "Aren't you ashamed of that?" Clarifying responses are accepting and illuminating, not rejecting and moralizing.

3. How did you feel when that happened? This response helps people understand that their feelings are part of their understandings and awareness and that feelings should be considered in decision making. Children need to know that feelings are important, that we respect their right to have their own feelings, and that feelings do not have to be suppressed.

4. Did you consider any alternatives? Note how this question tends to widen, to open up the thinking of children (and adults). With this response, as with *all* the others in this list, teachers will need to accept whatever the student replies without judgment. After the question is answered, leave the student with an honest "Oh. Now I see," or "I understand," or "You stated your views clearly," or "I appreciate hearing what you say," or some nonjudgmental phrase or gesture.

5. Have you felt this way for a long time? Questions that get at the same ideas as this question are, "When did you first begin to believe in that idea?" and "How have your ideas or understandings changed since the time you first considered this notion?" Here people are pushed to examine the history of their beliefs or attitudes, to look at origins, and to see if the beliefs are the result of personal reflection or if they have been absorbed unthinkingly. Note how the next response might follow after a student replies to this one.

6. Was that something that you yourself selected or chose? This reminds people that they *can* make their own choices, if they want to do so. An affirmative reply to this response might well be followed by response 7.

7.   Did you have to choose that? Was it a free choice? Here, no matter what the student says, it is probably wise to say no more but to discontinue the conversation with some nonjudgmental closing.

8.   Do you do anything about that idea? This response helps people see the responsibility for incorporating choices into actual living. A verbalization that is not lived certainly has less import than one that is lived, and it would not be called a value according to our definition. Another way of saying the same thing: "How does that idea affect your daily life?" or "In what ways do you act upon it?"

9.   Can you give me some examples of that idea? This helps push generalizations and vague statements of belief toward clarity. Note also the relevance of the next response.

10.   What do you mean by_____? Can you define that word? This approach also pushes understanding to clarity and helps prevent the mouthing of words students cannot really mean because they do not really understand them.

11.   Where would that idea lead? What would be its consequences? This encourages the student to study carefully the consequences of ideas. No meaningful choice can be made unless the consequences of alternatives are understood. Therefore, it is often very useful to help children examine the consequences of each available alternative. Accordingly, a teacher could also ask, "What would be the results of each of the alternatives?" or "How would those ideas work out in practice?"

12.   Would you really do that or are you just talking? Again this question provides the encouragement to see the importance of living in accordance with one's choice.

13.   Are you saying that . . . [repeat]? It is sometimes useful merely to repeat what the student has just said. This has the effect of reflecting his ideas and prompting him to ask himself if he really meant that. It is surprising how many people seldom hear what they say. Sometimes the phrase "Did I hear you correctly?" can be used for this purpose.

14.   Did you say that . . . [repeat in some distorted way]? Sometimes a teacher does well to twist purposely what a student has said. Will the student attempt to correct the distortion? After trying it, you may sense that the effect is much the same as response 13.

15.   Have you thought much about that idea (or behavior)? Of course the teacher accepts whatever reply a student makes to this. It is destructive to the valuing process to attack a negative answer to this question with something like, "Well, in the future it would be wise to think before you speak (or act)." An accepting and nonjudgmental mood is vital for the valuing process.

16.   What are some good things about that notion? A simple request for justification of expressed ideas in some such nonjudgmental words often brings dramatic reevaluation of thinking on the part of students. Many people rarely realize that there could or should be good, desirable, worthwhile aspects of ideas they hold. The ideas are just there, unexamined and unevaluated.

17.   What do we have to assume for things to work out that way? Many persons have neglected to examine the assumptions upon which their ideas, aspirations, and activities rest. This probing helps persons understand better, make choices more wisely, and make valuing more possible. It is sometimes useful, in this context, to suggest an assumption that the student seems to be making and ask whether she or he has considered it—for example, "Are you assuming that there was *nothing* good about the depression?"

18.   Is what you express consistent with . . . [note something else the person said or did that may point to an inconsistency]? To present such a disconcerting challenge, to note an exception, to relate things with other things, can produce real clarification *if* it is not done with an "I think I have trapped you in an error" tone of voice. The idea is not to slap students down, but to open things up for them so that they can think with new insight, if they want to do so. Happily, teachers trying this approach seem to find that most students do want to do so.

19.   What other possibilities are there? This raises alternatives to students and thus it aids them in valuing. Sometimes this question is posed to a group and all alternatives are listed on the board, again without judgment. Of course, other students and the teacher, too, can say which alternative *they* prefer, but there is no judging a child because she chooses a different alternative. No teasing or otherwise deriding others' choices is tolerated or else there is no free choice.

20.   Is that a personal preference or do you think most people should believe that? To inquire whether a statement is intended as a personal preference or whether it is something that should be generally endorsed is one way of helping to distinguish an attitude or prejudice from a social principle. "Is this idea so good that everyone should go along with it?" is another way to get at this.

21. How can I help you do something about your idea? What seems to be the difficulty? These questions remind the student that *action* is a component of life and intentions are incomplete until acted upon. Sometimes such questions uncover suppressed feelings or misunderstandings. Obviously, they locate real or imagined obstacles, too. Also try: "Where are you stuck?" or "What is holding you up?" (But be prepared to offer help if it is requested.)

22. Is there a purpose behind this activity? Asking students what, if anything, they are trying to accomplish, where they are headed with ideas or activities, sometimes brings the realization to students—and for the first time—that they might really have purposes and goals and that they might relate their ongoing activities to those purposes and goals.

23. Is that very important to you? This gets students to consider more seriously what is and what is not important to them. It is also often useful to ask students to put several things in order of rank. Assigning priorities is a useful variation.

24. Do you do this often? "Is there any pattern to your life that incorporates this idea or activity?" one might inquire. The idea here is to help students see what is repeated in their lives and what is not and to leave them with the decision of whether or not to build a pattern.

25. Would you like to tell others about your idea? Inviting students to explain their ideas to the class or others provides two challenges. It tests to see whether they are committed to the beliefs strongly enough to affirm them in public. It also puts the student in the position of thinking through ideas well enough to explain them, and perhaps justify them, to others.

26. Do you have any reasons for saying (or doing) that? This question tests whether or not a choice has been made and to what extent that choice is based on understanding. DANGER: Avoid using this question to pull a student up short when he or she is obviously not thinking. If you want to tell a student that you believe he is not thinking, tell him so. But use the above question when you really want to have a student consider personal beliefs or actions.

Incidentally, when a student does (or says) something and the teacher inquires, "Sonny, why did you do that?" the student often hears "Sonny, now why in the world did you ever do something as foolish as that?" "Why" questions are usually to be avoided when attempting to help students clarify their values. "Why" questions tend to make students defensive, prodding them into making up reasons or excuses when they really have none in mind. Besides, the question "Why did you do that?" carries with it the assumption that the student *knows* why, and that is perhaps the reason she tends to concoct a reason when she has none. It is much more effective, for value-clarifying purposes, to ask "Do you *have* a reason?" and then sometimes follow up an affirmative reply with, "Would you mind telling me?"

27.   Would you do the same thing over again? This question helps students to evaluate things that they have done, to consider why they did them, and perhaps to affirm the wisdom of doing such things in the future. Do not use this question everytime someone does something that *you* do not like. That would be an example of not-so-subtle moralizing. Use the question when you want to stimulate thinking, and strive to keep it nonjudgmental.

28.   How do you know it's right? When a child makes a moral or ethical judgment about something by saying that a thing is right or lovely or good, it is useful to ask how he knows that that judgment is correct. Sometimes we ask how he was able to decide. Note this dialogue.

Teacher: "I see you're hard at work on that project, Jean."

Student: "It's not good to be lazy, you know."

Teacher: "How do you know it's not good?"

Student: "Everybody knows that. My parents always say it."

Teacher: (Walking away) "I see."

Thus may a teacher subtly and persistently suggest that a person might think about such matters as rightness, or beauty, or goodness if she wants to do so.

29.   Do you value that? Merely picking out something a student has said or done and asking "Is that something that you value?" helps to stimulate clarifying thinking. Perhaps such a question could have been added by Jean's teacher in the above dialogue, for example

Teacher: "I see. Is working something that you value then, Jean?"

Student: "Huh? I suppose so."

Teacher: "O.K., Jean. Thank you."

30.   Do you think people will always believe that? Or "Would Chinese peasants and African hunters also believe that?" Or "Did people long ago believe that?" Such questions are useful to suggest to a student that beliefs may be unknowingly influenced by a person's surroundings, by the social milieu. It helps students gauge the extent to which they may be conforming. See also response 5.

Refer to Chart 1 for examples of how some of the above clarifying responses and others are related to the seven components of the valuing process. Those seven criteria are helpful for thinking of other useful clarifying responses and for keeping in mind the ones above. All clarifying responses in one way or another encourage the student to choose, prize, or act in terms outlined by the value theory.

Chart 1   *Clarifying Responses Suggested by the Seven Valuing Processes*

1. Choosing freely
a. Where do you suppose you first got that idea?
b. How long have you felt that way?
c. What would people say if you weren't to do what you say you must do?
d. Are you getting help from anyone? Do you need more help? Can I help?
e. Are you the only one in your crowd who feels this way?
f. What do your parents want you to be?
g. Is there any rebellion in your choice?
h. How many years will you give to it? What will you do if you're not good enough?
i. Do you think the idea of having thousands of people cheering when you come out on the field has anything to do with your choice?

2. Choosing from alternatives
a. What else did you consider before you picked this?
b. How long did you look around before you decided?
c. Was it a hard decision? What went into the final decision? Who helped? Do you need any further help?
d. Did you consider another possible alternative?
e. Are there some reasons behind your choice?
f. What choices did you reject before you settled on your present idea or action?
g. What's really good about this choice which makes it stand out from the other possibilities?

3. Choosing thoughtfully and reflectively
a. What would be the consequences of each alternative available?
b. Have you thought about this very much? How did your thinking go?
c. Is this what I understand you to say . . . [interpret statement]?
d. Are you implying that . . . [distort statement to see if the student is clear enough to correct the distortion]?
e. What assumptions are involved in your choice? Let's examine them.
f. Define the terms you use. Give me an example of the kind of job you can get without a high-school diploma.
g. Now if you do this, what will happen to that . . . ?
h. Is what you say consistent with what you said earlier?
i. Just what is good about this choice?

Chart 1 *Continued*

j. Where will it lead?
k. For whom are you doing this?
l. With these other choices, rank them in order of significance.
m. What will you have to do? What are your first steps? Second steps?
n. Whom else did you talk to?
o. Have you really weighed it fully?

4. Prizing and cherishing
a. Are you glad you feel that way?
b. How long have you wanted it?
c. What good is it? What purpose does it serve? Why is it important to you?
d. Should everyone do it your way?
e. Is it something you really prize?
f. In what way would life be different without it?

5. Affirming
a. Would you tell the class the way you feel some time?
b. Would you be willing to sign a petition supporting that idea?
c. Are you saying that you believe . . . [repeat the idea]?
d. You don't mean to say that you believe . . . [repeat the idea]?
e. Should a person who believes the way you do speak out?
f. Do people know that you believe that way or that you do that thing?
g. Are you willing to stand up and be counted for that?

6. Acting upon choices
a. I hear what you are for; now, is there anything you can do about it? Can I help?
b. What are your first steps, second steps, etc.?
c. Are you willing to put some of your money behind this idea?
d. Have you examined the consequences of your act?
e. Are there any organizations set up for the same purposes? Will you join?
f. Have you done much reading on the topic? Who has influenced you?
g. Have you made any plans to do more than you already have done?
h. Would you want other people to know you feel this way? What if they disagree with you?
i. Where will this lead you? How far are you willing to go?
j. How has it already affected your life? How will it affect it in the future?

7. Repeating
a. Have you felt this way for some time?
b. Have you done anything already? Do you do this often?
c. What are your plans for doing more of it?
d. Should you get other people interested and involved?
e. Has it been worth the time and money?
f. Are there some other things you can do which are like it?
g. How long do you think you will continue?
h. What did you *not* do when you went to do that? Was that alright?

Chart 1 *Continued*

i.   How did you decide which had priority?
j.   Did you run into any difficulty?
k.   Will you do it again?

TOPICS FOR
CLARIFYING RESPONSES

Let us consider now what kinds of student expressions might fruitfully be followed by clarifying responses. We would not want to follow all student statements and behaviors with clarifying responses. They are not for teaching subject matter, for example. They are for promoting student thought of a particular kind, the kind we call *valuing*. But when should clarifying responses be used?

We have arrived at eight important categories having a relationship to values: goals or purposes, aspirations, attitudes, interests, feelings, beliefs or convictions, activities, and worries, problems or obstacles. We call these *value indicators,* and they are just that: they point out that the expression (a statement or an action) indicates something about values.

Of course, we save the precious word *value* itself only for those expressions which meet all seven of the valuing criteria outlined in previous chapters. Value indicators are expressions which are *headed* toward values, but they have not yet "arrived." They are, however, ideal matter for value-clarifying responses.

The teacher who would help students must learn to listen for the specific comments students make which are in the realm of value indicators. With just a little practice, most teachers can hear these indicators. After a while, they come at a teacher with red flags flying. Below are some charts showing several value indicators and some examples of the kinds of things students are apt to say which tell a teacher that conditions are ripe for a clarifying response.

No value indicator operates alone, but a teacher who listens for those comments from students that fall in the several categories and who then responds within the framework of the valuing methodology should do much to advance the clarification of values and, in turn, should witness significant behavioral changes. Students who had been listless and apathetic should become more purposeful and self-directed. Students who had been over-conforming should more often stand on their own two feet and come closer to discovering their own identity. So it will be with other students with value-related behavior problems. This is part of the reward for the teacher who begins to work in the area of value clarification.

On Attitudes

As seen in Chart 2 people express an attitude when they reveal what they are *for* and what they are *against*. Beliefs, opinions, and convictions are often similarly expressed. Such statements are ripe for a clarifying response.

Chart 2 *Value Indicators: Attitudes*

Statements students have made:

1. "If you let in too many immigrants, I believe it just makes it tough for everyone else."
2. "When I sold him my bike, I didn't feel I had to tell him *everything* that was wrong with it."
3. "I think we just have to overcompensate Negroes at this time, because they're so far behind."
4. "You wouldn't catch me playing with dolls."
5. "I don't see why we have to wait until we're eighteen to drive."

Typical keywords that signal the statement of attitudes:

I'm for . . . .
I'm against . . . .
I feel that . . . .
I think if . . . .
The way I see it . . . .
If you ask me . . . .
In my opinion . . . .
My choice is . . . .
My way of doing it is . . . .
I'm convinced that . . . .
I believe . . . .

It may be helpful for you to try to match up the expression of an attitude, such as those in Chart 2, with a reasonable clarifying response, such as one from the list of 30. Responses 10, 11, and 12, among others, are often suited to expressions of attitudes. You need not, of course, commit these lists to memory. After trial-and-error practice, you are likely to develop enough of a sense of the process to let you improvise freely.

One useful tool for teachers to work with in the area of attitudes is careful listening to what students say followed by a mental "plusing" and "minusing" of their statements. We count as a "plus" what they are *for* and "minus" what they say they are *against*. This is particularly easy to do in students' written work, but we will discuss that more later.

We have found that students are not always aware when they have revealed that they are for or against something. And sometimes our clarifying responses make them wonder if they *should* have those attitudes or perhaps if those attitudes are not inconsistent with other things they have said or done. We must be careful to avoid making our students feel they will lose face as these attitudes are exposed. It is important, terribly important, to maintain an accepting atmosphere and to say perhaps over and over again, and mean it, "All of us are inconsistent from time to time, and all of us tend to be confused about certain things that we are for and against. One of the things we hope to learn is how to think about our attitudes and clarify them."

On Feelings

Chart 3 contains some statements that suggest feelings or emotions in a student. Often we would want simply to listen carefully and empathetically to a student's feeling statement. That may be the best response at the moment. For some students, and for those who have special emotional needs especially, we might try to say something or do something that would be emotionally nourishing to the child: "I know it felt awful to lose that game. I hope you know that I don't think you're a loser at all. I like you very much."

But sometimes a teacher might want to try a clarifying response, especially for those students who give no indication of emotional disturbances: "I can see you hate that work. I wonder if we could think of another way to approach that job." Or "You seem to get real excited each time that comes up. Are you clear about what might be behind that excitement, how come that excites you so much?" Or "You want Johnny to quit it. Can I help you find a way to get that message to Johnny in a way that won't upset him further?" Or "Yes, it sure did make you feel guilty. I wonder if you often suffer guilt." Or "Good news, is it? Have you shared your good news with others?"

A teacher can respond to feeling statements in many ways. We are suggesting that one clarifying response be added to the teacher's repertoire of available responses.

Chart 3   *Value Indicators: Feelings*

Statements students have made:

1. "I'm bored."
2. "I hate this work."
3. "I'd be scared to do that myself."
4. "We got a beautiful puppy yesterday!"
5. "I sometimes think I'll never amount to anything."
6. "I wish Johnny would quit it."

Typical key words that signal a statement involving feelings:

I'd feel bad if . . . .
I got angry when . . . .
I heard good news about . . . .

Chart 3   *Continued*

I had a hard time when . . . .
Listen to what Sally did . . . .
I would like . . . .
I feel guilty when . . . .

On Aspirations

As seen in Chart 4, students express an aspiration when they reveal some long-range plan or goal. You can see how such statements invite a value clarifying response.

Sadly, without help from sensitive teachers, so many plans never can come to fruition. And when a series of hopes goes down the drain, it becomes difficult for a person to continue to aspire. From such disappointment grows listlessness, indifference, and apathy. One of the most important things we can do when we deal with aspirations is to bring some of the dreamers face to face with the necessary steps between the first dream and the final achievement, and we must introduce this greater reality without dampening those aspirations. Such tasks remind us that there are no right answers in clarifying. Such a realization cultivates in the clarifier a quiet humility.

Chart 4   *Value Indicators: Aspirations*

Statements students have made:

1. "Someday I'd like to join the Peace Corps."
2. "If only I were better in math, I'd try for engineering."
3. "My hope is someday to buy a summer home on a lake and to have my own boat."
4. "My dream is someday to run a little nursery school of my own."
5. "We want to have six kids, three boys and three girls, eighteen months apart."

Typical keywords that signal the statement of aspirations:

In the future . . . .
When I grow up . . . .
Someday, I'm going to . . . .
My long-range plan is . . . .
In about ten years I'm . . . .
If all goes well . . . .
One of these days . . . .

On Purposes

As seen in Chart 5, students express purpose when they reveal some short-range goal or hope. They require help in planning, sometimes in writing letters or making phone calls, in getting commitments from others occasionally, and almost always in getting some money (working for it, saving it, borrowing it). When students have plans, their excitement often spills over. Plans and goals give a much needed lift to life in general, and people with many plans (if they don't get frenetic) tend to be zestful and purposeful. The teacher can help students test the consequences of some coming adventure, can pose alternatives for what else might use this energy, time, and money, and can help the student see what else could grow from the coming event. These are legitimate clarifying efforts. Moralizing, preaching, and generating guilt are not.

Chart 5   *Value Indicators: Purposes*

Statements students have made:

1. "This weekend we're going to play."
2. "At the end of the month three of us fellows are going skiing."
3. "If I can find the right rear end from an old car, I'm going to make a trailer."
4. "I called my buddy and he's going to write for the appointment to see this man about the summer job."
5. "When I save up the twenty dollars, I'm going to buy that guitar."

Typical keywords that signal the statement of purposes:

We're thinking about doing . . . .
On the fifteenth, I'm going . . . .
On the way downtown we're . . . .
I wrote for the plans . . . .
When I get this . . . I'm going to do that . . .
We're waiting to hear from him . . . .
Boy! Will Saturday ever come?
I'd like to . . . .

On Interests

As seen in Chart 6, students express interest when they reveal some of the things they like to do in their spare time. Included in the realm of interests are those things which excite us, which occupy our minds and hands, and which cause us to spend time, money, and energy on them. Hobbies are the most obvious expressions of interests, but so too are our reading and what we go out of our way to see or experience, such as sporting or theatrical events.

One of the interesting side effects for a teacher when he or she begins to listen and really show an interest in something a student is excited about is that the teacher's own life can take on some added flavor, for students have many delightful and really creative pastimes. Not all of them are values, however, and this is one of the ways we can help students, by getting them to clarify which are those that are merely passing whims or thoughtless behaviors and which are headed well along the road to becoming values.

Chart 6   *Value Indicators: Interest*

Statements students have made:

1. "I read everything I can lay my hands on about nursing."
2. "I'd rather listen to Bach than almost anyone else."
3. "I'm saving up to subscribe to this photography magazine."
4. "I'm going to enter this glider in the contest."
5. "No, I won't be home Saturday. I'm going to the town drag strip."

Typical keywords that signal a statement about activities:

I love making [or doing] . . . .
My hobby is . . . .
Yes, I subscribe to . . . .
I really enjoy reading about . . . .
If I had my choice I'd take the ticket to . . . .
Most weekends I'm over at the . . . .
Every night after school I . . . .
Boy, nothing makes me feel better than . . . .
I got this catalogue on . . . .

On Activities

As seen in Chart 7, students express activity when they reveal how they use time. Actually, the activity category is a part of many of the other value indicators. When one has attitudes, often activities will follow, and so it is with aspirations, purposes, and interests. In short, what we *do* with our waking hours hints at what values we may have. As an ideal, we might strive to value everything we do and to do only what we value.

Merely to kill time might be a value for some people, but for most of us the measurement of how we survive the onslaught of time tells much about the values we hold.

It is common to mouth the right words but to do very little about them. We must come, more of us, to do more about what we value. A list of our activities tells us more about what we prize and cherish than does an eloquent statement of beliefs. As teachers we do well to hold up a mirror to our students, to help them reflect on what they do with each day's 86,400 seconds, and to help them clarify the issue of the use of time and energy.

To summarize a bit, a teacher learns to spot value indicators and to follow them up, at least part of the time, with clarifying responses—sometimes in brief one-legged conferences, sometimes in written comments in the margins of student papers, and in other ways to be discussed. Expressions, verbal or behavioral, that are value indicators include attitudes, aspirations, purposes, interests, activities, opinions, convictions, beliefs, feelings, appreciations, and worries. The general intent is clear: Find value indicators and help students use the valuing process to see if they want to raise them to the value level.

Chart 7   *Value Indicators: Activities*

Statements students have made:

1. "I took my dog for a long walk."
2. "I worked five hours Saturday waxing the car."
3. "Friday night we watched the late show and then the late-late show."
4. "These two fellows and I made a hut."
5. "I lay down to take a nap, but just slept right through the night."

Typical keywords that signal a statement about activities:

After school, I usually . . . .
Last weekend, we . . . .
On my day off, I went . . . .
One of the best things we did Halloween . . . .
. . . all yesterday afternoon
We just like to play . . . .

SOME EXAMPLES

In this section we will offer some additional examples which show how the clarification process operates. Several cautions should be reiterated first, however. For one thing, there is no set formula for clarifying. It is a very personal and individualized process, both in the ways clarifiers proceed and in the range of problems that come up for clarification. There is a danger in seeing clarifying incidents in print. The model response is not to be taken as the only way an incident could have been handled. There are easily a dozen variations on each theme, and all could readily be said to advance clarification.

Another danger occurs to us. Seeing the dialogue in print sometimes makes it seem bland or even silly. We ask you to accept the idea that these conversations are held, on the contrary, in dead earnestness. The person being "clarified" usually senses the power of this methodology and generally does not fritter away an opportunity to get clear on something related to his or her values. In other words, the dialogues are not as moving in print as in person.

Finally, we might remind the reader that the examples we cite do not stand alone. Clarifying is not a one-shot business. Each incident may stand by itself, but the sensitive teacher is constantly looking for other incidents, and especially if a teacher uses some of the techniques noted in the following chapters, there will be more incidents than can ever be used.

Let us look at this dialogue,

Teacher: You were late again today. Do you like coming to school late?

Student: Well, no.

Teacher: How long have you been coming to school late?

Student: Quite a while. I guess most of the time since I've been coming to school.

Teacher: How do you feel about being tardy?

Student: Well, I feel funny about it sometimes.

Teacher: What do you mean by "funny?"

Student: Well, that I'm different from other kids. I feel embarrassed.

Teacher: As I get it, you feel uncomfortable about being late.

Student: That's right.

Teacher: What can I do to help you get here on time?

Student: Well, my mother usually calls me in the morning—but sometimes she oversleeps.

Teacher: Do you have an alarm clock?

Student: No.

Teacher: Could you get one? I could help you get one if that is what you think you need.

Student: It would be kind of fun. I'll try to get one.

Later in the semester, this student's mother said: "What have you and my son been talking about? He is getting to school on time and he hustles around to get ready. When I asked him what had been happening, he said, "Oh, my teacher and I have been talking."[1]

John

Here is dialogue which grew out of a classroom discussion in a high-school social studies class.

1. James Raths, "Clarifying Children's Values," *National Elementary Principal,* November, 1962, pp. 37—38.

John: If you let in too many immigrants it just makes it tough for everyone else.

Teacher: Tough in what way, John?

Here great courage was needed on the part of the teacher not to leap in with the usual chestnuts, such as "Was not your grandfather once an immigrant?" or "Don't you know that this country was founded by immigrants, that George Washington was an immigrant." and so on. The sum effect of that kind of question would have been to make John wish he had not brought up the topic. This is a most important point; every effort must be made to cull out of our questions those which moralize, get preachy, or back a student against a wall so that what appears to be a question is in reality a statement. Too often a question is asked in a way that tells us that only one right answer is acceptable. For example, "Don't you think . . . ?" or "Wouldn't you agree . . . ?" or "Is it not true that our ancestors were all immigrants?" Instead, this teacher has asked a real clarifying question, "Tough in what way?" It is a clarifying question for several reasons:

1. It keeps open the invitation for dialogue.

2. It talks to the real concern, which is probably more closely related to some problem about money than it is to immigration.

3. It works at making things clearer.

Back to our dialogue.

John: Well, they work so much cheaper that a decent American can't get a job.

Teacher: Can you give me an example of that happening, John?

John: Well, I went to this supermarket which had an advertisement, but this kid with an accent got there first.

Teacher: And he was willing to work cheaper?

John: Well, I don't know that for sure.

Again, the teacher resists the temptation to make John feel like a naughty boy, for she knows that would not advance clarification. Instead she offers a clarifying question.

Teacher: What did you feel when you found out that you didn't get the job?

John: Boy I was mad.

Teacher: Would you have been mad say if Pete over there had gotten the job?

John: I guess I would have been just mad at anybody, because I really
            need that job.

Teacher: Have you tried any of the other markets? Maybe we could
            make a list of them together and you could check them out one
            at a time.

Teacher makes a mental note: Why does John want that job after school?
Is he going to buy a car? Does he have one already and must work for it? Big
dance coming up? Saving for college? Perhaps explore these in some future
clarifying contacts; for money, what we spend it on, and what we don't
spend it on, becomes one important indicator of values.

What about the prejudicial statement about immigrants which John made
and which started off this dialogue? Can a teacher, in good conscience,
ignore such poor critical thinking? One answer is that a frontal attack is not
always the most effective. The teacher in this dialogue worked under the
assumption that the statement about immigrants, although obviously not
entirely innocent, was triggered more by John's frustration over not getting
the job he needed. At another time, in another context, the teacher may well
pursue the prejudice expressed.

Clara

Here is another example, this time based on expression of an aspiration.

Clara: Some day I'd like to join the Peace Corps.

Teacher: What are some good things about that, Clara?

Clara: Oh, the chance to be of service excites me and going to
            faraway places does too.

Teacher: Of those two, which would you put in first place?

Clara: I guess the faraway places part.

Teacher: Are you glad that that one is first?

Clara: No, I guess people would respect me more if the service part
            was first.

Now, the teacher has some interesting alternatives at this point. Which of
the following should he pursue?

1.   The area of how important it is for Clara to feel respected.

2.   The area of what services she has performed and might perform right
now.

3.   The area of what other possibilities does she have for getting to
faraway places?

4. The teacher also has the possibility of not going forward at all and saying, "Well, it's been interesting talking with you Clara, but I must get back to my papers. Perhaps we can talk about it another time."

In the transcript of the incident above, the teacher did end the clarifying discussion. When questioned, the teacher said that he felt that Clara had been a bit embarrassed when she realized what she had been doing and was anxious to terminate the conversation herself. The teacher's sensitivity must always be alert.

Other directions this discussion could have taken might have been equally as productive. You might want to look back at the list of clarifying responses and think about which of those might have reasonably followed Clara's opening statement.

A teacher may wonder when these conversations take place and where they are held. One obvious place is after school or between lessons. Other conversations occur in the morning before school, or in line in the cafeteria, or before class starts, or even when a teacher sees students downtown. Often they grow right out of the subject matter during class, as did the incident about immigration mentioned above.

More such dialogues would occur, we feel, if teachers cared more about them and went out of their way to hold them. Students seem to welcome them. Certain teachers have already established such rapport with students that they can talk often and easily with them. We advocate that such talks more often focus upon values via the clarification process. For example, a young teacher was walking down the hall and overheard this snatch of conversation:

Jerry: When I save up the twenty dollars, I'm going to buy that guitar.

The teacher heard the expressed purpose, turned and said that she overheard the comment.

Teacher: Can you play a guitar, Jerry?

Jerry: A little, but I'm going to really learn when I get my own.

Teacher: Is playing the guitar important to you, Jerry?

Jerry: Yes, very.

Teacher: What are the possibilities for making the twenty dollars?

Jerry: Not too good right now, I'm afraid.

Teacher: Any chance of cutting down on what you now spend and saving it?

Jerry: You mean giving up smoking?

Teacher: That's one alternative.

Joe: (Jerry's friend): Or staying out of the bowling alley for three weeks.

Teacher: Well, good luck to you, Jerry. See you later.

The school day is really full of opportunities for these "one-legged conferences," for they are not interviews and not therapy. (We do *not* recommend the brief clarifying response for the solution of emotional problems.) The clarification methodology is concerned only with values and as such it seems to be a process well within the boundaries of teachers' work.

Sometimes a student will view a clarifying response to something he has said or done as an intrusion.

Teacher: I see, Vic, that you are still hard at work on that map. Is that something that you are very happy to do?

Victor: (No clear response. Appears to want to avoid a conversation. Continues to work at map.)

Teacher: Just thought I'd ask. See you later, Vic.

This example shows what often happens with clarifying: sometimes some children just do not seem to want to respond and the teacher, ever respectful and permissive about the clarifying process, attempts to let the student off the hook without any embarrassment or pressure. A clarifying teacher encourages the valuing process but does not insist upon it. In fact, teachers should be pleased whenever a student shows that she knows she is respected enough to be able to say to a teacher, "I'd rather not talk about it." The wise teacher walks off with something like a "Well, bring it up again someday if you would like," knowing that at least the child has passed the point of total acquiescence.

Must the teacher be neutral in all situations? Although when we deal with values, we emphasize the need for a nonjudgmental approach, for acceptance, for students to arrive at their *own* ideas on the basis of their *own* critical thinking and evaluation, we do not mean to suggest that the teacher must remain neutral. The teacher may well take a clear position on a value-related issue. After all, we ask students to take positions, so it would only be fair for the teacher to do so. Besides, students often can make good use of the teacher's ideas and information. The trick is for the teacher to share his or her thinking *without* short-circuiting student thinking. The aim should be to have the students consider the teacher's wisdom as they think for themselves and not to adopt the teacher's words as a substitute for independent thought. Some teachers accomplish this by voicing a judgment and then saying, "But others have different positions" or, "But I didn't always think this and I may yet change my opinion again."

The following conversation is an example.

Teacher: June, it seems to me that you very seldom talk in class discussions. Does it seem that way to you? (In this case, the teacher was picking up on something that a student did, or failed to do, and working at clarifying it.)

June: Yeah. I suppose so.

Teacher: Is that a pattern in your behavior? I mean are you pretty quiet in other groups and outside of school?

June: Well, maybe. Yes, usually.

Teacher: It seems to me that it would be more fun participating and getting your ideas into the group, and I would like to see you do that; but I guess there is nothing wrong with not participating if you don't want to. Have you thought about this?

June: Well, no, not much I guess.

Teacher: Well, I won't interrupt your studying any longer, June. You can get back to your work.

In this exchange, the teacher clearly stated her position—it seemed to her that more participation was desirable—but also left open the possibility that others could disagree. Hopefully, the teacher did not leave the student with the feeling that there was a "right" way to behave, but rather left the student with a bit of food for thought. We would hope that June reflected somewhat like this: "Now, I usually am quiet aren't I? I wonder why. Should I push myself to talk up and participate? Would Ms. Nelson want me to? I guess she would accept me either way. But what do *I* want?"

If this teacher did not maintain an open and accepting atmosphere and if the students were not accustomed to hearing the teacher's opinions and knowing that those were only some of many possible opinions, it might have been better for the teacher to omit the statement of her position in the above exchange. The conversation could have been exactly the same, except that the sentence preceding "Have you thought about this?" would be omitted.

It seems to us very desirable that a teacher's ideas, feelings, and opinions are made known to students. This demonstrates that any person can talk openly about such things. And this provides mature alternatives for students to consider when making up their own minds. But if the teacher cannot do this without fear that students will copy those ideas, feelings, or opinions unthinkingly, their expression might better be held back until students have at least begun their own value-clarifying thinking. To accomplish this, sometimes we will tell a group, "Let's hear your thoughts now. Later I'll tell you what I think about all this."

Incidentally, we believe it is usually unwise for a teacher to appear neutral when in fact he or she is not neutral. When we decide to withhold our position, for whatever reason, we prefer to announce candidly that we are doing that and, whenever possible, to give our reasons for doing so. "I'd rather not talk about my thoughts today," a teacher might say, "Somehow I'd feel more comfortable keeping them to myself." This, incidentally, is a good reminder to students that they too may always choose to keep their thoughts to themselves.

QUESTIONS, QUESTIONS

Students are accustomed to having teachers ask questions. The standard recitation lesson is basically a question-and-answer process. In value-related areas, many teachers also use questions to guide student behavior and thinking—for example,

- Johnny, didn't I tell you to be quiet?

- Don't you think it would be a good idea to wash your hands before lunch?

- Why do you tease the girls? When are you going to stop? Do I have to punish you again?

- Don't you think it would be good for you to get higher grades?

- You know that the way you're going you'll never get into college, don't you?

However, these questions have very little to do with the clarifying approach we are discussing. A clarifying response respects the right of the individual to make decisions; the above questions seem to us not questions at all but statements of the teacher's decisions. We would guess that they are not likely to trigger a clarification process.

Because of this common practice in questioning (not limited to teachers), because many students expect that when a teacher asks them a question it is really a concealed directive, it is wise to begin to use clarifying questions at times when the student knows that you are *not* disapproving of what he or she is saying or doing.

Do not begin the use of clarifying responses by saying "Have you thought of any alternatives to what you are doing?" after a student hits another student. Such a question will most likely be interpreted as a rebuke. When you must control a situation or inform students of behavior limits, we prefer clear statements to leading questions: "Stop that, Harry," rather than "Harry, do you enjoy doing that?" After all, a teacher has more responsibilities than clarifying values. We would prefer that clarifying strategies not be confused with strategies more appropriate to instruction or to the administration of classrooms. If they *do* get confused, we fear that comments designed to stimulate students' thought about values will be interpreted by students as directives in disguise: "Wonder what point teacher is *really* trying to make?"

When you first try clarifying responses, use them after a student has helped another student, worked hard to pass a test, volunteered to do extra work, or done something else he or she knows that you are not likely to disapprove of. The point here is that it is wise to begin using clarifying responses only in situations that will prevent students from equating those responses with criticism or rebuke. The simplest way to do this is to use clarifying responses, in the beginning, in situations of which you either approve or have no preferences.

Incidentally, after students become familiar with the clarifying responses, they will begin to use them on one another and on other friends, and that is a delightful development. Somehow, people like to have genuine clarifying responses directed to them. It does not threaten, and they know it helps clarify ideas and feelings.

IN CONCLUSION

Basic to the approach to values offered in this book is the clarifying response. The clarifying response is usually aimed at one student at a time, often through brief, informal conversations held in class, in hallways, on the playground, or any place else where the teacher comes in contact with a student who does or says something to trigger such a response. Clarifying responses are also used during whole-class discussions and as comments written in the margins of students' papers.

Especially ripe for clarifying responses are such things as expressions of students' feelings, beliefs, convictions, worries, attitudes, aspirations, purposes, interests, problems, and activities. These sometimes indicate a value or a potential value and thus we refer to them as *value indicators*. A teacher who is sensitive to these expressions finds many occasions for useful clarifying responses.

The purpose of the clarifying response is to raise questions in the students' minds, to prod them gently to examine their lives, their actions, and their ideas, with the expectation that some will want to use this prodding as an opportunity to clarify their understandings, purposes, feelings, aspirations, attitudes, beliefs, and so on.

Participating in such exchanges, some students may choose the thoughtful consistency between words and deeds that characterizes values. But not everything need be a value. Beliefs, problems, attitudes, and all the rest are parts of life too.

It may be useful to list some things that a clarifying response is *not*.

1. Clarifying is not therapy.

2. Clarifying is not used on students with serious emotional problems.

3. Clarifying is not a single one-shot effort, but depends on a program consistently applied over a period of time.

4. Clarifying avoids moralizing, preaching, indoctrinating, inculcating, or dogmatizing.

5. Clarifying is not an interview, nor is it meant to be done in a formal or mechanical manner.

6. Clarifying is not meant to replace the teacher's other educational functions.

If clarifying is none of the above, what is it? It is an honest attempt to help students look at their lives and to encourage them to think about life, and to think about it in an atmosphere in which positive acceptance exists. No eyebrows are raised. When a student reveals something before the whole class, he or she must be protected from snickers from other class members. It is essential to maintain an environment where searching is highly regarded.

We emphasize that students will probably not enter the perplexing process of clarifying values for themselves if they perceive that the teacher does not respect them. If trust is not communicated—and the senses of students for such matters can be mystifyingly keen—students may well play the game, pretending to clarify and think and choose and prize, while being as unaffected as by a tiresome morality lecture. This is a difficult and important problem, for it is not easy to be certain you are communicating trust, whether or not you believe you are doing so. (A moot point is whether some people can communicate a trust that they, in fact, do not have.) One must be chary about concluding that a teacher who says the right words is getting the results desired. There is a spirit, a mood, required that we cannot satisfactorily describe or measure except to say that it seems related to a basic and honest respect for students. It may be fair to say that a teacher who does not communicate this quality will probably obtain only partial results.

For many teachers a mild revolution in their classroom methodology will be demanded if they are to do very much with the clarification of values. For one thing, they will have to do much less talking and listen that much more, and they will have to ask different kinds of questions from the ones they have asked in past years. Teachers usually favor questions that have answers that can be scaled from "right" to "wrong." No such scoring can be applied to answers to clarifying questions.

The rewards for giving up the old patterns may not come right away, but there is mounting evidence that teachers who act responsively begin to have small miracles happening in their classrooms. They often see attendance go up, grades rise, and interest and excitement in learning crackle. They witness students who had been classified as apathetic, listless, and indifferent begin to change. In the words of one teacher, "students get their heads off their elbows and use those elbows to wave hands in the air."

In brief, one might see the clarifying response fitting into the value-clarifying method in the following way.

1. First, look and listen for value indicators, statements or actions which suggest that there could be a value issue involved.

It is usually wise to pay special attention to students who seem to have particularly unclear values. Note especially children who seem to be very apathetic or indecisive, who seem to be very flighty, or who drift from here to there without much reason. Note, also, children who overconform, who are very inconsistent, or who play-act much of the time.

2. Secondly, keep in mind the goal: children who have clear, personal values. The goal therefore requires opportunities for children to use the processes of (a) choosing freely, (b) choosing from alternatives, (c) choosing thoughtfully, (d) prizing and cherishing, (e) affirming, (f) acting upon choices, and (g) examining patterns of living. We provide these opportunities with the expectation that the results of these processes are better understandings of what a person stands for and believes in and more intelligent living.

3. Thirdly, respond to a value indicator with a clarifying question or comment. This response is designed to help the student use one or more of the seven valuing processes listed above. For example, if you guess that a child does not give much consideration to what is important to *him,* you might try a clarifying response that gets at prizing and cherishing. Or the form of the value indicator may suggest the form of the clarifying response. For example, a thoughtless choice suggests responses that get at choosing, and a fine-sounding verbalization suggests responses that get at incorporating choices into behavior.

The rest of the chapters in part three provide additional techniques that teachers can use to get students involved in value-related discussions, thinking, and activities. Each of these, of course, provides threads for a teacher to use in helping children clarify values.

6

A Writing Strategy

The clarifying response technique presented in the last chapter is used to help one student think more clearly and independently about something he or she has said or done. Other students may well overhear the exchange and profit indirectly—as they learn to use the valuing process themselves and as they hear talk about an issue that may also be relevant to their lives—but the clarifying response is essentially a strategy focused on the individual. The strategy presented in this chapter, the value sheet, focuses on group discussion.

THE VALUE SHEET

There are many things in our complex world that are worth getting clearer about,[1] and the value sheet is one strategy for bringing some of these to the attention of students in a nonthreatening and stimulating way. This is consistent with our value theory because each student is faced with the issue and its alternatives. Each person is encouraged to make an intelligent choice freely and thoughtfully and to act in ways consistent with that choice.

A value sheet in its simplest form consists of a provocative statement and a series of questions, which are duplicated on a sheet of paper and distributed to class members. The purpose of the provocative statement is to raise an issue that the teacher thinks may have value implication for students. The purpose of the questions is to carry each student through the value-clarifying process with that issue. Since valuing is an individual matter, each student completes a personal value sheet, preferably by writing answers on a separate sheet of paper. Later, that writing may be shared with other students or the teacher or it may be used as a basis for large- or small-group discussions.

Examples of Value Sheets

Value sheets can also be used as programmed instructional material But perhaps some examples will help make this clearer.

1. The question of finding topics for the valuing process is further discussed in Chapter 11.

Value Sheet 1

THE MEDITATION ROOM AT THE U.N.

Directions: Please answer as many of the questions below as you wish, but answer them thoughtfully and honestly. I will collect the papers at the end of the study period and return them to you with occasional comments later in the week. This is an optional assignment and has no effect on grades, of course.

There is a chapel or meditation room at the U.N. General Assembly building in New York that has had all symbols of particular religions removed. There is nothing there but some rows of chairs, a potted plant, and a shaft of light. Marya Mannes writes of this room:

> "It seemed to me standing there that this nothingness was so oppressive and disturbing that it became a sort of madness, and the room a sort of padded cell. It seemed to me that the core of our greatest contemporary trouble lay here, that all this whiteness and shapelessness and weakness was the leukemia of noncommitment, sapping our strength. We had found, finally, that only nothing could please all, and we were trying to make the greatest of all generalities out of that most singular truth, the spirit of man. The terrifying thing about this room was that it made no statement whatever. In its capacity and constriction, it could not even act as a reflector of thought.

1. Write your reaction to this quotation in just a few words.

2. What emotions does it produce?

3. Are there some reasons for believing that Mannes' quotation is "antireligious"? If not, why? If yes, in which ways?

4. In your mind, does Mannes, in the quotation above, exaggerate the danger which she sees? Explain.

5. Can you list some more examples in our society which tend to support Mannes' point?

6. Can you list any which tend to refute her point of view?

7. If this quotation suggests a problem which worries you, are there some things you might personally do about it? Within yourself? With some close friends? With the larger society?

8. Is there any wisdom from the past which you can cite to ease Mannes' concern? Is there any wisdom from the past which might alarm her even more?

9. What do you get aroused about? Are you doing anything about it?

* From M. Mannes, "Meditations in an Empty Room," *The Reporter,* February 23, 1956; republished in M. Ascoli, (ed.), *Our Times: The Best From The Reporter Magazine* (New York: Farrar, Straus & Giroux, Inc., 1960).

The second value sheet has directions that indicate that it is to be completed in a study period. This is only one of several ways it could be used, of course. Value sheets are suitable for homework assignments and for individual class work, for example. The important consideration in the use of value sheets is that each student has an opportunity to grapple with the questions *before* getting involved in any discussion that might tempt him to avoid thinking for himself and listen passively to others. Once each student has done some independent judging and thinking, a discussion is often useful. In any case, the directions given for the value sheets in this chapter are meant to be merely suggestive. Value sheets are used differently by different teachers.

The second example is a controversial one. It confronts the student with something that can be highly charged. Perhaps because of this, many students have found that this sheet provides a rich educational experience.

It would be useful for you to count the number of times the questions on this sheet use the words "you" or "your." "You" questions are the hallmark of an effective value sheet.

There was an effort in the sheet, as in all value lessons, to allow for the fullest range of opinions, to avoid loading the dice in favor of any one point of view. There is no position taken by the teacher, although we hope each teacher does indeed know where she or he stands on this issue. When a teacher is seriously concerned with the clarification of values, she does not moralize, preach, indoctrinate, or inculcate. She must rely upon the informed and considered thought of students, while feeling free, of course, to confront students with alternatives not yet recognized and consequences not yet considered.

Question 7 on Value Sheet 1 deserves particular attention. In many sheets, we strive to move students toward the recognition that there is a large gap between most of our words and our deeds. If values are to be part of who we are, then we must constantly strive to close that gap. We need to do what we value. We need to value what we do.

Question 8 on that same sheet recognizes the subject matter responsibilities each of us as teachers have, and question 9 simply and directly asks, "What do *you* get aroused about?" It is frightening to realize how few things most of us do indeed care deeply about. We believe students need to examine such a position, and the next sheet illustrates that point further.

Value Sheet 2

ILLEGAL BEHAVIOR

Directions: Write out answers to the questions below. Later, you will have a chance to discuss your answers with a small group of students. You need not reveal your answers to anyone if you choose not to do so.

New Rochelle, N.Y., Oct. 27*—When the red light turns to green and reads "Thank you" at any one of the automatic toll booths of the New England Thruway here, it does not always mean what it says. At least not if the motorist has short-changed the machine or dropped lead washers or foreign coins into it.

The state police reported today after a two-week campaign against toll cheaters that they had arrested 151 persons. They have been fined in City Court from $25 each for first offenders to $250 for multiple offenders.

Lieut. Thomas F. Darby reported that the offenders included a clergyman, a doctor, a dentist, an atomic scientist, lawyers and quite a number of engineers, advertising men, and salesmen.

What the offenders did not know, the lieutenant said, was that new toll-booth glass with one-way vision prevented them from seeing watchful troopers inside.

Neither did they know, the lieutenant continued, that the license plate of each offender was recorded, along with the objects he dropped into the machine.

1. Under what circumstances would *you* try to pass a toll machine without properly paying the fee? Check the most applicable reply below.

_____Only if I was certain that I would not be caught.

_____If I felt I had a good chance of not getting caught.

_____Never, under any circumstances.

_____Only if I needed the money desperately, like for family food supplies.

_____Write any other choice that better suits you:

2. Among the 151 persons arrested, there was only one clergyman, doctor, dentist, and atomic scientist. On the other hand, there were several lawyers, engineers, advertising men, and salesmen. Do you think this means that persons in the first group of occupations are more honest than those in the second group? Discuss.

3. Do you think this behavior is serious? Do you think these persons are likely to be dishonest in other ways that would be more serious? Discuss.

4. Return to Question 1 and put an X by the reply that you would make to this: Under what circumstances would you keep a dime that was returned in error in a phone booth?

5. How do you account for any differences in your answers to Questions 1 and 4, if any?

6. Are you clear about how you feel about illegal behavior? Discuss.

* Date line "New Rochelle," *The New York Times,* October 28, 1961. ©1961 by The New York Times Company. Reprinted by permission.

Value Sheet 2, appropriate for young and old students, shows how a little news item can be tied into a general theme, in this case illegal behavior. Note how the sequence of questions leads the student into the theme gently but interestingly.

Question 1 gets the student to take a position, often a useful clarifying tactic. Question 2 calls for a bit of critical thinking and takes the heat off the student for a moment. Question 3 is similarly impersonal and calls for thinking about some of the consequences and correlates of slug passing. Question 4 and 5 bring the issue back home, often dramatically, and point up possible inconsistencies in a person's stance. Noting inconsistencies is another important clarifying tactic and is especially useful before posing the jackpot question, number 6.

This sheet has directions that lead from individual thinking to small-group deliberations, but other directions could be used, of course.

Value Sheet 3

LEISURE

Directions: Please respond in writing to the questions below and turn your work in on Monday. I will pick a few of the responses to read to the class, anonymously, and we may have time for an open discussion of a few of the questions after our other lessons.

The cartoonist, Osborn, has said:

If we are to have any Leisure—we must set limits to our efforts and to do this requires some truly adult decisions and no fudging or blurring of the outlines!

How much *lawn* are we going to *mow?* If we choose too little, we have lots of Leisure, but a vapid face. If we choose too much we become tired, irritable, dislocated, insensate.*

1. Just what is Osborn saying? What is this "lawn" he mows?

2. Can you expand on your own observations of "vapid faces"? What are some of the things people with vapid faces *do*?

3. What does Osborn say to *you*, personally?

4. Are you in basic agreement with him? In what ways would you change what he says so that it more nearly describes what *you* actually believe (or value) in this area?

5. Well, what do you actually DO about changing the way you operate in the realm of this problem? How do you begin? What do you do first? Second? Third? When do you start? What are some things you can do over the next three months? Six months? Next year? Today?

6. What about your own lawn? Do you seem to be mowing too little? How do you measure if you're mowing too much? In what ways can you cut down? In what ways can you mow more? How do you decide? (Please tell us later if you make any changes in your life on the basis of this sheet.)

* From R. Osborn, *On Leisure* (New York: The Ridge Press, Inc., 1956), p. 58.

The sources for value sheets are varied and, in a sense, endless. Teachers who use them tend to read with scissors in hand. Value Sheet 3 came from a cartoon book which was distributed to doctors by one of the large pharmaceutical firms. However, it discusses a problem of concern to people other than members of the medical profession. Each teacher will discover just which sources of ideas are most effective for his or her approach and for particular children.

Ideas that lend themselves to value sheets are those that directly or indirectly touch the lives of the students. Some topics touch students mainly in their current stage of growth, such as bicycle safety and cheating on tests, and these are *less* significant than topics that will face students throughout their lives, such as carefulness in general and honor in general.

Value Sheet 3 deals with the question of the worthy use of leisure time and, as such, is a question which persists throughout life. It also reflects well our activities and thus gets at a useful value indicator.

SUBJECT MATTER AND VALUE SHEETS

It may be apparent by now that there is a viable connection between value sheets and the standard subject matter of the schools. Of course, we believe that there is good reason for having "pure" value lessons—that is, lessons that stand all by themselves. We know that boys and girls need to have time and help to think through certain issues in life, and that they enjoy and seem to profit from such thought. Consequently, we believe a teacher would be wise to use value sheets just for the sake of value clarity. But we have also found that they provide an exciting and provocative *introduction and motivation* for typical subject-matter lessons.

Look at the sheet on the Meditation Room at the U.N. (Value Sheet 1). That sheet could lead to units in social studies on the great religions of the world, on prejudice, on the history of religious tolerance, or on the United Nations, for example. In mathematics, the teacher might use such a value sheet to lead, via the arcs and lines found in classical church designs, to a unit on geometry. The alert English teacher could tie such a sheet to units on symbolism, religious poems, modern fiction, journalistic objectivity, and so on. Other teachers might well find other ways to use that sheet to carry over student enthusiasm and involvement to a subject-matter unit.

The following areas for value sheets to be introduced occur to us:

- *Social studies.* Exploration. Westward expansion. Invention and discovery. Immigration. Geography. National banking system. Big business and big government. Public utilities.

- *Mathematics.* Division. Graphs. Percentage. Extrapolation. Analysis of data. Large numbers. Place value of numbers.

- *Science.* Space Astronomy. Disease. Nature of research. Newton's laws. Nutrition.

- *Reading and English.* Add new words to vocabulary lists and spelling lists. Find grammar errors or examples of certain usage forms. Use to motivate stories dealing with travel, money, exploration, science fiction, etc. Require that written responses to questions use topic sentences, gerunds, the semicolon, colorful verbs, etc. Have the passage read for speed and then for detail.

- *Foreign language.* Translate the opening passage into the foreign language. Translate the questions into the foreign language. Respond to the questions both in English and in the foreign language. Have the students respond in English, but have the value sheet written in whole or in part in the foreign language.

As a value sheet can lead into a subject-matter unit, so can it *culminate* such a unit. A number of teachers have given out value sheets as the last assignment in each unit, to help students go beyond the information to the values concerned. The examples above would be generally suited to that approach.

Finally, value sheets can be *incorporated* into the middle of subject-matter lessons. They can be used merely as interesting interludes in the unit. Or they can be an integral part of the subject matter itself.

For example, an arithmetic unit on weights and measures used a value sheet on deceptive packaging. In this case, the teacher did not begin the sheet with some dramatic opening, but wrote a few sentences saying that such practices do exist. Then the sheet asked questions that probed the students' thinking about such packaging (and deceptions in their own lives) and had students calculate weights and sizes from sample boxes and cans, seeking examples of packaging that might be called deceptive.

A social studies teacher made up her own value sheet during a unit that, in part, dealt with the Chinese Exclusion Acts. The teacher wrote out a few questions to stimulate students' thinking about exclusion, for the nation and for themselves, then went on with the history lesson.

For reading, English, literature, and foreign language teachers, the value sheet is a natural teaching device. For reading, there are few things more stimulating for reluctant readers than value sheets. Most slow readers show new interest when so confronted. For English, value sheets provide a neat and exciting way to present vocabulary and grammar illustrations and practice. For foreign language classes, motivation and learning can be increased immeasurably when what the students read in the foreign language is, in whole or in part, a value sheet, and/or what writing practice there is comes in response to value questions.

Literature and reading lessons are bursting with value possibilities. Note, for instance, how Value Sheet 4 presents literature and then connects it to the lives of the children. Perhaps this is the richest use of literature—to help the readers better understand themselves and their relationships to their world. Since this is the purpose of value sheets, they are well suited for use with reading and literature lessons.

Value Sheet 4
WORKSHEET:
"SILAS MARNER" BY GEORGE ELIOT*

Instructions: Read chapters V through VIII for Monday, March 2. Write out answers to the following questions, ready to be turned in and/or discussed in class.

Chapter V
1. What is the focus of the narrative in this novel?

Chapter VI
1. What is the function of this chapter? How is it different from other chapters?

2. Briefly characterize the major people you meet at the Rainbow.

3. Do you know any people who are similar to those at the Rainbow? Discuss briefly.

4. Consider the topics of conversation at the Rainbow. Do those topics persist to this day with the people you know? How much of your discussions involve those topics?

5. How would you define *gossip?* Why do you think we gossip?

6. How much time do you spend in gossip in an average week?

7. What are some alternative ways of spending this time?

8. Compare the consequences of time spent in gossip to the consequences of time spent at the alternative you listed and make some judgment as to which consequences you would want for yourself.

Chapter VII

1. What reasons can you think of for the people being glad that the "reality of ghosts remained still an open question"?

2. Any implications in question 1 for your thinking and your life?

3. Some people say that Macey and the farrier do not remain true to their character in questioning Silas on page 652. Discuss the assertion.

Chapter VIII

1. Consider Godfrey's statement about Dunstan, "He'll never be hurt—he's made to hurt others." Do you know of a person who could never be hurt? Is it possible to be that way, do you think?

2. Do people ever consciously hurt you? Can you explain this?

3. Do people ever unconsciously hurt you? Can you explain this?

4. Can you think of something you can do to help persons understand what they are doing when they are hurting you and how they might cease this kind of behavior?

5. Will you do it? (Please let me know if and when you do such a thing and how it works out. Write me a brief note.)

* From Joyce Cox, Connetquot High School, Long Island, N.Y.

Often when the class is all reading the same story or textbook, there is no need to write out an opening passage. Merely refer to it at the top of the sheet and then list the questions, as in Value Sheet 4.

Note also how "subject-matter" questions and "value" questions are interspersed. Teachers are responsible for teaching both of these, and each type of learning reinforces the other. Children cannot develop clear and workable values without some understanding of alternatives and the consequences of each alternative; providing this understanding is the responsibility of the teacher. But children can make little real use of their understanding until it is given some personal meaning for actual living, and that is the role of the valuing process, which teachers also must nourish. Both are indispensable for an educated person.

You may infer that we do not believe that the learning of understanding has to precede the valuing process. We feel that they usually *both* proceed best when they proceed together. Valuing is superficial without understanding. Understanding is superficial without valuing. And neither can wait until the other is accomplished. Thus we reject the position that says that children should learn their subject matter first and do their valuing later. Knowledge not turned into values has a short half-life in memory and can be almost as easily used destructively as constructively (witness the informed Germans of World War II and the educated social irresponsibility reflected in our own newspapers today). Thus we recommend that teachers consider moving valuing right along as a part—a vital and exciting part—of the learning process. Besides, unless children learn to use the valuing process when they are growing up, they may have a much more difficult time finding their way to the process, and thus to clear, independent thinking about moral issues, when they are older.

Value Sheet 5

CIVIL LIBERTIES

Below are several paragraphs relating to one issue. Select the paragraph that comes closest to your own position and change the wording in it until it represents your thinking as exactly as possible. Or you may write a new position if none of the ones listed is close to the one you prefer. The idea is to get a statement about which you can say, "This is where I now stand."

A useful way to decide between alternatives is to identify the *consequences* of each of the positions and then to decide which set of consequences you prefer would come about. You may, of course, use other sources of information before committing yourself to a position.

1. Freedom is basic to the existence of a democratic society. This does not mean license to do as one sees fit. Within the limitation of not interfering with someone else's freedom, it is desirable for the individual to pursue his own self-interest.

2.   In our society, everyone has freedom. One may do, think, and say that which he believes. We draw the line at a point, however. In the best interests of our society, we cannot permit anyone to hold doctrines or to preach anything that might undermine our society as it stands now. Erroneous beliefs, therefore, cannot be treated with the same tolerance as the normal and accepted doctrines, since their sole purpose is to destroy the very foundation of our society. Any dangerous opinions and beliefs must, therefore, be curbed.

3.   Many persons think of freedom as the right of suffrage, but this is only an illusion that one is free. He who thinks that his power of freedom comes from his vote has only to compare the power he has with that of the international financier, or a big business person; voting provides freedom only in a flimsy parliamentarian sense. It is an illusion in which each person is like the trained dog who thinks he learned the tricks by himself.

4.   The only true freedom that can ever exist comes about when we allow so-called truth and error to clash in the open market place of ideas. We cannot suppress any heresies nor can we censor thoughts, ideas, or practices; *nothing* is heretical. We must promote and encourage differences of opinion, and we must discourage uniformity of thinking. It is only this way that we can prevent a tyranny of the mind and body from ever imposing itself.

5.   True freedom is nonexistent. Each of us acts out a plan that is set for us before we are five years old. Our emotions reflect the society into which we are born. All our actions also reflect that society and are determined by it. Even our conception of freedom is one which has been drummed into us by the particular society. Convinced that we are free, it never occurs to us to question the fact that even in the ability to leave society, we are a slave to its laws.

This is the last value sheet upon which we will make specific comments, and it is a valuable one. It is a clear and effective form.

The directions for this kind of value sheet can remain unchanged, no matter what the topic. Students are asked to examine a number of alternative positions on a given issue, in this case "civil rights," and each is asked to frame her own position. No questions are needed when you use this format. The challenge to examine alternatives and choose a position is built into the directions.

These value sheets are easy to construct. Choose any issue that penetrates the lives of people in our society. Examples are:

1. Selfishness vs. altruism

2. Sloppiness vs. neatness

3. Individual initiatives vs. governmental controls

4. The role of advertising

5. Independence vs. dependence

6. Sexual promiscuity vs. abstinence

7. Acting on emotions vs. acting on intellect

8. Capitalism vs. socialism

9. Democracy, autocracy, and anarchy

10. Wealth vs. pleasant life

11. Tardiness vs. promptness

Write out a few paragraphs identifying possible positions on an issue. Ask each student to study the alternatives (and other available data) and to write out her own position. Finally, collect the papers and/or discuss the issue. The teacher can use the students' positions when revising the sheet to add to her original list of alternatives. It is, of course, important that all conceivable and identifiable alternatives—not just the "acceptable" ones—be brought to the attention of the student if she is to make a choice that can lead to a value.

Value Sheet 6

FRIENDSHIP

1. What does friendship mean to you?

2. If you have friends, did you choose them or did they get to be your friends by accident?

3. In what ways do *you* show friendship?

4. How important do you think it is to develop and maintain friendships?

---

5. If you plan to make any changes in your ways, please say what changes you will make. If you do not intend to make any changes in your ways, write "No changes."

Value Sheet 7

MINDING YOUR OWN BUSINESS VS. HELPING THOSE IN NEED

I. Some people say that human beings are basically selfish, that you must watch out for yourself, that it's best to serve your own purposes, avoid hurting others, and "mind your own business."

II. Others say that people must stick together and help one another, or they will fall separately, that no man is an island, that each person's fate is intertwined with other people's fates, and you should "help those in need."

1. What label might be appropriate for each of those positions?

2. Is this a case of "either-or," *either* you support one position *or* the other? Are there other positions that you could take concerning this issue? If possible, identify some other positions.

3. Professor Laurence Hopp of Rutgers University suggests that people who have experienced social injustice, who have experienced feelings of being unfairly treated, are likely to take the second position. Would you agree? Have you any evidence for your ideas?

4. It has also been suggested that those who have experienced success, who have power and privilege, would likely take the first position, regardless of whether or not they have earlier experienced social injustice. Would you agree? Have you any evidence for your ideas?

5. What other explanations might account for people preferring one position over the other? List them and discuss each briefly.

6. Read each of the eight situations below and try to identify *what you would do* in each case. Although not all the information is provided for any of the situations, make the best estimate you can of *what you would do if you were faced with such a situation in the future.* Try to be as realistic as possible in your choice of actions.

When you are finished, try to summarize *your* position regarding the issue minding your own business versus helping those in need.

Situation A

You are walking down a busy shopping street in the middle of the afternoon. You hear screams across the street and see a man choking a woman in a doorway. Several persons on both sides of the street notice, but nobody moves as the woman continues to scream and as the man tries to drag her indoors by the throat.

Situation B

You are in a group of persons with whom you would like to be friends. Two members of the group begin to tease a nearby girl who has a very strange face. Others in the group join in, although a few are silent.

Situation C

The young married couple that lives next to you has a little boy three years old. During a friendly visit with them, you observe that they are energetically teaching that boy to hate a minority group.

Situation D

An unpleasant-looking man approaches you on a corner and asks you for a dime for a cup of coffee.

Situation E

Someone asks your advice on a tax law that must be voted on in the forthcoming election. The proposed law would not change the total amount of money collected, but it would increase taxes for those in the middle- and upper-income brackets and decrease taxes for those in the lower-income brackets.

Situation F

You hear that the Indians on the reservation in the next state are suffering from severe poverty and that nobody is doing much about it.

Situation G

You read that blacks in some areas of the South continue to suffer discrimination and that they are sometimes beaten or even murdered and that the white persons in those areas are angry with those trying to interfere with the way things are.

Situation H

You are asked to make a judgment about U.S. foreign policy. The leaders of country XYZ are about to be thrown out by the citizens there because they are not doing the kind of job that the majority of the citizens want. Those leaders appeal to the United States for armed support, to keep the citizens from removing them. The United States government is concerned because the current leaders vigorously support the United States in international disputes, while the new leaders that would probably emerge in that country are not expected to support the United States in international questions and would probably ask for the removal of a large American air base on their territory.

Value Sheet 8

ON THOMAS JEFFERSON

His duplicity sinks deeper and deeper into my mind. His hatred of Hamilton was unbounded; of John Marshall, most intense; of my father, tempered with compunctious visitings, always controlled by his ambition . . . he died insolvent, and on the very day of his death received eleomosynary donations from the charity of some of those whom he had most deeply injured.*

1. In what ways does this picture of Jefferson differ from the one you have been taught?

2. How do you explain the difference?

3. What *is* the truth and how do you know it?

4. Is it possible for one to go through life without making enemies? Explain.

5. How much of your life should you live so you don't make anyone critize you? Is criticism good? Is it bad? Explain?

6. Take some well-known person living in our world today. Write three different paragraphs expressing three different points of view about this person, and base each paragraph on facts.

7. How can we judge people? It has been said that the purpose of education is to know a good man when you see one. How has your education helped you in this?

* Joseph Berger, "Diary of John Quincy Adams," *The Times Magazine*, March 13, 1960. © 1960 by The New York Times Company. Reprinted by permission.

Value Sheet 9

ON CIVIL LIBERTIES

The National Defense Education Act of 1958 stipulated that a student wanting a federal loan for education purposes had to sign an affidavit stating that he or she "does not believe in, and is not a member of and does not support any organization that believes in or teaches, the overthrow of the United States Government by force or violence or by any illegal or unconstitutional methods."

1. What do you think of such a requirement? (Check one)

_____Seems reasonable. I would not mind signing such an affidavit.

_____Seems unreasonable, but not seriously so. Not worth making a fuss over.

_____Seems unreasonable, and seriously so. I would not accept money under such conditions and believe the law should be changed.

_____(Any other position; write it out here:)

2. Some people did think such a "loyalty oath" serious and refused to accept money on that basis. In fact, some 32 of the nation's leading colleges and universities had officially notified the Office of Education that they had withdrawn from or declined to participate in the program specifically because of that requirement. Another 63 institutions participated, but under protest.

Why do you think some schools protested that oath?

3. The provision was repealed by Congress in the 1962 session. President Kennedy said when he signed the repeal that the oath was "offensive" to college students. Under what conditions do you think the government should change laws when the people object?

4. Discuss your feelings about this matter further. Perhaps you will want to discuss the general relationship between citizens and government, or what you would have done in the specific situation described above, or what you will do in the future under such circumstances.

Value Sheet 10

COURAGE*

"Courage is generosity of the highest order, for the brave are prodigal of the most precious things."—C. C. Colton

"True courage is to do without witness everything that one is capable of doing before all the world."—La Rochefoucauld

"Courage is like love: it must have hope to nourish it."—Napoleon

"Courage leads starward, fear toward death."—Seneca

"Brave men are brave from the first."—Corneille

"The courage of the tiger is one, and the horse another."—Ralph Waldo Emerson

"Ultimate bravery is courage of the mind."—H. G. Wells

"Grace under pressure."—Ernest Hemingway†

1.   What does the word "courage" mean to you?

2.   Do you think courage manifests itself? How?

3.   Do you think everyone possesses courage? How? If not, why?

4.   Are you proud of your level of courage? Discuss.

* By Sima Schuman

† Peggy Streit, editor, *The Times Magazine*, November 24, 1963. © 1963 by The New York Times Company. Reprinted by permission.

Value Sheet 11

HOME OF THE BRAVE?

I used to be an idealist. When there was a picket line, I would picket. When there was a sitdown, I would sit. When there was a demonstration, I would demonstrate. I sat for two days in front of a store that wouldn't hire "minority type" people—I felt that they should have a fair chance in the land of opportunity, that all men are created equal. They told me to go to Russia. I was born in Brooklyn!

Then there was the time I marched around the U.N. and handed out leaflets saying that we shouldn't use bombs to kill each other, and that man should study war no more. They called me an atheist!

Once I was arrested for going into a school with a sign saying that all children are entitled to an equal opportunity to education, like the Supreme Court says the Constitution means. They called me a Communist!

Soon I got tired of being called all these names, so I gave up. I don't care if half of them starve. I don't care if they don't all get educated. I don't care if they kill each other with bombs. I don't care if their babies die from radiation. Now I'm a good American.*

To think on and to write on:

1. What is this writer for and what is he against?

2. Have you had any experiences like his?

3. Who are some people who should be concerned about the problems he mentions?

4. Are there any things which *you* are working to change, to set right, to improve? Discuss briefly.

* Gary Ackerman, *Castle,* Oct. 8, 1963.

Value Sheet 12

ON MEXICO

"After the taking of Mexico, Cortez divided the land among the conquerors and on the ruins of the Aztec City he began to build the Spanish city of Mexico, proclaiming its future greatness. He organized a city corporation, established markets, repaired the aquaduct of Chapultepeo, which had been cut during the siege, laid down moral laws, thus beginning the government of the colony whose wealth he protected by wise measure. . . .

"Then Pizzaro showed his admirable gifts as organizer and colonizer; he divided the land into districts, he organized the administration of justice and the working of the mines . . . and in short time, thanks to his energy and will, the church, town hall, palaces, and houses formed a beautiful city (Lima) which grew and prospered."*

"Pizzaro, in imitation of Cortez, laid hands on the Inca Atahualpa, and held him as security for the good behavior of his people.

"In return for his freedom the Inca promised to fill a large room with objects of gold to a depth of nine feet. Almost immediately porters began to come in bearing golden vases, goblets, and jars; miniature gold birds and beasts, golden leaves, flowers, beads, and roots. Melted down, this mass yielded 1,326,539 pesos de oro, the equivalent of $15,500,000 in American money. Having secured this treasure, the Spaniards treacherously led their prisoner out to the plaza of Caxamarca and strangled him with a bowstring."†

1. How do these accounts differ?

2. Speculate on the probable reasons WHY they differ.

3. Which account seems most reasonable to you?

4. How do you know what to believe?

5. Are there any implications here for your reading or believing?

* From Bleye Pedro de Aguado, *Compiedo de Historia de Espana* (1933), II, 115, 123–24, as quoted in A. C. Walworth, Jr., *School Histories at War* (Cambridge, Mass.: Harvard University Press, 1938).

† T. J. Wertenbaker and Smith, D. E., *United States* (New York: Charles Scribner's Sons, 1931), pp. 18–19.

Value Sheet 13

*COPERNICUS**

Some 400 years ago, a mathematician named Copernicus studied the earth and the heavens and concluded that the conception of the earth as the center of the universe was incorrect. Calculations showed him that it was more reasonable to see the sun as the center and the earth as rotating around it. The German mathematician Johann Kepler confirmed and refined the findings of Copernicus; but this new idea was too revolutionary to be considered dispassionately, on its scientific merits.

"Because man is conservative, a creature of habit, and convinced of his own importance, the new theory was decidedly unwelcome. Moreover, the vested interests of well-entrenched scholars and religious leaders caused them to oppose it," write Morris Kline in his *Mathematics in Western Culture.*†

Martin Luther called Copernicus an "upstart astrologer" and a "fool who wishes to reverse the entire science of astonomy." Calvin thundered: "Who will venture to place the authority of Copernicus above that of the Holy Spirit?" Do not Scriptures say that Joshua commanded the sun and not the earth to stand still? The inquisition condemned the new theory as "that false Pythagorean doctrine utterly contrary to the Holy Scriptures," and in 1616 the Index of Prohibited Books banned all publications dealing with the idea.

Galileo was thought to believe the new theory to have some merit, and was called by the Roman Inquisition and compelled on the threat of torture to declare: "The falsity of the Copernican system cannot be doubted, especially by us Catholics . . ." On hearing of Galileo's persecution, Descartes, a nervous and timid individual, actually destroyed one of his own works on it.

Writes Kline: "Indeed, if the fury and high office of the opposition are a good indication of the importance of an idea no more valuable one was ever advanced."

1. Can you understand how people of good will might react violently to new ideas that they see as threatening some of their values?

2. Has there been another situation in history that you can recall in which the advance of knowledge was resisted by partisans with similar vigor?

3. Can you imagine something like that happening in the future in the United States if some new idea, say in sociology or some other discipline, were to seriously challenge the status quo?

4. What methods do you think might be used to fight new ideas?

5. What methods might be used to fight for the right to consider new ideas?

6. How receptive are *you* to new ideas, and how resistant are you? Can you think of conditions under which you would try to repress truth?

* This material comes from the work of Arnold Rothstein of Hofstra College.

† Morris Kline, *Mathematics in Western Culture* (New York: Oxford University Press, 1953).

Value Sheets 6 through 13 provide examples that have been used by teachers both as "pure" value lessons and in relation to subject-matter units. They represent a few of the different forms that these sheets can take. Each of those sheets was written with a particular age of children in mind, but a simple modification of the language could adapt the sheet for students of other ages, or for adults for that matter.

Incidentally, any topic is suited to any grade level as long as the children have enough information or can get enough information to examine the alternatives intelligently. Most teachers are delighted by the surge of interest and intelligence shown by children when they are given important adult-sounding choices to reflect upon. The problem with most children is not that they face choices which they cannot handle, but that they are not given enough choices and the kind of help the value theory recommends to permit them to develop their choice-making abilities. We would encourage teachers to resist a temptation to keep young children away from "sophisticated" topics. Having seen primary-grade children deal thoughtfully and seriously with racial prejudice and methods of teaching, intermediate children similarly deal with problems of war and peace and what makes for a successful marriage, junior high-school children reflect intelligently on matters of sex and on religion, and high-school children of very average ability tackle creativity and wisdom issues that deal with self-delusions, parent-grandparent relationships, and government policy in complex circumstances, we are convinced that many children wait only to have their minds and interests freed by teachers who dare trust them with important choices.

The following value sheets treat some fairly sophisticated topics, but they may be discussed at different levels depending on what responses students make.

Value Sheet 14

PRESIDENT TRUMAN TO HIS BIOGRAPHER*

"I think I told you, in school we usually had only one man's point of view of the history of something, and I'd go to the library and read three or four, sometimes as many as half a dozen, versions of the same thing, the same incident, and it was always the *differences* that interested me. And you had to keep in mind that they were all telling what for them was the truth.

"And that is one of the reasons that when I got into a position of power I always tried to keep in mind that just because I saw something in a certain way didn't mean that others didn't see it in a different manner. That's why I always hesitated to call a man a liar unless I had the absolute goods on him."

To have only *one* alternative is to be weak. We should seek out others to have a more adequate basis for choice. In your history courses, have you had more than one point of view represented? Give some examples.

* Merle Miller, *Plain Speaking: An Oral Biography of Harry S. Truman* (New York: Berkeley Publishing Co., 1974), p. 231. Used by permission.

Value Sheet 15

SWEET ADVERSITY

Sweet are the uses of adversity,
Which, like the toad, ugly and venomous,
Wears yet a precious jewel in his head;
And this our life, exempt from public haunt,

Finds tongues in trees, books in the running brooks,
Sermons in stones, and good in everything.
I would not change it.

> William Shakespeare
> *As You Like It*
> Act II, Scene i
> The Forest of Arden

At times we seem to believe that all of life should be a continuing sweet and happy song. What are some of the uses of adversity? And what are some of the uses of good fortune in your own life?

Value Sheet 16

EISENHOWER AND HIS SON

In his most recent book,* Bob Considine tells of a conversation he had with General Eisenhower. They had been together in Korea and there Considine had noticed that the General made it a point to take his son aside and talked to him. Meeting him again in Hawaii, Considine asked the General to share what he had told to his son. The General replied, "I said, John, if you get killed in this war it'll be a terrible thing for your mother and for me, but that's a soldier's life. We take that risk when we put on the uniform. Somehow, your mother and I would live through a thing like that.

"But for God's sake don't get captured. Don't let them capture you. If you should be captured and they held you over my head, I wouldn't be able to serve as President of the United States."

Perhaps you should read this page several times. We don't know, *for sure,* what President Eisenhower was trying to say to his son. Make some guesses, and later we'll share our guesses with each other.

*Bob Considine, *They Rose Above It* (Garden City, New York,: Doubleday & Co., 1977).

Value Sheet 17

ALCOHOLISM

What are some of the facts and some of the myths about alcoholism?

Myth: Alcoholism is a minor killer in the world.

Fact: Alcoholism is the third largest killer in the world.

Myth: A majority of alcoholics are "bums" who live in seedy, rundown hotels known as "flop-houses."

Fact: Skid-row alcoholics represent only 3 to 5 percent of all known alcoholics.

Myth: Most known alcoholics are either unemployed or hold jobs for only short periods of time.

Fact: Ninety-five percent of all alcoholics are in the work force with their services averaging from 5 to 22 years.

Fact: There are 95 million people in our country who use alcohol. Nine million are known alcoholics and another 1.3 million Americans between the ages of 12 to 17 have serious drinking problems.

Write an imaginative essay on automobile safety; on safety in the air; on safety in the home; and in industry with this knowledge as background.

Value Sheet 18

THE COMMUNICATIONS INDUSTRY

According to Marc U. Porat, an economist now working with the Aspen Institute, more than half the wages paid in the United States and nearly half of the nation's $1.8 trillion gross national product originate with the production, processing, and distribution of information goods and services.

Porat recently stated that while "information occupations" accounted for only 10 percent of the work force at the turn of the century, they now represent 45 percent of all jobs in the United States. "Information occupations" include all newspapers, magazines, books, all radio, all television, all advertising employees, all of the bureaucracy getting out propaganda of one kind or another, the National Letter Carriers Association, The International Business Machines Corporation, all those instruments used in making copies of all kinds, all computers and the people who use them.

When new jobs or professions or careers are created, men and women are often unemployed—those people are being replaced by persons in the *new* jobs. What are some of the sad features of this social transformation? What are some of its advantages for society?

Value Sheet 19

THE WOMAN IN A CAGE*

By way of background: the hero (detective) and a young girl with whom he seems to be falling in love are talking about an older woman (middle-aged) who has revealed some rather harsh features of character.

The girl:	She seems to be improving.
The detective:	She escaped from her hexington cage.
The girl:	That heavenly house . . . a cage?
The man:	Uh-huh.
The girl:	The new one isn't half so beautiful.
The man:	It will be when she has finished. And then the walls will close in again.
The girl:	Another cage, do you mean?
The man:	Another cage, I agreed.
The girl:	Life can't be just escaping from one cage and ending up in another!!
The man:	Everyone lives inside bars. The trick is not to want to get out.
The girl:	Stop it! I don't want to hear that.

What is the detective saying about life? Does he prize life the way it is? The girl does not prize what he is saying. What is it, do you suppose, that she objects to?

* From a detective story, *Blood Sport,* by Dick Francis (New York: Harper and Row, 1967), p. 151.

Value Sheet 20

SEVEN AGES ON STAGE

All the world's a stage,
And all the men and women merely players.
They have their exits and their entrances,
And one man in his time plays many parts,
His acts being seven ages. At first the infant,

Mewling and puking in the nurse's arms.
And then the whining schoolboy, with his satchel
And shining morning face, creeping like snail
Unwillingly to school. And then the lover,
Sighing like furnace, with a woeful ballad
Made to his mistress' eyebrow. Then a soldier,
Full of strange oaths, and bearded like the pard,
Jealous in honor, sudden and quick in quarrel,
Seeking the bubble reputation
Even in the cannon's mouth. And then the justice,
In fair round belly with good capon lined,
With eyes severe and beard of formal cut,
Full of wise saws and modern instances;
And so he plays his part. The sixth age shifts
Into the lean and slippered pantaloon,
With spectacles on nose and pouch on side;
His youthful hose, well saved, a world too wide
For his shrunk shank; and his big manly voice,
Turning again toward childish treble, pipes
And whistles in his sound. Last scene of all,
That ends this strange eventful history,
Is second childishness and mere oblivion,
Sans teeth, sans eyes, sans taste, sans everything.

William Shakespeare
As You Like it
Act II, Scene vii

This was written by William Shakespeare almost 400 years ago.
Does it still have sound and sensible meaning for our times? Are *you*
an actor on the world's stage, and if so, what is your part—this year?

Are these seven ages just as appropriate now as they were long
ago? In what ways? How would *you* change them?

Value Sheet 21

THE DIFFICULT CHOICE

The Road Not Taken

Two roads diverged in a yellow wood,
And sorry I could not travel both
And be one traveler, long I stood
And looked down one as far as I could
To where it bent in the undergrowth;

Then took the other, as just as fair,
And having perhaps the better claim,
Because it was grassy and wanted wear;
Though as for that, the passing there
Had worn them really about the same,

And both that morning equally lay
In leaves no step had trodden black.
Oh, I kept the first for another day!
Yet knowing how way leads on to way,
I doubted if I should ever come back.

I shall be telling this with a sigh
Somewhere ages and ages hence:
Two roads diverged in a wood, and I—
I took the one less traveled by,
And that has made all the difference.

Robert Frost

From THE POETRY OF ROBERT FROST, edited by Edward Connery Lathem. Copyright 1916, © 1969, by Holt, Rinehart and Winston. Copyright 1944 by Robert Frost. Reprinted by permission of Holt, Rinehart and Winston, publishers.

Some decisions are hard to make and some unhappy in our memory. Discuss one of *your* experiences like this.

Value Sheet 22
INTERNATIONAL TRADE IN MILITARY ARMS
Statistics on Arms Trade

Exports 1961–75 (in billions):

United States	$40.9
Soviet Union	26.5
France	3.8
United Kingdom	3.2
China	2.3
West Germany	1.8
Czechoslovakia	1.7
Poland	1.6
Canada	1.5
All others	5.0

Source: World Military and Social Expenditures, 1977.

Exports to the Third World (in millions):

	1974	1975
United States	$1200	$1769
Soviet Union	1540	1652
United Kingdom	481	503
France	357	477
West Germany	101	118
Italy	106	65
China	80	48
Netherlands	25	32
Sweden	5	16
Canada	1	5
Czechoslovakia	11	5
Japan	2	—
Third World	211	141

Source: Stockholm International Peace Research Institute Yearbook, 1976.

Major purchasers of U.S. weapons,
fiscal year 1973–76 (in millions):

Iran	$10,900
Saudi Arabia	7800
Israel	4400
West Germany	952
South Korea	935
Greece	812
Netherlands	762
Belgium	761
Australia	759
Taiwan	628
Jordan	601
Norway	559
Kuwait	538
Switzerland	516

Source: Department of Defense, DSAA,
December 1976.

1.   In the top two tables the United States is the leader. Is this an honor? Should we prize this? Choose to be leader in the next decade?

2.   In what ways is the arms trade related to our economy? To our way of life?

3.   If we reduce significantly the manufacture of armaments many people will be unemployed. Is this an adequate reason for making armaments?

4.   In the bottom table, notice carefully the countries buying the most armaments from the United States. What does this mean for the probability of war in the Middle East?

Value Sheet 23

TEENAGE DREAMS*

Confronted with the same uncertainties as their American counterparts, West German teenagers have some clear ideas about what they'd like their future to bring.

The majority would like to own their own car by age 20 or 21, their own apartment or house between 22 and 24, and by 25 to have married their life's partner. The first child should then ideally come within the next three years.

"The 'Youth Study '76,' published by the McCann Advertising Company, finds that most West German teenage girls hope to fulfill all their dreams by the age of 33. The young men give themselves a few more years. They want their life desires met by age 37."

In our meetings with parents as individuals and in very small groups, we were told that young Americans were very much like these West German teenagers. Young people, it is said, want everything—and quickly. They do not want to work and save their money for future satisfactions. Can these dreams really come true, or is this "pie in the sky?" Is it like asking for the moon? What do you have to say about this question? Write two or three paragraphs which reveal your point of view.

* Pamela Swift, "Teenage Dreams," *Buffalo Courier Express*, July 10, 1977.

Incomplete Value Sheets

We have said that value sheets can be built in many forms. The simplest form consists of a provocative and value-laden opening statement followed by a series of thought-provoking questions. Alternatively, a sheet might be a list of questions prepared from a reading the class has done, such as Value Sheet 4 on *Silas Marner*. Or it might simply be a series of questions on a concept, much like Value Sheet 6 on friendship. Value sheets can also present alternatives and ask a student to choose, as does sheet 5 on civil rights. Sheets might be constructed to add information and insights to the issue as a student progresses through the questions, as demonstrated by sheet 2, "Illegal Behavior," and the "mind your own business" sheet 7. Cartoons, poetry, music, and any other form that accomplishes the purpose of helping students to clarify their values might also be used.

Below are five possible openings for value sheets. You might want to use them to practice making value sheets.[2]

1.   "Merry-Go-Round"*

Where is the Jim Crow section
On this merry-go-round, Mister,
Cause I want to ride?

* Langston Hughes, *Selected Poems* (New York: Alfred A. Knopf, Inc., 1959). Copyright © by Langston Hughes, 1959. Used by permission.

2. See Appendix A for value sheets based on these openings.

Down South where I come from
White and colored
Can't sit side by side.
Down South on the train
There's a Jim Crow car.
On the bus we're put in back—
But there ain't no back
To a merry-go-round!
Where's the horse
For a kid that's black?

2. The human being is made up of oxygen, nitrogen, phosphorus, hydrogen, carbon, and calcium. There are also 12½ gallons of water, enough iron to make a small nail, about a salt shaker full of salt, and enough sugar to make one small cube. If we were to put all of this together and try to sell it, the whole thing would be worth about one dollar.

3. Louis Armstrong writing on his art: "I don't want a million dollars. See what I mean? No medals. I mean, I don't feel no different about the horn now than I did when I was playin' in the Tuxedo Band. That my livin' and my life. I love them notes. That why I try to make 'em right. See? And any part of the day, you liable to see me doing something toward it for the night.

"A lot of musicians, money make a damn fool out of them. They get famous and can't play no more. They spend their time counting the customers. Me, I don't play no louder or no softer, and I ain't goin' play no less. I might play a little *more*, but always up to par."

4. Shuttlesworth's civil-rights biography reads like something out of Horatio Alger: Christmas, 1956, Shuttlesworth home bombed and completely demolished; winter, 1957, his church dynamited by racists; late 1957, Shuttlesworth and wife, mobbed, beaten, and stabbed; jailed eight times—four times during the Freedom Rides; sued for 3 million dollars by state officials of Alabama; car and personal property sold at public auction; driver's license revoked for a whole year; the three Shuttlesworth children illegally arrested and beaten.

5. "In Germany they first came for the Communists, and I didn't speak up because I wasn't a Communist. Then they came for the Jews, and I didn't speak up because I wasn't a Jew. Then they came for the trade unionists, and I didn't speak up because I wasn't a trade unionist. Then they came for the Catholics, and I didn't speak up because I was a Protestant. Then they came for me—and by that time no one was left to speak up."—Pastor Martin Niemoller.

AN OUTLINE OF THE STRATEGY

Let us see if we can now succinctly outline the strategy that we call "value sheets."

Content

As the clarifying response aims at a particular expression of a particular child, the value sheet aims at students in general and thus deals with ideas that are important for most students. Such ideas often emerge from topics related to:

1. *Money,* how it is apportioned and treated.

2. *Friendship,* how we relate to those around us.

3. *Love and sex,* how to deal with intimate relationships.

4. *Religion and morals,* what we hold as fundamental beliefs.

5. *Leisure,* how it is used.

6. *Politics and social organization,* especially as it affects the individual.

7. *Work,* vocational choices, attitudes toward work.

8. *Family,* and how we behave within it.

9. *Maturity,* what we strive for.

10. *Character traits,* especially as they affect a person's behavior.

Value sheets take different forms. Often they are based on a single provocative statement. Sometimes two or more divergent positions open a value sheet. Sometimes the questions and statements are woven together so that the value sheet has a dramatic development, with the student becoming increasingly involved in a complex issue. Sometimes value sheets consist of nothing more than a series of probing questions that are keyed to a common reading done from a text, a current events reading, or a piece of literature, or keyed to a common experience like an assembly program, a class problem, or a major public event. Cartoons, films, recordings, television shows, and other stimuli can also be used to begin a value sheet.

The questions on a value sheet should be in the style of the valuing theory. That is, the questions should not try subtly to convince a student to believe what the adult believes, but rather the questions should help the student take the issue at hand through the value criteria. The crucial elements, of course, are *choosing* (freely, thoughtfully, from alternatives), *prizing* and willingness to affirm, and *acting* (living personal choices in some pattern, not just talking about them). The thirty clarifying responses of the preceding chapter illustrate this style.

Methods for Using Value Sheets

The value sheets are used in a variety of ways, the *least* effective of which is as discussion lessons. Values do not easily come out of the business of a classroom discussion, especially a heated discussion. A person needs quiet, hard thought, and careful decisions to produce clear, persistent, and viable values.

A discussion is inappropriate for value lessons for the following reasons:

1. A value discussion tends to move toward argumentation, with participants becoming defensive of positions they may not exactly hold after the heat of the talk is finished. Value development requires a nondefensive, open, and thoughtful climate.

2. Participants in a discussion often perform in ways that are partly motivated by factors irrelevant to the issue being discussed, such as desires to please other students or the teacher, and thus the thoughtful, deliberative aspects of valuing often become diluted with emotional considerations.

3. Valuing is an *individual* process; a person does not develop values from a group consensus. We must each choose, prize, and act; and this is difficult to do in a room in which a lot of talking is going on.

4. Although valuing is an active process requiring much individual intellectual energy, most people are passive most of the time in a discussion. In fact, many people are passive almost *all* of the time in discussions. In most discussions, the bulk of the talking is done by a certain predictable few.

5. Finally, a discussion tends to generate pressure on individuals to accept the group consensus or the strong leader's arguments or the teacher's suggestions, and values cannot arise from pressures to accept something. The free choice must, in this value theory, be truly free if it is to lead to a meaningful personal value.

For those reasons, we have found that the most effective ways to use value sheets begin with individuals responding to the questions privately and deliberately. Usually, we insist on written responses. Writing elicits more careful thought than just speaking about something. Sometimes, however, the teacher will find it advisable to make the value sheets in whole or in part optional, or to permit students to write their responses anonymously. This is especially helpful when students might fear being completely candid in a certain area or when the teacher does not feel confident in insisting that a student deliberate about certain ideas, such as religion. Each teacher will find a comfortable personal approach, but the approaches in the following list are those we have found useful.

Students do value sheets for homework or during study times. They may even be handled as programmed instructional material. A number of teachers have found value sheets to be especially appropriate for weekend assignments, when students feel somewhat fewer pressures and have more time for unhurried thought. Then, several alternatives are possible:

1. Students discuss their written answers in small groups without the teacher's presence. This forces the students to think through issues without looking to the teacher for "the right way."

2. Students turn in their writings and the teacher later reads, without comment or evaluation, selected viewpoints that raise interesting alternatives or illuminate the issue in a special way. This is best done without the teacher identifying the writer, however, with the writer having the opportunity to claim credit for what is read to the class if he or she so wishes. Discussion may follow.

3. Students turn in their writings and the teacher returns them with occasional comments in the margins. The comments should, of course, be in the style of the value theory and should ask further questions that help the student rethink certain aspects of what was written originally. For example, asking students if something they wrote came after considering alternatives, asking them to define a word or an idea, or asking them if they really live in ways consistent with what they write are all valuable comments to use in reacting to what students write for a value sheet. Naturally, teachers do not evaluate the students' values. They may, however, evaluate the language usage, spelling, and so on.

4. Students turn in their writings to a committee which selects representative ones to be read to the class or posted on the bulletin board.

5. Each student completes written answers and then the class has a general discussion about the topic. This is useful inasmuch as it raises new alternatives and ideas for some students. It is harmful inasmuch as pressures for conformity tend to develop. In any case, it is preferable for group discussion to *follow* individual thought on value sheets and teachers should strive to protect the right of dissent. In fact, they themselves should present alternative arguments if such are not forthcoming from the group. Without individual commitment to a position after full examination of the alternative arguments, no values can be very firm or intelligent.

6. After a while, the teacher may find that some students will want to make up value lessons for the class. This will occur after the sense of the value process is absorbed, and it is to be encouraged. We recommend, in fact, that students be taught the criteria for values and how to make effective value sheets.

Do's and Don'ts

As was discussed earlier in the chapter, value sheets can be used apart from subject matter, or they can be used to initiate subject lessons, to close subject lessons, or in the midst of and as a part of subject lessons. The *Silas Marner* sheet is an example of this last approach. More about the relationship between subject matter and value approaches appears in chapter 9.

Ten do's and don'ts may help teachers begin to develop their own value sheets and put them to use.[3]

• DO try an adaptation of one of the sheets presented in this book for a starter, if you like.

• DON'T moralize, no matter how subtly, when you make your own value sheets or during value discussions. It is contrary to the theory. An easy way to check yourself is by asking two questions of your sheets: (1) "Can the reader be fairly sure from this sheet what my position is?" If so, it is a sign that your beliefs are shining through and will affect those tractable children who need, more than the rest of the class, the experience of thinking things out for themselves. (2) "Are there any questions that have implicit in them 'right' answers?" Asking a question such as "Don't you think that it is good to be neat and clean?" is not asking a question at all for most students. Moralizing has not worked in the past; do not be afraid to abandon it as a classroom practice.

This does not mean that you should never make your personal views known to students.[4] We think that teachers should be quite candid about their viewpoints, while making it very clear that students are not to accept those viewpoints uncritically. For most classes, however, it may be wise to conceal many of your viewpoints until students realize that they will be expected to find their own values and not to mimic the positions of others, even the teacher's. And in all classes, it is wise to keep the questioning

---

3. Appendix B contains a form useful for helping to predict the effectiveness of value sheets.

4. Smith (1958, p. 34) argues that it is not *possible* for a teacher to remain completely neutral in presenting issues.

section of the value sheet as neutral as possible. When you communicate your positions, you should do so openly and forthrightly. Declare "This is how I see the issue." Try not to let your viewpoints slant and load value sheets, for that makes it more difficult for students to choose freely and intelligently and, thus, more difficult to obtain values.

• DO avoid "yes-no" and "either-or" questions, for both limit value-related thinking. And avoid "why" questions for they push children who have no clear reasons for choices to make up reasons for the benefit of the question. Some substitutes for "why" questions are: "Do you *have* a reason for your choice? If so, please mention it." "What alternatives did you consider before you arrived at your choice?" "List the consequences that you desired from your choice and also the consequences from alternative choices that you rejected."

• DON'T worry unnecessarily about parents. Experience tells us that most of them will respond to value sheets with feelings of relief that important issues are being raised in a nondirective, serious way. The user of value sheets will likely get many times more accolades than complaints.

• DO get into sensitive areas, important areas, as soon as you dare. They are the ones students like to think about and need to think about.

• DON'T ask too many questions. If there are more than three or four complex questions, permit students to answer only the ones that interest them or that they have time for. You don't want value sheets to be a chore or a bore.

• DON'T try to give the students grades on the basis of what they say, for that will squelch honesty faster than almost anything. You can, naturally, grade the usage of language.

• DO include many "you" questions on value sheets, for that is the essence of the value process.

• DO make certain that every value sheet contains a choice to be made, alternatives to consider, and that the consequences of each alternative are pointed to. Sheets without choices, such as those that have students reflect on their feelings about situations, do little to advance value clarity. The purpose of the value theory, and the strategy of these value sheets, is to help children think through important areas of their lives and eventually to learn to respect their own decision-making abilities.

• DO ask many questions about actual behavior, about what a person does or intends to do about a personal choice. So very many of us have learned to talk a good game, but to let it go at that. Unfortunately, as Paul

Goodman so aptly put it, "When we do nothing, we run the risk of becoming nothing."[5]

OTHER WRITTEN STRATEGIES

In addition to value sheets like those presented earlier, we can use other written strategies in our sheets to stimualte value-clarifying thinking and discussion. These include compositions based on decision-making situations, questionnaires that call for rating of values along with expansion and clarification, listing and rating value-laden preferences, writing messages in various forms (such as a telegram) to a person who has an important influence on the student's life, and creating a values coat of arms.

The remaining sections in this chapter give some examples of these approaches which you may want to try.

Decision-making Situations*

1. If you were at the Constitutional Convention, how would you have voted on the question of slavery? What have students your age done about the race problem in America today? If you care about that problem, have you done anything to help?

2. Compare the ways in which decisions are made in the U.S. government with the ways decisions are made in your family. Are there checks and balances in your family? What part do you play in family decisions?

3. If you wanted to change something in our society or in this school, what are some ways you would go about it? Have you ever tried any of these ways?

4. The First Amendment affirms the right of freedom of speech. Have you recently made use of that freedom in a way you are proud of?

5. Do you consider the Civil War a just war? If you had been there to choose, on which side would you have fought, if either?

6. What would have been your reaction if you were drafted to fight on one side but did not sympathize entirely with that side? If this happened to you in the future, what would you do?

7. Under what circumstances would you kill a person?

8. What kinds of living things would you kill without concern?

* From M. Harmin, H. Kirschenbaum, and S. B. Simon. *Clarifying Values Through Subject Matter.* Minneapolis: Winston Press, 1973. Pp. 50—51, 53. Used by permission.

5. See Appendix C for examples of other value sheets.

9. How are disputes settled in your family? What can you do to experiment with better ways of settling disputes?

10. Have you ever acted—written a letter to an editor or congressman or tried to influence someone else's thinking—to help prevent a war or other conflict? What *can* persons your age do?

Listing Strategy— Things I Love to Do[6]

Ask students (teacher does it with them) to number from 1–20 on a paper. Then suggest they list, as rapidly as they can, 20 things in life which they really, *really* love to do. Stress that the papers will not be collected and "corrected," and that there is no right answer about what people *should* like. It should be emphasized that in none of values strategies should students be forced to participate. Each has the right to pass. Students may get strangely quiet; and, at first, they may even be baffled by such an unschoollike task as this. Flow with it, and be certain to allow enough time for them to list what they really love to do. Remember, at no time must the individual's privacy be invaded, and the right of an individual to pass is sacrosanct.

When everyone has listed 20 items, the process of coding responses can be started. Here are some suggested codes which you might ask the students to use:

1. Place the $ sign by any item which costs more than three dollars each time you do it.

2. Put an *R* in front of any item which involves some risk. The risk might be physical, intellectual, or emotional. (Which things in your own life that are things you love to do require some risk?)

3. Using the code letters *F* and *M*, record which of the items on your list you think your father and mother might have had on their lists if they had been asked to make them *at your age*.

4. Place either the letter *P* or the letter *A* before each item. The "P" is to be used for items which you prefer doing with people, the "A" is for items which you prefer doing alone. (Stress again that there is no right answer. It is important just to become aware of which are your preferences.)

5. Place a number 5 in front of any item which you think would not be on your list 5 years from now.

6. Most of the following strategies are adapted from S. B. Simon, L. W. Howe, and H. Kirschenbaum, *Values Clarification: A Handbook of Practical Strategies for Teachers and Students*. New York: Hart Publishing, 1972.

6. Finally go down through your list and place near each item the date when you did it last.

The discussion which follows this exercise argues more eloquently than almost anything else we can say for values clarification.

Expansion and Clarification Strategy—
"I Learned That I . . . "

This strategy fits in with the preceding one. After students have listed and coded their 20 items, the teacher might say, "Look at your list as something which tells a lot about you at this time in your life. What did you learn about yourself as you were going through the strategy? Will you please complete one of these sentences and share with us some of the learning you did?"

> I learned that I. . . .
> I relearned that I. . . .
> I noticed that I. . . .
> I was surprised to see that I. . . .
> I was disappointed that I. . . .
> I was pleased that I. . . .
> I realized that I. . . .

The teacher must be willing to make some "I learned that I . . ." statements, too. And they must not be platitudinous, either. Every effort is made for the values-clarifying teacher to be as honest and as authentic as possible.

"I learned that I . . ." statements can be used after almost any important value-clarifying strategy. It is a way of getting the student to own the process of the search for values. It should be clear how diametrically opposed "I learned that I . . ." statements are from indoctrination, although it is possible to misuse this or any clarification strategy to get kids to give back the party line. On the other hand, using this strategy can begin to build that lifetime search for personal meaning into all of our experiences.

Listing Strategy—
Baker's Dozen

This is a very simple strategy which teaches us something about our personal priorities. The teacher asks each student to list 13, a baker's dozen, of his favorite items around the house which use plugs, that is, which require electricity.

When the students have made their lists, the teacher says, "Now, please draw a line through the three which you really could do without if there were suddenly to be a serious power shortage. It's not that you don't like them, but that you could, if you had to, live without them. O.K., now circle the three which really mean the most to you and which you would hold onto until the very end."

It should be clear that again there is no right answer as to what "good" people *should* draw lines through and circle. The main thing is for each of us to know what we want and to see it in the perspective of what we like less.

Message Strategy— "I Urge" Telegrams

The teacher obtains blank Western Union telegram blanks or simply has students head a piece of paper with the word *Telegram.* He or she then says, "Each of you should think of someone in your real life to whom you would send a telegram which begins with these words: "I urge you to. . . ." Then finish the telegram and we'll hear some of them."

A great many value issues come out of this simple strategy. Consider some of these telegrams:

To my sister: "I urge you to get your head together and quit using drugs." Nancy. (All telegrams must be signed. It is our affirmation of the need to name your name and to stand up for what you believe in.)

To my Sunday School teacher: "I urge you to quit thinking that you are the only person to know what God wants." Signed, your student Rodney Phillips.

To my neighbor on the North Side: "I urge you to see that we have no other place to play ball and that you not call the cops so often." Signed, Billy Clark.

One of the things that students working with values clarification learn to do is to find out what they really want. "I urge" telegrams help do that. Just think of the people in your own lives to whom an "I urge" telegram needs to be sent. The second thing students working with values clarification learn to do is to find *alternative* ways of getting what they need and want. Take the case of Billy Clark's neighbor. The class spent some time brainstorming ways of approaching that neighbor. They talked about how to negotiate with a grouch, and how to try to offer alternatives in your drive to get what you want.

"I urge" telegrams are used several times during the semester. The students keep them on file and after they have done five or six, they are spread out on the desk and "I learned" statements are made based on the pattern of the messages carried by the telegrams.

Students also learn to use the "I urge you to . . ." model to get messages across between student and student and between student and teacher.

An assignment I like to use, related to the "I urge" telegram, is to have each student get a letter to the editor published in a magazine or newspaper.

Drawing Values Strategy— Personal Coat of Arms

Each student is asked to draw a shield shape in preparation for making a personal coat of arms. The teacher could go into the historical significance of shields and coats of arms, but the exercise is primarily designed to help us learn more about some of our most strongly held values and to learn the importance of publicly affirming what we believe—that is, literally wearing our values out front on our shields.

The coat of arms shield is divided into six sections (see accompanying figure). The teacher makes it clear that words are to be used only in the sixth block. All the other spaces are to contain pictures. He or she stresses that this is not an art lesson. Only crude stick figures, etc., need be used. Then the teacher tells what is to go in each of the six sections:

1. Draw two pictures. One to represent something you are very good at and one to show something you *want* to become good at.

2. Make a picture to show one of your values from which you would never budge. This is one about which you feel extremely strong, and which you might never give up.

3. Draw a picture to show a value by which your family lives. Make it one that everyone in your family would probably agree is one of their most important.

4. In this block, imagine that you could achieve anything you wanted, and that whatever you tried to do would be a success. What would you strive to do?

5. Use this block to show one of the values you wished all people would believe, and certainly one in which you believe very deeply.

6. In the last block, you can use words. Write in four words which you would like people to say about you behind your back.

The teacher can do several different things at this point. He can have the students share among themselves in little trios or quartets. He can also get the pictures hung up on the walls and get people to take each other on gallery tours to share the coats of arms. A game could be played which would involve trying to guess what the pictures represented. The class might try to make a group coat of arms to represent their living together in that classroom. In any case, the value expressions elicited in this nonverbal way are very exciting and lead to discussions which range far and wide. Incidentally, this strategy is a good one to use with parents to illustrate to them the

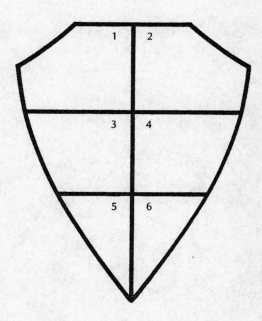

power of the values-clarification methodology. It makes a meaningful exercise for an evening PTA meeting.

The Coat of Arms strategy illustrates quite well some things common to all of the values-clarification strategies. The teacher sets up an interesting way of eliciting some value responses. She establishes that there is no right answer. The strategy is open-ended and allows students to take the exploration to whatever level they want to take it. Finally, there is a chance to share with each other some of the alternatives that emerge from our searching. This whole process allows each student to focus on areas where some work has yet to be done in order for the student to keep growing. The Coat of Arms can be done several times during the school year and the various shields compared and seen as measures of a student's search.

A Discussion Strategy

Large-group discussions often fail to meet a teacher's expectations. Teachers enter them with good intentions—to get students involved, to stimulate thinking, to encourage students to learn from one another, and to spark interest in a topic. But too often discussions wind down into private conversations among a few big talkers, with the bulk of the students becoming disinterested observers. When it comes to discussions that have a values focus, there are the added problems of minimizing senseless argumentation and avoiding peer pressure toward mindless conformity.

Careful planning is, thus, very important to a large-group discussion. Consider these four steps the next time you want a rich, *reflective* discussion on a values issue: select a topic, encourage students to think before talking, structure sharing, and help students extract learnings.

STEP 1:
SELECT A TOPIC

Sometimes a values discussion will naturally grow from ongoing activities. At other times, you may want to offer a topic that has important value implications for your group. To identify such a topic, listen carefully for issues that confuse your students. Or, depending on their ages, consider fashioning a question around a value-rich topic, such as friendship, money, rules, family, siblings, chores, religion, love, sexuality, work, careers, goals, leisure, or politics.

Some ways to initiate a discussion you may want to consider are using quotations, a picture without a caption, a scene from a play or movie, provocative questions, and other idea sources to generate interest.

Quotations

Write out a provocative quotation or read it to the class. For example, Gustave Flaubert said, "Nothing great is done without fanaticism. Fanaticism is religion; and the eighteenth century 'philosophers' who decried the former actually overthrew the latter. Fanaticism is faith, the essence of faith, burning faith, active faith, the faith that works miracles . . ."

After making sure that the class understands the quotation, the teacher might proceed with some questions to spur the discussion.

1. Are *you* a fanatic about anything?

2. What groups of people in our society seem fanatical to you? Why would you or wouldn't you join them in their efforts? What is better about *your* alternative?

3. How did you arrive at your decision about what to do?

4. Have you done anything lately about what you believe?

Here are several other quotations which have brought about exciting discussions:

> Thoreau: "The mass of men lead lives of quiet desperation. What is called resignation is confirmed desperation."

> Confucius: "To see what is right and to do nothing, that is cowardice."

> Hemingway: "I know only that what is moral is what you feel good after and what is immoral is what you feel bad after . . ."

A teacher's own portfolio of quotations will grow with experience in this approach. For hundreds of examples, see the Oxford Dictionary of Quotations. One warning we would make is that the teacher must be prepared to be disagreed with, perhaps to have a personal understanding of a favorite quote vastly increased. Further, the teacher must realize deep down that there is no one right answer to how one lives by the words of another person.

The Picture without a Caption

Using this approach, the teacher brings in a picture which tells a story of some kind. The picture should be large enough to be seen from all parts of the room or the teacher should use an opaque projector or transparency device. Students are asked to supply a caption describing what is going on in the picture. After various captions are examined, an attempt might be made to see what the students would have *done* in a similar situation. In one class, photographs of a street fight were used. In another, photographs of a group of pickets provoked a heated discussion.

A Scene from a Play or a Movie

To generate discussion, a teacher obtains the script from a play, television show, or a movie and duplicates a small part of it. Students act it out, but action is cut off before there is any solution to the problem. The students then take over and discuss what *should* have been done, how this situation was like something in their own lives, and so on. Showing films which are cut prematurely can also lead to interesting discussions. It is usually better to obtain excerpts from something students have *not* seen. Below we have an example, a brief scene from a play from the early 1940s, Maxwell Anderson's *High Tor.* A value-sensitive teacher will delight in the responses that an excerpt like this elicits.

The setting: a section of the broad flat traprock summit of High Tor, a mountain overlooking the Hudson River. Van, who lives by himself on the mountain, is having a picnic supper with his sweetheart, Judith, who has come to see him.

Judith: Van, I want to talk to you seriously.

Van: Can't be done. Listen, things get serious enough without setting out to do it.

Judith: Van, this spring you had three weeks' work, laying dry well. You could have had more, but you didn't take it. You're an expert mason . . .

Van: I'm good at everything.

Judith: But you work three weeks in the year . . .

Van: That's all I need . . .

Judith: And all the rest of the year you hunt or fish or sleep, or God knows what . . .

Van: Ain't it the truth?

Judith: Last fall I came looking for you once, and you were gone . . . gone to Port Jervis hunting . . . deer, you said on the postcard . . .

Van: Sure, I was hunting deer . . . didn't I bring you half a venison?

Judith: But not a word to me till I got the postcard ten days later . . .

Van: Didn't have a minute . . .

Judith: Then last winter there's a note nailed to a tree and you're in Virginia, down in the Dismal Swamp tracking bear. Now, for God's sake, Van, it's no way to live.

Van: Jeez, it's a lot of fun.

Judith: Maybe for you.

Van: You want me to take the job?

Judith: Why don't you, Van?

Van: Porter in a hotel, lugging up satchels, opening windows, maybe you get a dime, I'd choke to death.

Judith: I'd see you every day.

Van: Yeah, I could see you on the mezzanine, taking dictation from the drummer boys, all about how they can't get home. You can stand it, a woman stands that stuff, but if you're a man I say it chokes you.

Judith: We can't live in your cabin and have no money, like the Jackson Whites over at Suffern.

Van: Hell, you don't need money. Pap worked that out. All you need's a place to sleep and something to eat. I've never seen the time I couldn't find a meal on the mountain here, rainbow trout, jugged hare, something in season right around the zodiac.

Judith: You didn't like the Chevrolet factory, either?

Van: (walking toward the cliff edge). Look at it, Judy. That's the Chevrolet factory. Four miles down, and straight across, that's Sing Sing. Right from here you can't tell one from another; get inside and what's the difference? If you're in the factory you buy a car, and then you put in your time to pay for the thing. If you get in a hurry and steal a car, they put you in Sing Sing first, and then you work out your time. They graduate from one to the other, back and forth, those guys, paying for cars both ways. But I was smart. I parked at a police station and rung the bell and took to the woods. Not for your Uncle Dudley. They plugged the dice.

Judith: But one has to have a car.

Van: Honest to God now, Judy, what's the hurry? Where are we going?

Judith: If a man works hard, and has ability, as you have, Van, he takes a place among them, saves his money, works right out of the ruck and gets above, where he's safe and secure.

Van: I wouldn't bet on it much. But suppose it's true. Suppose a man saves money all his life, and works like hell about forty years, till he can say: goodby, I'm going, I'm on easy street from now on. What's he do? Goes fishing maybe? I'm on vacation now. Why should I work forty years to earn time off when I've got it?*

Provocative Questions

Provocative questions, such as the following, often stimulate rich discussions.

1. How often do you consider the consequences of what you do before acting?

2. How do you know when something is good or right?

3. Why should we give high salaries to some and low salaries to others?

4. How come so many of us want to get ahead and are never satisfied?

5. Consider examples, such as honest journalism or local democracy, in which a discrepancy exists between reality and what people say is supposed to be.

6. Should we do what we like to do? When and when not?

---

* *High Tor,* Copyright 1937 by Maxwell Anderson. Copyright renewed 1964 by Gilda Anderson, Alan Anderson, Terence Anderson, Quentin Anderson, and Hesper A. Levenstein. All rights reserved. Reprinted by permission of Anderson House, Hinsdale, N.Y.

7. When, if at all, is it right to tattle?

8. When, if at all, is it right to take dares?

9. What is *good* about teasing, war, thievery, prejudice, etc.?

10. Should the majority of the people be able to do *anything* with society?

11. What is *not* good about being law-abiding, generous, confident, obedient, wise, etc.?

12. How often do you do things you are not proud of?

13. How often do you do things just because others expect you to do them that way?

Other Idea Sources

Briefly, here are other suggestions for sources of materials to spur discussion having a value-clarification focus.

1. Editorials

2. Letters to the editor

3. Literature passed around at election time

4. Popular song lyrics

5. Tape recordings of news broadcasts and other programs

6. Tape recordings of interviews students have obtained from various persons in the community with strong viewpoints

7. Excerpts from speeches

8. Materials from embassies of foreign countries

9. Advertising

10. Cartoons, comic strips, etc.

11. Films

The list is endless, for the teacher will soon be deluged with materials which students begin to bring in because they know that discussion in their class often leads to an examination of things which are terribly important. If it is desirable, the teacher can select from the items brought in by students those which fit most fully into existing plans for subject-matter lessons and then relate the two. Such discussions have very valuable contributions to make toward motivating a study of a unit. For example, the *High Tor* discussion was used by a teacher to motivate a unit on mass production and automation. An English teacher made use of the Confucius quote and the discussion which followed to lead her students toward both a unit on biography and an examination of the opportunities in peoples' lives to turn their backs upon the wrongs they have witnessed.

Humorous Stories

Humorous stories like the following can also be used to initiate discussion.

1. President Carter once said that one day the preacher gave a sermon with the title "If you were arrested for being a Christian, would there be any evidence to convict you?"

2. The first woman said to the second woman, "How's your husband?" and the second woman replied, "Compared to what?"

3. The father was getting ready to pay the paper boy and did not have the correct change. He turned to his young daughter (three years old) and said, "Denise, will you lend me a dime? I'll give it back to you after I've been to the store." She consented, but when the father returned and gave her a dime, she examined it closely and said: "The dime I loaned to you had a five on it. You said you'd give it back, but you didn't. This is a different dime and I want my dime back."

STEP TWO: THINKING BEFORE TALKING

The second step of this sequence is to start individual thinking *before* the air gets filled with spoken words and students are thereby torn between listening and reflecting.

• Sometimes a teacher may ask all students to sit quietly and to think about the question for a minute or two.

• Sometimes it is best to ask all students to jot down some notes as they consider their initial reactions to the issue.

Without this space for individual reflection and thought, it is very difficult for the slow thinker, for those with an inclination to conform, or for those who think in complicated patterns to play a thoughtful role in a discussion.

STEP THREE:
STRUCTURE SHARING

Sometimes a discussion may be held including the whole class without any particular structure. A teacher might start a discussion by saying, "The floor is open to comments by anyone. No need to raise your hand." But usually some structure is desirable if the discussion is not to be dominated by a few big talkers. So you might say, "Let me call on a few people. Just say 'I pass' if you have no comment to make." Or say, "In this discussion, I'd like each person to speak only once until everyone who wants to has had a chance to make a comment."

Some teachers like to use small groups for discussions, both to facilitate involvement and to give more time and space for thoughtful comments. It is often hard for a student to be thoughtful in a large group where each person is thirsting for a chance to jump into the conversation or is afraid to participate. Small-group work is especially useful for limiting the influence of antagonistic students. Here are some procedures to try:

• Put students into pairs, trios, or quartets. Groups larger than four or five invite nonparticipation by the more timid students. Try to avoid friendship groups (see Chart 1, *Eight Ways To Form Small Groups*). Ask the small groups to *start* by whipping around the circle, giving each student a chance to make one initial comment about the topic. Groups are then to continue to discuss the issue informally until you call time.

• Do not give small groups too much time; it is often preferable to leave things unfinished rather than risk tedium. Call the class together and invite anyone to offer comments to the class. You might tell students, "You may give your own thoughts or report some of the thinking of your group."

Chart 1   *Eight Ways to Form Small Groups*

1. Any non-friends. "Without speaking, walk around until you find two others whom you do not know too well. Then the three of you sit together . . ."

2. Stand up continuum. "Stand along the walls according to birthdates, starting with January 1 in this corner." Adjacent students are then formed into groups. (Other criteria for lining up: alphabetically, according to height, according to how much a student enjoys television commercials, how much each one favors capital punishment, etc.)

3. Slips of paper. "I passed out slips of paper, each of which has a number (or animal, color, city, etc.). All the persons with the one's (or all the fish, etc.) sit in this spot, all the two's here . . ."

4.   Silly criteria. "I need three people who hate their brothers. O.K., you three will be group one. Now I need three persons who know how to ride a horse . . . (or wear glasses, like pizza, can't ride a bike, have grandparents in their home, are left-handed, love singing, play basketball, etc.)."

5.   Selection chain. "Harry, pick one person you do not know too well." Harry says, "Do I have to?" You say "yes" and Harry selects Beatrice. "Now Beatrice, you point to someone whom *you* do not know too well." And so on, the student just chosen in turn selecting the next student, until all students are placed in one group or another. This procedure usually takes a lot of time.

6.   Boy-girl groups. Boys and girls line up separately and both lines number off, one to whatever. Boy-girl pairs are formed. For quartets, two pairs are joined.

7.   A student committee does it. "Who would like to volunteer to take the class list and form quartets for us, trying to mix the groups as much as possible?"

8.   Counting off. Ask students to count off. For example, if you have thirty students and want to form trios, ask students to count off by tens. Then say, "One's sit here. Two's here . . ."

It is probably best not to let this large-group discussion go too long either. And don't always try to give someone from each group a chance to report, or the discussions can become everlasting.

• If a discussion is very lively after large-group recapitulation, with many students anxious to join in, the teacher might re-form the small groups or form new small groups so that students can interact with different people.

• Move on to step four.

STEP FOUR:
HELP EXTRACT LEARNING

Our last step is often to ask students to sit alone, this time to consider what they were able to learn from the experience. Perhaps ask each student to jot down endings to sentences such as these:

• I learned that. . . .
• I rediscovered that. . . .
• I'm beginning to wonder. . . .
• I was surprised that. . . .
• I never knew that. . . .

Then ask volunteers to share some of their learnings, either in small groups or with the class as a whole. Or ask students to record their learnings in a notebook or to turn in learnings to you for your information (preferably not to be graded).

Whenever possible, invite students to continue to explore any issues that dangle in their minds, if they care to do so: "Write your ideas more carefully and post them for all of us to see," Or perhaps say, "Read such-and-such if you want more information." You might help students who wish to pursue something further to write a learning contract, to form a study group with others, or to identify an individual project they can carry out.

Chart 2   *A Sample Discussion Lesson Plan (based on a class reading)*

Working alone	Sit for a moment and think back to the situation we just studied. Consider how Mr. X could have done things differently. Make some notes for yourself about what he might have done differently and what would probably have happened if he did that.
Trios	Now form into trios. Give each person a few minutes to tell his or her ideas. Then pick *one* of those ideas, and working together, develop it more fully. Be ready to tell us about one different thing Mr. X could have done and—this is important—tell us what the consequences would be for all the important persons in that situation.
Pairs of trios	Each trio now pairs with another trio. Each of your groups has developed a new ending to that situation. Take a few minutes and share those two endings with each other.
Whole class	Anyone want to share with the whole class some thoughts or learnings or an idea they particularly liked?
Working alone	Try to write an "I learned" statement. In a moment, I'll ask if a few persons would be willing to read aloud some of their "I learned" statements. Consider also whether you want to write up your personal idea or your group's idea and post it for others to see.

AVOIDING INDOCTRINATION IN VALUES DISCUSSIONS

The four-step discussion sequence—select a topic, start thinking before talking, structure sharing, and help students extract learnings—is suitable for any kind of class discussion. When the intent is to clarify values there should be one special focus: to avoid subtle indoctrination.

First let us distinguish two kinds of discussions. Some discussions have as their purpose the teaching or review of subject matter. In such discussions, the teacher can point to errors in data, make judgments about the adequacy of answers, and provide standards of rightness and wrongness.

Other discussions have as their purpose the clarification of student values. When discussions have this purpose, teachers must be willing to accept judgments they do not favor. If the teacher—no matter how subtly—were to restrict contributions in a value-clarifying discussion, he or she would be risking depriving students of the privilege of making their own decisions about the topic under consideration. Moreover, the teacher would be implying that students cannot do their own thinking and their own valuing, an implication that, if frequently repeated, would tend to convince students that it is so. The result would be a perpetuation of the conformity, apathy, indecisiveness, and overdissenting of which we spoke earlier.

The importance of this point cannot be overstressed. Many teachers habitually use leading questions in a discussion to help the student see, for example, that honesty is the best policy. This kind of guided discussion is well suited to the teaching of subject matter but disastrous for consideration of values. If the teacher thinks students are not ready to judge the issue of honesty, to use the same example, the teacher should not pretend to permit them to do so. He or she should tell them openly, "Students, we cannot let you decide this for yourselves right now. This decision is one that is too complicated (or dangerous) to give you. Most adults around here believe that honesty is the best policy, and you can expect to run into trouble if you behave in ways that contradict this. When you are older, you will certainly have a chance to think this through for yourself. Any questions?"

But when we *do* intend to give students a value choice, we must avoid leading the students to our values (or to any values). We must avoid using such a leading question as "Would you like *me* to be dishonest to *you?*" That question virtually demands one answer and reflects one position. When we have one answer in mind for a question, that question is unlikely to produce clarifying thought.

Below is an excerpt from a discussion between a class and a teacher who is concerned with value development but yet who will not permit dishonest behavior in the classroom. The problem here is maintaining standards while not denying that students must learn to think for themselves.

Teacher: So some of you think it is best to be honest on tests, is that right? (Some heads nod affirmatively.) And some of you think dishonesty is all right? (A few hesitant and slight nods.) And I guess some of you are not certain. (Heads nod.) Well, are there

	any other choices or is it just a matter of dishonesty *versus* honesty?
Sam:	You could be honest some of the time and dishonest some of the time.
Teacher:	Does that sound like a possible choice, class? (Heads nod.) Any other alternatives to choose from?
Tracy:	You could be honest in some situations and not in others. For example, I am not honest when a friend asks about an ugly dress, at least sometimes. (Laughter.)
Teacher:	Is that a possible choice, class? (Heads nod again.) Any other alternatives?
Sam:	It seems to me that you have to be all one way or all the other.
Teacher:	Just a minute, Sam. As usual we are first looking for the alternatives that there are in the issue. Later we'll try to look at the consequences of the alternatives we've identified. Any other alternatives, class? (No response.) Well, then, let's list the four possibilities that we have on the board and I'm going to ask that each of you do two things for yourself: (1) See if you can identify any other choices in this issue of honesty and dishonesty, and (2) consider the consequences of each alternative and see which ones you prefer. Later, we will have buzz groups in which you can discuss this and see if you are able to get clear about this.
Ginger:	Does that mean that we can decide for ourselves whether we should be honest on tests here?
Teacher:	No, that means that you can decide on the value. I personally value honesty; and although you may choose to be dishonest, I shall insist that we be honest on our tests here. In other areas of your life, you may have more freedom to be dishonest, but one can't do *anything any time,* and in this class I shall expect honesty on tests.
Ginger:	But then how can we decide for ourselves? Aren't you telling us what to value?
Sam:	Sure, you're telling us what we should do and believe in.
Teacher:	Not exactly. I don't mean to tell you what you should value. That's up to you. But I do mean that in this class, not elsewhere necessarily, you have to be honest on tests or suffer certain consequences. I merely mean that I cannot give tests without

the rule of honesty. All of you who choose dishonesty as a value may not practice it here, that's all I'm saying.

Thus in this discussion a teacher who is concerned that students develop an intelligent and viable relationship with their worlds—that is, develop clear values—(1) helps them to examine alternatives and consequences in issues, (2) does not tell them, directly or indirectly, what is "right" for all persons and for all times, (3) is candid about personal values but insists that they not be blindly adopted by others, (4) sometimes limits behavior that he considers ill advised but never limits the right to believe or the right to behave differently in other circumstances, and (5) points to the importance of individuals making their own choices and considering the implications for their own lives.

Value discussions do not end in ways similar to subject-matter discussions. There are no conclusions to draw, no consensus to identify, no test items to take. The teacher ends a value discussion merely by asking students to write "I learned" statements, by having somebody summarize what has gone on, by pointing to some next steps—such as the setting up of subgroups of those who are interested in talking further about the issue, or by offering an invitation to the class to raise the issue again at some appropriate time.

We often close our value discussions with the simple comment, "Well, class, *so what?* What use has this discussion been? Has it helped you in any real way? Think about this for a moment." After a long moment's pause we are apt to add, "If any of you adjust your life on the basis of the thought generated by this discussion, if you really live differently, I'd like to hear about it and how things work out. Please give me a note sometime, and also let me know if you would be willing for me to share it with the rest of the class."

8

Strategies to Expand
Awareness of Consequences

It is easy to stew in frustration when we see a young person acting with grand disregard for the consequences of her or his behavior. The person may be leaving materials messy. Or stealing. Or refusing to invest energy in work. Or driving recklessly. Or violating health requirements. Or ignoring social responsibilities. We are quick to carp, "Can't you see what will happen? What if everyone did that? Stop and think about the consequences of your acts."

This is probably not a very productive message, we suspect. Yet the intent is important: to get young people to look more broadly or further ahead and to consider more carefully what will result from their actions. The assumption, which we believe to be a sound one, is that the more we anticipate the future, the more intelligent our decisions and actions will be.

According to Dewey, anticipating consequences fully not only measures intelligent behavior but moral behavior as well. When we focus narrowly on one goal, such as one that suits us personally, and start acting to achieve that goal, we are more likely to act as if our end will justify any means, and we are more likely to neglect a whole host of other ends that just as certainly will result from our actions. The antidote is to reflect broadly and open-mindedly on anticipated outcomes, to "stop and think about the consequences of your acts," to use our earlier phrase.

> We all tend to relapse into this non-moral condition whenever we want any one thing intensely. In general, the identification of one end which is prominent in conscious desire and effort with *the* end, is part of the technique of avoiding a reasonable survey of consequences. The survey is avoided because of a subconscious recognition that it would reveal desire in its true worth and thus preclude this action to satisfy it—or at all events give us an uneasy conscience in striving to realize it. (Dewey, 1922, p. 230)

But the question we face here, and it is the question of this chapter, is what a teacher or other adult can *do* to help a young person become better at anticipating consequences. Let us look at some options.

The first option is so obvious that it is often overlooked: We might stop and consider whether or not something is pushing the student to disregard consequences. Too often, we find that the student is full of anger, is feeling hopeless, or is otherwise without the patience necessary for careful deliberations about future events. So the first step is diagnosis. Are some current emotions preempting thoughtfulness and perhaps even encouraging destructiveness? If so, helping the student with emotional needs is the logical step to take.

But many students who are not emotionally preoccupied will neglect to look ahead as far as they might. Sometimes this is because we have not encouraged the anticipation of consequences more frequently or modeled it more consistently. How might we do better? Here are some ideas:

- When reading a story, ask students about the extent to which a character thought about consequences *before* acting.

- Ask students to keep a consequence diary. "Keep track of all the times next week when you stop, think ahead, and then decide to do or *not* to do something."

- From time to time, have the class develop a list of possible consequences. "What will happen if we do this? If we don't do it?" "Let's list what would have happened if this machine was not invented?"

- Talk about experiences in your life when you did and did not anticipate consequences accurately.

- Have students list three alternative choices in a problem situation (academic or personal) and then have them list some key predictable consequences for each choice.

- Play some "guess what will happen" games in which the winner is the person who most fully anticipates the consequences of some action, experiment, or decision.

- Talk aloud about a decision while you are making it, mentioning the consequences that come to your mind, so young people can see the process in action. You might say, for example, "If we stop the discussion now we will probably forget about the issue. If we continue some people will get bored. Now let's see, what outcome do I think is preferable . . ."

Such activities bring the idea of consequences to the attention of students. Some of the activities of course also give students practice in anticipating consequences.

But we can do more. We can help students understand and appreciate more of the tangle of consequences that exist in our complex world. We can expand their awareness of the range of effects that spiral out from everyday acts. The trick to doing this seems to be to talk to students about types of consequences that they do not yet fully appreciate but are able to appreciate at that point in their development.

To identify what consequences students are capable of appreciating, we might look at the developmental sequence through which people typically acquire such understandings. This sequence, outlined in the following sections, is an interpretation of the research reported by Lawrence Kohlberg and his colleagues (1975).

LEVELS OF AWARENESS OF CONSEQUENCES

Unaware of Consequences (Level 0)—

Very young children are largely unaware of the consequences of their acts. Impulsiveness is the mode.

- "I just did it because I wanted to."

Punishment (Level 1)—

Soon enough, punishment comes into awareness. Children become aware that they might be punished for their acts. Especially if they feel vulnerable, they will tend to be obedient and to defer to power once they reach this level of awareness.

- "I don't want to get into trouble."

Self-interest (Level 2)—

Next comes an awareness of our own self interest, of what meets personal needs, of what gives gratification. Immediate gratification is often sought first at this stage. Awareness of the needs of others is also growing, but others are mostly used to trade off pleasures; the focus remains on self-interest.

- "I need others to take care of me."
- "I helped you last time. This time you should help me."

Approval from Others (Level 3)—

There next develops a clear awareness that others observe us and judge us. And with it comes an interest in winning the approval of others. A person now can find satisfaction in being seen as a "good guy" or a "good gal." We can now also appreciate more of others' internal states and can thus consider the consequences an act might have on anothers' feelings as well as on our own.

- "I hope I was a good boy today."
- "Sally was trying to help us even though she messed up the game."

Stability and Structure (Level 4)—

The next new element added seems to be an awareness of social structures and the importance of those structures in controlling behaviors. People who have reached this level make reference to specific rules and sometimes place great value on law and order. They are often ready to punish severely those who violate stability. Their interest is in keeping things steady rather than in progress. People at this level can appreciate the importance of loyalty to a group.

- "Everyone should believe in the Ten Commandments."
- "We've got to have law and order."

Individuality (Level 5)—

Human variability seems to be the next element to be appreciated. We begin to appreciate people different from ourselves. There is a willingness to bend laws to allow for individual needs. There is also a willingness to change individual laws to meet the needs of the group better. Freedom becomes highly regarded. This stage develops with a flexibility and an openness to change not seen at earlier stages. There is more tolerance for ambiguity and uncertainty. There also develops a respect for the processes by which issues are resolved. Due process and rational deliberation come to be seen as more important than existing laws or rules.

- "We should all cooperate and decide what's best."
- "There are exceptions to every rule."

Complex Wholes with an Emphasis on Justice (Level 6)—

We next see developed an appreciation and respect for interdependence. A person's view reaches for comprehension of all life. Any individual's rights are seen as dependent on the integrity of the complex whole. People who reach this level are able to feel the nobility of personal sacrifice performed for the good of the whole. They may feel proud to defy a law for a greater good. Often they can verbalize personal principles of life. No longer is law or even collective decision making seen as paramount; personal integrity and conscience are viewed as even more fundamental.

- "I try to live by treating others the way I would want others to treat me if our positions were reversed."

APPLYING
KOHLBERG'S IDEAS

Studies of many people in many cultures verify that people typically progress through the stages outlined one at a time and acquire new appreciations in the order of that list. Unfortunately, some people get stuck at one stage or another and never grow to be able to consider consequences on the most comprehensive levels.

The research also indicates that the best way to help a person move toward those more comprehensive levels is to identify the maximum level the individual can currently grasp and then to bring to attention ideas from the next higher level. Thus a person who has achieved level-three understandings, for example, would be best helped to grow by discussing ideas from level four, not ideas from levels five or six or from levels one, two, or three. The strategy is to lead a person ahead gradually and sequentially.

If, for example, we found children thinking on the punishment level (level one), we might look for an occasion to talk about the needs individuals have to find satisfactions in their lives or how we all can help each other to be happy (level two). Because of the developmental nature of these understandings, we would expect that these level-two ideas would be the next ones the children would be ready to grasp.

If we were talking to a child who seemed to appreciate his self-interest but not anything more (a level-two person), the next time an appropriate topic or issue emerged, we might ask him about being liked or approved by others and whether or not he cared about that. Since our intention would be to stimulate awareness and to invite growth and not to force change or to embarrass the student, we would do this as nonjudgmentally as we could.

If we were talking with students about stealing and the students took the position that it is alright to steal as long as everybody is doing it (level 3), we would talk about the importance of laws (a level-four idea). If the students were already able to appreciate law-level ideas, we would move to level five and talk about the advantage of not being arbitrary but of examining each stealing incident and the individuals who were involved before making a final judgment. If the students were already able to appreciate individual variability (level five), we would raise the issue of how stealing should fit into the whole picture of human relationships and if students believe that something more comprehensive might replace the absolute, "Thou shall not steal."

Thus, this developmental approach to appreciation of consequence aims to expand people's awareness gradually. The assumption is that the more consequences we can understand and consider when we make value judgments, the wiser our judgments can be.

To expand the range of consequences students appreciate, we can, as mentioned earlier, carefully pick which consequences to mention on the basis of an estimate of what stage students have already reached. But we can also promote growth by arranging for students to discuss morally problematic situations (situations in which we must balance several goods or bads to reach a judgment) by focusing attention on the consequences that would ensue from various alternative actions, and by asking students to judge the worth of those consequences.

If we can organize such discussions so that they proceed calmly enough, so that students do less arguing and more listening to each other's positions and reasonings, we can expect that the relatively mature students will communicate relatively mature awareness of consequences. Such expressions will have a leading effect on the thinking of the less mature students. Fortunately, students tend to grow upwards, not downwards, in awareness of consequences. When students share thinking, the lower-level students tend to grow. The higher level students do not tend to regress. Of course, it remains the teacher's responsibility to lead the thinking of the most mature students, unless—which is often the case—those students read or otherwise interact often enough with ideas more advanced than their own.

Also, teachers might consider having all students fill out value sheets from time to time that prompt them to consider ideas from various consequence levels—another method of bringing advanced levels to their attention. One example is included in this chapter as Value Sheet 1.

Value Sheet 1

SHOULD I HELP OUT?

1. Imagine that a teacher asked you if you wanted to help some other students. And imagine that you are trying to decide if you do want to help them.

Here are six things to think about at a time like that. Put a check mark by the one thought that would be *most like yours*. Which sounds most like you?

_____ Will I get punished if I don't do it?

_____ What's in it for *me?* Will *I* get help when I need it?

_____ If I help them, will the other students end up liking me more?

_____ Is there a rule about helping in situations like this one?

_____ What is best for all of us, all things considered?

_____ As I think about this situation and the kind of person I want to be, what is the best thing for me to do?

2. Then share your responses with some others. See if you can understand why others checked different things.

3. Now, after you had more time to think about this, go back to the original list. Want to change your check mark? Also, write a little about what you would *like* to be able to do, whether or not you would do it.

A final word about this notion of expanding students' awareness of consequences. This principle has much to do with the expansion of awareness of life itself. The more of the nuances of life we can appreciate, the more we will be able to appreciate and weigh the consequences of different behaviors. Of course, one of the best ways to expand a person's awareness of life is to involve the person in examples of the arts and humanities with which the person can identify emotionally, intuitively, or intellectually. That, after all, is what the arts and humanities are all about: messages about humanness. The finer the example, the deeper or broader or finer is the message communicated. We mention this impact because there is a trend in some schools away from arts and humanities. We would want to reexamine any such trend in our schools, especially to make sure that it is not a result of poor teaching—the exposure of students to examples of arts and humanities with which they cannot easily identify—or the use of teaching methods that do not, for example, expand awareness as much as they dull interest in the subject. Artists have exquisite messages about life for us, well told. It sometimes pains us to see those messages fogged by pedantic study.

Nineteen
Other Strategies

"No pleasure endures unseasoned by variety," said Syrus two thousand years ago, and there is plenty of variety for the teacher who would work at values. This chapter outlines nineteen miscellaneous strategies that can be used from time to time by any teacher, regardless of grade level or subject-matter specialty. Some of the strategies, such as voting and the public interview, take only a few moments and are perfect for occasional change-of-pace activities. Other strategies, such as value reports and action projects, can be blended directly into subject-matter units and made a part of the academic curriculum.

Each teacher will find different ways to use each strategy. But all the strategies do two things. First, they focus our attention on life. They bring to mind our attitudes, feelings, activities, goals, aspirations, interests, beliefs, and worries. Or they raise some of the confusing issues of life: relationships, money, hope, power, generosity, justice, and the rest.

Second, they help us deal with life more skillfully and more comprehensively. They give us practice in choosing freely, seeking alternatives, anticipating consequences, recognizing what we prize and cherish, standing up and affirming what we care about, acting on our choices and prizings, and doing so with some consistency.

In short, each strategy activates part of the values-clarification theory. Collectively they communicate the style of that theory in action.

1. RANK ORDERS

. . . to practice making decisions

A teacher says to the class, "Before we get into our work today, look at the three words on the board: *wealthy, wise, good-looking*. Let's go down the people in the first row and get to know them better by seeing how they would rank those words. Mary, you're first, which would you rather be, wealthy, wise, or good-looking? Say those three words in the order that shows your preferences."

After Mary, the teacher calls on the next person to say the three words. Explanation is avoided. The procedure has each person, one after another, say the three words, showing how each would rank the items personally.

After five or six people, or however many the teacher chooses, a moment or two of general discussion might be invited: "Anyone have a different ranking? Or want to say something about this?" But discussion is not necessary. The teacher may just explain the strategy a bit and then go on with other lessons.

"From time to time we may do something like this. It's just a chance to get to know each other better and to open up some issues you may want to think about further on your own, or with your friends or family. Besides, it gives you some practice in making choices."

Besides providing decision-making practice rank ordering also reminds us that different people have different preferences and that we can reveal those without a lot of argumentation, discussion, or loss of friendship.

Rank orders can be used simply as an occasional value-clarifying experience, without reference to subject matter. But they can also be used in connection with subject matter. Thus a physics or science teacher, introducing a unit on momentum, might talk briefly about how car accidents demonstrate the power of momentum and then, to exercise value skills, might ask students, "If an older brother were driving too recklessly to suit you, would you more likely (1) say nothing, (2) say that you prefer slower driving, or (3) complain or whine."

This exercise is not a time to settle complicated matters. Rank orders simply open issues, exercise our ability to make choices, and help us appreciate differences and get to know one another better. Used every once in a while, with or without a subject-matter connection, they add a dash of values-clarification to the group experience.

Here are some other possibilities:

1.   Which would bother you most: finding gum under your shoe in a movie theater, having the people behind you talking throughout the movie, or having the row in front stand up and file out before you finished watching the last scene?"

2.   Which do you like better: lectures, discussions, workbooks?

3.   Which would be easiest for you: telling someone he has bad breath, sending him a note about it, doing nothing?

4.   Which would you prefer: being told you had bad breath, receiving a note, not being informed in any way?

5.   Which is hardest: being rejected by a friend, being hit by a big boy, losing your wallet?

6.   Which do you prefer in a friendship: loyalty, generosity, honesty?

7.   Which would you rather be: a black American, a black African, or a black Mexican?

8. Who would be the easiest to live without: your parents, your friends, or your brothers and sisters?

9. Which would you rather have: a loving father, a cheerful father, or a famous father?

2. VALUE PAIRS

. . . to exercise value thinking and speaking

Here is a convenient, high-interest, endlessly repeatable activity that prompts students to reflect on their values, hear what others are thinking, and grow in respect and appreciation of their peers.

"We have fifteen minutes extra this morning," a teacher might say, "so I'd like to introduce a new activity, called *value pairs.* The first step is for you to pair yourselves up with someone in the room. Now in each pair decide who will be number one and who will be number two.

"OK, now everyone make a note of these three questions. What have you done recently that made you feel proud and good about yourself? What sometimes worries you? And what's a good way to handle a conflict when two people disagree about which TV program to watch?

"When I say start, I'd like person Number One to respond to any one— only one—of those questions. Person number two just listens quietly. Then person number two gets a chance to respond to any one of the questions. And number one just listens.

"Then number one gets a second chance. And continue to take turns that way until I call time. When it comes your turn, you can talk about any question you like, even if you have done it before. Sometimes you think of new things to add.

"Got it? You'll just have a few moments for this exchange, so don't use much time."

And then it begins. The students more-or-less think and share. The teacher keeps an eye on involvement, warns the group that 30 seconds are left when interest appears to start to wane, and calls time too early rather than too late. We want to start thinking here, neither exhaust it nor deplete student interest. Then the teacher says, "You may want to pick up the conversations again at lunchtime or after school. Be responsible for taking care of your own unfinished business. But now we need to move on. I'd like to give you a chance to share thoughts with someone new. In a moment I'll ask you to shift over to new partners. All the number one's will stand and find a new seated number two. Then you will have another few moments to take turns telling your answers to the questions and hearing what your new partner has to say. Same three questions. You can give your old answers or say new answers, if you like. As soon as you switch partners, begin your exchange of answers. But this time person number two takes the first turn.

Afterwards, time permitting, a third round might be held or even a fourth. It is almost always better to keep the pace fast and hold several brief rounds than to hold fewer slow-paced rounds. A fast pace keeps students alert and interested. It also allows students to get to talk with more of their peers, to hear more alternative thoughts and further expand their thinking, and to express more often their own thoughts and further refine their thinking.

For brief time periods, one round value pairs would be sufficient. Once the students learn the pairing and shifting procedures, it takes little time. A second round could be conducted a second day using the same questions or, if the original three generated only tepid exchanges, using different questions.

For variety the teacher might pose one question to groups of four sitting together. One person in each group starts by answering the question. The group then whips around the circle, each person in turn answering or saying "I pass," until time is called. Then the teacher gives a new question and the whip-around is repeated.

Where do you find good questions? The first guideline is to listen to the lives of the group, to see what issues are in their lives. Some general guidelines can also help you. Chart 1, *A Grid for Value Questions,* found on the next page, can be useful. Interesting value questions can usually start from any item in any column. The third column only suggests value-rich topics. Revise it to suit the age-level of your group.

For example, here is a question stimulated by the first item in each column:

- "Choosing freely": What was a choice you once had that gave you trouble, when you didn't know what to decide?

- "Goals, purposes": Do you usually make plans for doing things on weekends or do you just play it by ear, doing whatever comes along?

- "Friendship": What is a good or a bad thing you remember a friend of yours once did?

Excellent questions often come from connecting two or more items, within a list or across lists. See the examples at the top of page 155.

Chart 1   *A Grid for Value Questions*

Valuing processes	*Value indicators*	*Value-rich topics*
choosing freely	goals, purposes	friendship
searching for alterna-	aspirations	stealing
tives	attitudes	family
predicting conse-	interests	money
ąuences	feelings	impulsivity
clarifying what is	beliefs, convictions	hobbies
prized, cherished	activities	authority
sharing, affirming what	worries, problems, ob-	love
one cares about	stacles	dating
acting, doing some-	thinking	rules
thing about choices		school
and prizings		religion
building patterns,		sexuality
consistency in life		work
		cooperation
		poverty
		internationalism
		evironmentalism
		peace
		racism
		sexism
		marriage
		tenderness
		loyalty
		honesty
		change
		machines
		television
		workmanship
		generosity
		pets
		censorship
		propaganda
		abortion
		bureaucracy
		corruption
		jealousy
		fears
		envy
		guilt
		violence

- "Alternatives" and "aspirations": What are three different things people sometimes aspire to but that you will probably not have for your life?

- "Aspirations" and "stealing": If you get married and have your own family some day, how would you like to react to your child being caught stealing? How would you like *not* to react?

- "Consequences" and "family" and "money": In the long run, which do you think would have the best outcomes: giving children an allowance if they promise to help around the home, giving them an allowance whether they help or don't help, insisting that they earn their spending money by working outside of the home?

The most intriguing questions often are created out of a general area suggested by those columns:

- How do you feel about swearing?

- Tell about a dream you once had.

- What are some things you like (dislike) about yourself?

- What names do you like as well or better than your own?

- Give some examples of when you would probably put your foot down and *not* follow the crowd?

- Might you ever get hooked on smoking or drugs, do you think?

- How do you go about making friends or meeting new people?

- What questions would you like to hear the answer to?

Many questions, of course, can be repeated with a new focus:

- What thoughts do you have about (television commercials, brushing teeth, etc.)?

- What do you do or feel when (you lose something, your life get complicated, it rains, etc.)?

- Tell about some of your (patterns in life, strong beliefs, risks attempted, etc.).

- What are some things you sometimes wonder about (marriage, work, teachers, dating, etc.)?

- What might you want to whisper to (your mother, father, the president, a person who bugs you, etc.)?

With the grid for value questions as a guide, you might brainstorm a list of possible questions with other teachers or with the students themselves. Eventually you will accumulate a file of more thought-provoking questions than you can ever use.

Use some of those questions in the strategy called "value pairs," perhaps when your group is weary and in need of revitalization, and you can expect an increase in hard thinking on life issues, more openness and sharing among the students, and a generally warmer group climate as a bonus.

Finally, there is nothing wrong with building academic lessons onto the value-pair experience. You might have students write compositions or read in literature or history for a greater perspective on topics. (Additional thoughts about subject matter and values are to be found in Chapter 10.) But we find that such strategies as value pairs work fine as group revitalizers, climate builders, and value clarifiers, and we recommend you consider trying them simply for those purposes. See if the results you get do not easily justify the time required.

3. THOUGHT SHEETS

. . . for private value sharing

When we enter into value clarification, we need to be on the lookout for ways to elicit value expressions consistently. One of the most effective techniques for doing this and for getting to know each student as an individual involves giving students the opportunity to write freely about anything in their lives. This gets directly at the students' concerns and does not rely upon topics initiated by the teacher.

Using this strategy, each week a student turns in a single sheet or perhaps a four-by-six-inch card upon which has been written some thought of importance to *the student*. It is written after due reflection and should indicate something of the quality of living in the preceding week. These are called "thought sheets." To introduce them, the teacher may say something like this:

1. A thought sheet is due every week on Monday. It is to be your ticket of admission to class on that day.

2. Thought sheets may be of any length, any style, any form. Prose, poetry, skit, drawing, etc. —all are acceptable. However, a few words are enough. Long statements are not necessary.

3. A thought sheet may be on *any* topic as long as it represents *your* thoughts, feelings, interests, and so on.

4. Your thought sheets will not be graded or corrected in any way. They are treated as sincere expressions of some of your deepest concerns and are not to be written as "compositions" to impress the teacher. They are yours.

5. If you do not have anything to tell about your life some week, just turn in a slip of paper with your name saying, "No thought for this week."

Students are also told that from time to time excerpts from some of the thought sheets will be read to the class anonymously. The first week the teacher should be careful to read a selection of them to illustrate the different forms and styles and kinds of topics that are possible. This is healthy stimulation to those students who wait cautiously to see if the teacher is kidding in saying that students can write anything important *to them*.

It is fun for teachers to read over the thought sheets. We get to know the complex realities, lovely and sad, behind some of the familiar classroom faces. And that allows us to be helpful to individuals sometimes, to offer empathy often, and to appreciate almost always.

Here are some excerpts from thought sheets that students have written:

I can see why you brought up the point yesterday about whether feeling alone in the world might be a horrible experience or an exhilarating one. Now that I think about it . . .

. . . A bright flash emanated from the object in the shop. The watchman lay dead. Another tape clicked from the computer, "IT'S ALL RIGHT. THE HUMAN IS DEAD, COMMENCE WORK." The shop came to life again.

Exams to me are a waste of time. After all, what is an exam? What does it show? Nothing! It doesn't prove whether I have learned anything over the year, because I could study before the test and probably a few days later I wouldn't remember a thing. If a final is given, it might not be a bad idea to give it unannounced without letting the students "prepare" for it.

> . . . As I watch the space up high
> In my mind I wonder why
> I ever thought big was I
> For if big am I what is the sky?

The other day, coming home from school, I saw a very bad fight. I wanted to stop it, but I didn't know what to do. I didn't do anything and I am ashamed.

When thought sheets are read, the classroom usually comes to a most respectful hush. Students like to hear the thoughts—honest thoughts—of fellow students. Comments following the reading are usually lively and direct. The unidentified author frequently takes part in the verbal exchange. Everyone listens to and experiences contact with students who may be doing exciting and important things. We hear of alternatives or consequences in life we had **never** considered. It is a mirror held up to our own lives. A thought-sheet reading time is one of the most vibrant of schoolroom activities, and one of the most productive in terms of values clarification.

Often a teacher will return thought sheets to students with notes penned in the margins. "Interesting," we might write. Or "Thank you for sharing it with me." Or "I'll bet you were angry that day." Or "I wish I could have seen your happy face."

Sometimes a teacher will think of a comment that might produce some clarifying thought: about free choices, about alternatives, about consequences, about being proud, about sharing feelings, about taking action, or about building patterns in life.

We may simply choose to commend the writer on her or his thoughtfulness. We may suggest something to read on the topic, something which may be in direct opposition to the student's expression. We do this because we know that a value must be chosen from among alternatives and that we must be able to stand up and affirm our position, even in the face of another strong opinion. Sometimes reading a thought sheet provides us with an important contact for value-clarifying discussion with a student.

Thought sheets may be valuable in other uses also. The teacher may hold thought sheets for students or ask the students to save them and then, after 10 or 12 weeks, may pose some questions to help students clarify the lives revealed by their sheets. Some questions to use in such an exercise include:

   1.   Which of your sheets reflect your most cherished beliefs or attitudes?

   2.   Which sheets would you drastically rewrite at this point?

   3.   Can you spot a pattern to the things you stand for as they are revealed in your thought sheets?

   4.   Which of your sheets would make worthy "editorials" for the school paper?

   5.   Pick the one sheet which you would most like the class to know you wrote.

   6.   If your thought sheets have not yet made you proud, what can you do about it?

7. Pick one sheet in which you expressed a very strong, positive opinion. Have you done anything about it?

8. Why do you or do you not like to write these sheets?

One English teacher, William Dell, whose students wrote the excerpts quoted earlier, used thought sheets as a means not only to exercise value thinking but to practice more formal writing. Chart 2 shows an assignment sheet he distributed to his classes.

Chart 2   *Thought Sheet Theme Assignment*

Read over *all* of the thought sheets that you have written so far. Then write a theme on *one* of the following topics.

1. Summarize what you seem to be saying in your thought sheets. What seems to be the direction or trend of your thinking and feelings? You may find that you might be concerned with one or more of the following questions.

- What is my outlook on life?
- What do I value in life?
- What are my goals and purposes?
- What do I believe in?
- What are my problems?
- What things am I interested in?
- How do I spend my time?
- What do I think about?

2. Take one or more of your thought sheets and compare it in terms of style, form, and content to one or more of the rest of your thought sheets. Be thorough.

3. Take one or more of your thought sheets and expand the content into a theme, story, or poem.

4. Sort through your thought sheets and notice if they seem to classify themselves into certain groups. What headings would you give to these groups? Discuss what these headings tell you about your life—such as your thoughts, feelings, concerns, observations, awareness and so on.

5. Select your *best* thought sheet and your *worst* thought sheet. What is good about your best? What is bad about your worst?

Thought sheets provide an amazingly accurate gauge of how intense the search for values has become in an individual classroom. One of the most rewarding things to a teacher is to see how many students continue to write thought sheets on their own when they have ceased to be an assignment. Indeed, some teachers make the writing of thought sheets optional as soon as the idea is grasped, which usually takes at least four weeks. Making the writing optional greatly reduces the number written, but insures that those that are written are truly thoughtful, deeply and personally. Try thought sheets several ways and see which approach suits you best.

4. WEEKLY REACTION SHEETS

. . . for looking at our daily lives

A time to sit down and look back very systematically at a week just lived is helpful to value growth. Upon reflection, many youngsters are surprised to see the absence of activities which are personally satisfying, and some may come to question just how many weeks have passed in this manner.

Five copies of a weekly reaction sheet are passed out to each student, and students are then asked to fill out one sheet for each of the next five weeks, sometimes in substitution for the thought sheet. Among the questions which we have included on the weekly reaction sheets are:

1.   Did you act on any of your values this week? What did you do?

2.   Did you do anything this week which required more than three solid hours?

3.   What, if anything, did you do this week of which you are proud?

4.   Did you work on any plans this week for some future experience you hope to have?

5.   List one or two ways in which the week could have been better.

6.   Were you in emphatic agreement or disagreement with anyone this week?

7.   What did you learn this week, in or out of school, that you are likely to use in your later life?

8.   What did you do this week that made you very happy?

9.   What was the best day of the past week? What made it the best?

10. Are you happy with the way you spend your weekends? How could you improve them?

11. Identify three choices you made during the week.

12. Were there important contradictions or inconsistencies in your week?

13. How was this week different from the previous week?

A teacher would need to select a few questions from this list and, of course, include other questions to encourage the process of values clarification. We would not use thirteen questions at one time.

The purpose of the weekly reaction sheet is to promote value thinking. Thus, useful questions are those that touch on choosing freely, choosing from alternatives, and choosing after consideration of consequences; prizing choices and being willing to affirm them; and acting on choices and acting in some pattern of living. Regular attention to questions such as those on the reaction sheets encourages people to take hold of their lives and live them more positively, enthusiastically, purposefully, and proudly.

A variation on the weekly reaction sheet is the *daily reaction sheet.* For this strategy, the teacher poses one question everyday or every other day and each student takes a moment or two of class time to write a response to it. For example, one fifth-grade teacher asked students every morning to complete a sheet headed, "Things I did since yesterday morning of which I am proud." After a few weeks of this practice, the teacher noted new awareness of behavior among children.

It is important to realize that there will be some resistance from students who feel that this kind of questioning borders on prying or invading privacy. We inform students that they have the right to leave any questions blank at any time. However, to leave any particular question blank for three or more times may also bring forth a gentle "why" from the teacher.

What does the teacher do with these reaction sheets as they come in? Although the main purpose of the reaction sheets is served when students think about the questions and answer them, the sheets become even more valuable (and motivation to do them thoughtfully is increased) when teachers use them in some way. Here are three ideas:

1. We may simply read them to look for any pleas for help or guidance. We may comment on some of the points made. We may ask questions, either directly of the student or in the margins of the student's paper. We may call a conference if one seems to be wanted or needed.

2. We may mimeograph several student responses to one particular question or read them aloud and give the class an opportunity to discuss these responses.

3. We may have the students exchange reaction sheets and then interview each other about how life is going, about what is being learned, about what each would change, and about how students can help one another think through problems or support one another's efforts to change. (Note that the students' anonymity would be violated with this approach. In most circumstances they should be warned of this ahead of time.)

Whatever we do with these reaction sheets, they are one of the important ways we have of helping students examine in some consistent manner the relationships between thoughts and the ways in which we spend our time.

5. OPEN-ENDED SENTENCES

. . . for beginning clarifying thinking

The two preceding strategies—the thought sheet and the weekly reaction sheet—are best used regularly in a patterned way. On the other hand, open-ended questions can be used anytime to help students clarify and share some of their activities, attitudes, beliefs, and other "value indicators."

The teacher starts by giving one or more open-ended sentences orally, on a duplicated sheet, or written on the chalkboard. Two examples are "If I had twenty-four hours to live . . ." and "Three of the most important things to me are . . ." Students might then be invited to share their endings in small groups. The class, for example, could be randomly formed into groups of four. Groups then whip around the circle, starting with the person wearing the most red, giving each person a turn to complete the sentence or say, "I pass." After all students have had a turn, they can be instructed to chat informally about the issue or each other's responses until the teacher calls time and perhaps offers a new sentence for the groups.

Another approach is to have students write responses to the sentences, perhaps as homework. The teacher then can write a single comment on each paper. This comment need take very little time. A simple question will help students reflect on their writings.

The teacher may also read several papers aloud anonymously to the class and ask any class members if they have any questions or comments they would recommend to this anonymous author. This is one of the ways we have of teaching our students the value-clarifying process. Often students' questions reveal more sensitivity than the teacher's.

A subject-matter unit might grow out of such writings. For students who are studying a person's life or reading literature, a rich lesson grows from asking them to try to deduce how that person might answer certain open-ended questions. A comparison of results and the justification of answers provides depth understanding and exciting thinking.

Here are some other open-ended questions which have been productive:

1. With a gift of $100, I would. . . .

2. If this next weekend were a three-day weekend, I would want to. . . .

3. My best friend can be counted on to. . . .

4. My bluest days are. . . .

5. I can hardly wait to be able to. . . .

6. *My* children won't have to. . . , because. . . .

7. People can hurt my feelings the most by. . . .

8. If I had a car of my own. . . .

9. I've made up my mind finally to learn how to. . . .

10. If I could get a free subscription to two magazines, I would select. . . , because. . . .

11. Some people seem to want only to. . . .

12. The night I stayed up later than ever before I. . . .

13. If I could have seven wishes. . . .

14. I believe. . . .

15. Secretly I wish. . . .

16. My advice to the world would be. . . .

6. CODED STUDENT PAPERS

. . . to reexamine what we have said

All of us are familiar with the ways teachers "go over" students' papers for grammar, spelling, and other errors in expression or thinking. It also seems important to help students face the nature of the value they express. Coding student papers for values does this.

First, the teacher asks students to do writing which is apt to elicit value-related expression. Papers on controversial topics, thought sheets, weekly reaction sheets, or open-ended questions can, of course, be used for this. The teacher then marks a plus sign on the paper over those expressions which indicate something the student seems to be *for* and a minus sign over those *against*. It is a simple process. A teacher can come to do it with great speed. For students there often is a quiet impact. For the first time they may become aware of what they say they are for and against.

When the paper is returned, students are asked to change any statements they have made and wish to change. They are also asked to rewrite any parts to say more fully what they really want to say. Furthermore, they are asked to comment on any grouping pattern, or any serious inconsistency which emerges from the things they seem to be for and against.

The teacher may choose also to read the paper in a search for statements which reveal other value indicators: interests, activities, purposes, beliefs, feelings, aspirations, and so on. Students may be asked questions in the margin which attempt to clarify the value indicators. For example, "Have you *done* anything about this?" or "Where did you first get this idea?"

Since critical thinking is such an important part of the clarification process, the teacher may also, on some papers, call attention to students' statements which reveal that a serious *assumption* is made, or that *extreme* statements have been used, or that *either-or* thinking is in evidence, and so on.

Students have the option of answering or not answering the questions posed. They may or may not arrange for a conference to talk further about the questions. A short correspondence may result between the teacher and student. No one can *make* a student value, but a teacher can stimulate clarification.

It may seem that the teacher's volume of work would get to be overwhelming once this paper-coding routine began. We have found, however, that the coding adds very little time compared to the usual comments teachers make on students' papers, while the growth which sometimes takes place as a result of this clarification process can be dramatic.

The roots of a student's values can grow before they reach his or her awareness. By coding writings, we can hold the hints of a young person's thinking up to the light, so that the student can reflect on them and perhaps clarify them.

Here are some additional symbols you might want to consider using with this coding strategy.

E *Extremes* (all, none, every, never, always). Are you sure? Would you change this on reconsideration?

I *Indefinites* (some, seldom, sometimes, perhaps, a few, might). Is this unnecessarily vague? Can you be more specific?

VJ *Value judgments* (wasted time, a good lesson, it was unfortunate, a difficult job, a wonderful man). Are you making a judgment that others might not agree with? Do you want to be more objective here?

AT   *Attributing* a situation or a person's feelings on unstated evidence (she overlooked the student, he wanted to cry, she felt badly, he teased her, Sal likes reading, they were afraid to answer, a productive lesson). Are you sure? Have you made it clear to the reader that this is only your inference from the data? Would it be better to omit this, or state the basis for your interpretation?

Alt.   *Alternatives* (either we do this or that; if this happens, then that results; John should do thus and so; from the information we can conclude such and such.) Are there other alternatives? Have you considered other possibilities?

G   *Generalizations* (since our friends like it, boys everywhere will; after examining three towns, an authority states. . . ; after talking to him for five minutes I could tell what kind of person he was). Have you overgeneralized? Do you have enough data for the conclusions you are making?

OS   *Oversimplification* (money leads to happiness, a college education will make a cultured man, Japan started the war, we need more scientists to win the cold war). Have you oversimplified the situation? Have you inappropriately reduced a complex situation to simple terms?

PR   *Projection* (teachers deserve higher salaries, he should quit, they discriminate against people like me, bright students should get more attention than dull students, John cannot be taught anything). Have you examined your own motives here? Could it be that you are projecting your own feelings into the situation, perhaps not consciously?

D   *Dogmatic* Are you sure? Have you considered alternatives?

7. THE TIME DIARY

. . . to mirror our behaviors to us

At the highest level, the use of time is consistent with one's values. In effect, people do what they value and value what they do. But all lives are not lived at this level. For many of us, there is a terribly visible gap between our use of time and what we claim to cherish.

This gap can be illuminated and often partially closed for students by having them keep a time diary. A time diary is simply a chart of one week's activities broken down into perhaps half-hour segments. In each half-hour block, students record what happened in their lives. The teacher does not ask to see this record, for time diaries are often very personal. But the teacher does ask each student to analyze the completed diary with questions like these in mind:

1. How do you feel about how you spent your time?

2. What proportion of your time represents your life at a truly gratifying level?

3. What inconsistencies, if any, are there in the week's activities?

4. What proportion of time was used for things that you do not value highly?

5. When you are older, do you think that you will be proud of having used that week in your life in that way?

After individuals have examined their diaries from the perspective of questions such as those, a discussion that shares insight is useful, although not necessary. It would be more important for the student to summarize what has been learned from study of the time diary and give that summary (*not* the answers to the questions above) to the teacher for comment or simple recognition. Also very useful is a repeat of the time-diary assignment after some weeks, with the added assignment that a comparison be made of the two weeks' records.

8. AUTOBIOGRAPHICAL QUESTIONNAIRE

. . . to begin to tell our tales

Early in the term teachers can take a step to find out as much as possible, short of prying, about their students. A rather lengthy autobiographical questionnaire can be distributed. Students have the right not to answer any question; but again the tone is one of encouragement, support, and acceptance. The data that comes in can be reviewed or can be filed until such time as information about a particular student is desired, perhaps when value indicators are needed in order to work with a particular student.

Some sample questions for an autobiographical questionnaire follow; but each teacher should adapt, add to, and eliminate questions from this list to suit his particular class.

1. Name

2. Birthdate   Age in years

3. Address   Phone number

4. What other schools did you go to? Tell me something about them.

5. Who are the people in your family? If you had to use two sentences to describe each person, what would you say about each member of your family?

6. Have you ideas about what you would like to do when you grow up?

7. What possibilities have you talked over with your parents?

8. Does your father work? What does your father do for a living?

9. What are some of his interests, hobbies, etc.? What does he do when he isn't working?

10. Does your mother work? What does she do for a living?

11. What are her interests, hobbies, etc.? What does she do when she isn't working?

12. How do you spend your time after school?

13. Of all the things you do in your free time, which do you like most?

14. Which do you like least?

15. What does your family usually do for Thanksgiving? Christmas?

16. What have you done the last two summers?

17. What have you done the last two Christmas vacations?

18. What magazines do you read regularly?

19. Do you subscribe to any yourself?

20. What are your favorite television shows?

21. Have you seen any movies in the last few months which you particularly liked?

22. Tell me a sentence or two about each movie and why you liked it.

23. What are your favorite sports, if any?

24. If I were to ask you what books you've read which you've liked the best, what would you answer?

25. Do you work after school or on weekends? Where? What are you using the money for?

26. What do you like best about school?

27. What do you like least about school?

28. If you could change some part of your educational program, what would it be?

29. If you were a teacher, how would you teach your classes?

30. Have you a hobby which takes up a lot of your time? What is it?

31. How did you get interested in it?

32. Which of your friends are interested in it with you?

33. Who are some of your friends who aren't interested in this activity?

34. Is there an adult outside of school whom you dislike intensely? Why?

35. Are there some adults outside of school whom you admire intensely? Why?

36. Do you have some good ideas about things which you might like to mention?

37. Have you ever invented anything? What?

38. What is there about you which makes your friends like you?

39. Is there something you want badly but can't quite afford right now? What?

40. Of all the people you know who have helped you, who has helped the most? How did they go about it?

9. THE PUBLIC INTERVIEW

. . . to appreciate one whole person

One of the more dramatic value techniques is called the *public interview.* Let's look at one which took place in an elementary school class and see how it develops.

Teacher: Today, class, I would like to introduce the public interview. For this we need a volunteer, someone willing to be interviewed publicly, in front of the whole class.

The person interviewed comes up and stands or sits here at my desk, in front of the room. I will go to his or her seat and interview from there. The spotlight, you see, is on the person being interviewed.

Now, what I will do first is ask what topic the interviewee wants to talk about. You as the interviewee can choose one of the topics on our list of value areas, or any other topic—even a very particular topic, such as what you did over the weekend, or an idea you have, or a problem or decision you are facing. Anything you choose.

You can even choose "dealer's choice," and then I will just ask any questions that occur to me. Then I will ask you questions—questions that may help *you* get clearer on the topic of the interview or questions that I think may help the class to get to know you better.

If you volunteer, relax, you always have an out. If I ask you any question that is too personal or that you would rather not answer here in front of everyone, you just say, "I pass," and I will go right on to another question.

And if you want to end the interview, you just say, "Thank you for your questions." That's the signal for you to take your own seat and for the interview to terminate.

Got it? The volunteer picks the topics or can pick dealer's choice. You can say "I pass," whenever you want to pass a question. And say "Thank you for your questions," if you want to terminate the interview before time runs out.

Now how many brave souls would be willing to be the first one interviewed?

(There is a pause as, one by one, five or six hands emerge from laps. The teacher waits, finally selecting Paul, a rather secure boy, a safe bet for such a new venture.)

All right, Paul, you be the first. Others may have a chance another time. Take my seat, Paul. I'll sit in the back. How do you feel, Paul?

Paul: (In the teacher's chair.) O.K., I guess.

Teacher: Do you recall what you say if you would rather not answer a particular question? (Making certain the safeguards are understood.)

Paul: "I pass."

Teacher: And if you want to end the interview before time runs out?

Paul: I say, "Thank you for your questions."

Teacher: Fine, Paul, now on what topic would you like to be interviewed?

Paul: My sister.

Teacher: Would you care to tell us something about your sister, Paul?

Paul: Not especially. Except that we hate each other. I want to be interviewed, asked questions, rather than just to say something.

Teacher: O.K., Paul. What do you hate about your sister?

Paul: Well, she is two years younger than I am, and she always is in the way. Like she argues about what TV program to watch, and she hangs around me when I'm playing, and she . . . she is just a nuisance.

Teacher: Are there some times when you *like* having her around?

Paul: No, absolutely not. (Laughter.)

Teacher: How do you define *hate?* What do you mean by that word?

Paul: Terrible. Like I want to murder her. She should go away.

Teacher: What's the difference between hate and dislike?

Paul: One is stronger. Hate is stronger.

Teacher: What is the difference between hating someone and hating things that the person does?

Paul: Hmm. I just thought of a time when I didn't hate my sister. Once we were walking along and someone said how nice we looked together, we were younger and were walking hand in hand. It was a good feeling. But, I don't know. If you hate enough things a person does I guess you end up hating the person. Is that right?

Teacher: What do you think?

Paul: I don't know.

Teacher: Paul, what are you going to do about the situation between you and your sister? Apparently you don't like things the way they are.

Paul: What can I do? I know what I'd *like* to do . . . (Laughter.)

Teacher: Well, one thing you can do is keep away from her. Another is try to work things out so that there is less argument and conflict between you. What other alternatives are there?

Paul: I don't know. I don't know. But thank you for your questions. Can I go now?

Teacher: Certainly, Paul. That's the rule. Whenever you want. Thank you. (Moving to the front of the class.) Maybe we'll ask for another volunteer for a public interview tomorrow, but now let's get ready for our arithmetic work.

The purpose of the public interview is twofold: First, it gives one person the satisfaction and feeling of importance that comes from being the main attraction. Second, and more importantly, it gives the classroom teacher a vehicle for getting lives revealed to each other in more than a superficial what-did-you-do-over-the-weekend fashion.

The assumption here is that it is often useful for us to share our thoughts and ideas with others. Sometimes a view of another's life opens up ideas and actions worth considering for our own lives. It gives us alternatives to consider. Sometimes the public interview increases understanding of others, leading to increased empathy and appreciation of the complexity of their lives. Sometimes a view of another's life removes guilt from our own lives; this happens when we find that what we think or do is not so terrible or so unusual.

Furthermore, the public interview always demonstrates that a person can talk honestly about thoughts and experiences, even deeply personal ones, with a group that is supportive and nonjudgmental. The need for denial and suppression of feelings and concerns is reduced within the group and may well be reduced within each individual.

There is also, especially for the person being interviewed, the clarifying experience that may be stimulated by the teacher's questions. Paul, for example, may be stimulated to consider whether he hates his sister, the things his sister does, or something else, whether "hate" is what he really feels, and what, if anything, he might do about it. At the very least, Paul has now had an opportunity to get a bothersome issue off his chest. Other students might also find food for thought in that interview.

Needless to say, a public interview must be carried out in a classroom in which there is acceptance, security, and warmth. There can be no judging, certainly no ridicule. What we get is a glimpse of a real life, a life that must be respected. All our lives have both beauty and blemishes, and we use the public interview to raise some of this to the surface, to look at it, to understand it, to learn from it. The public interview is an effective technique for bringing more humanness into the classroom.

Public interviews are not everyday events. They are too potent for that. They are used on occasion, to fill a loose ten minutes, to give a spurt to a dull afternoon, or to recognize a person who has something to share with the class.

Students often select topics such as unusual experiences they have had, problems they face, plans for the future, and among older students, topics as profound as the use of nonviolent resistance, the role of revolution in the future, defects in ideal democracy, and the purpose of life. Many students will select "dealer's choice" and then a good part of the excitement is to see what topics the teacher hits upon. Often it is lively when the teacher flits from topic to topic, always, of course, giving the student being interviewed the opportunity to say "I pass." Some questions that have proven provocative are:

1.   Are there things you would not tell even best friends? What kinds if things, and why?

2.   Would you bring up your children differently from the way you are being brought up? How and why?

3.   How do you feel about going steady?

4.   Do you do things to make your parents feel good without them asking? What? When?

5.   How do you feel about the mixing of different racial or ethnic groups? How about you, personally?

6.   What do you see yourself doing five years from now? Twenty years?

7.   Did you ever steal something? Recently? How come?

8.   Do you receive an allowance? How do you budget it?

9.   Anything you would like to change about yourself that you would care to talk about in public?

10.   Ever get teased? Ever tease others?

11.   What does "love" mean to you?

12.   How has school been for you over the years?

13.   Can you think of something that you would be willing to say to the class and that you think might be good for them to hear?

The careful structure of the public interview also makes it useful for dealing with heated or emotional classroom issues. The teacher facing two fighting angry children finds it helpful sometimes to say, "Let's have a public interview about this. Who would be willing to take the interview seat?" Neither of the combatants would have to volunteer, and it might be best to start with someone else until they cool off. An onlooker or someone who participated in a similar fight in the past would be likely ones to start, perhaps, a series of interviews. The purpose, of course, is to understand the issue and help the children deal with it intelligently. The public interview is a convenient way to begin the process and to give the teacher control over the situation.

As to the mechanics of the public interview, a few comments may be helpful.

1. Although usually students choose the topic for an interview, sometimes—as in the case of the quarrel mentioned above—the teacher may select the topic and ask for volunteers to talk about their experiences, perceptions, or ideas about it. Thus, the public interview can be used not only to look more closely at one person's life, but to look steadily at one issue. As different students talk about the same issue, alternative ideas and understandings are evoked and the issue becomes more fully elaborated.

2. A classroom might well have two or three interviews at one time. Or one interview might extend for as long as thirty minutes, if the interest held. Some students have rich lives that are delightful and fascinating to look at.

3. Sometimes the interviewee is told in the middle of the interview that she may ask the teacher or any one member of the class a question on the topic under discussion, with the opportunity for the person to avoid answering by saying, "I pass." If it seems to be working out well, the student in front of the room might be permitted to ask another question or several more, thus temporarily turning the questionee into the questioner. Children like this opportunity for turn-about.

4. Another way to add variety and strength to the public interview is occasionally to ask if another student has a question for the person being interviewed. Take care not to permit another student to make a speech or embarrass the person up front; if a member of the class has something she feels she must contribute to the interview topic, permit *her* to be interviewed publicly later. But let students occasionally practice the art of questioning.

5. Usually students will not terminate interviews with a "Thank you for your questions," and teachers will find it wise to tie things up with something like, "That's all we have time for now" or "Let's see if someone else is willing to take the interview chair." And sometimes a topic chosen by the student does not lend itself to many questions of much interest and then the teacher might ask the student being interviewed to select another topic on which to continue the interview, or to give someone else a chance. There certainly is no reason to stick with one topic throughout one interview if it does not go any place.

6. Repeat the rules of the game frequently enough, especially in the beginning, so that the public interview keeps its structure and identity intact. Much of the structure, of course, is designed to make the interview dramatic and psychologically safe for the interviewee.

7. Naturally, the teacher does not moralize or take issue with the student being interviewed. The questions can be like those from the list of thirty clarifying responses earlier presented. And simple acknowledgment of answers is sufficient: "I see," "Uh huh," or "I understand you better now. Thank you."

8. The public interview is not the sole teaching strategy available to deal with an issue, of course, and teachers might do well to try not to settle complex matters merely through one or several public interviews.

Often a teacher will find it useful to give a brief lecture to a class about some aspects of a topic, to increase their understanding of the alternatives or the consequences of alternatives. This need not be done right after the interview and perhaps should not be done so promptly, lest the interviewed students feel as if they have merely been used to get at a lesson the teacher has in mind for the class. Note that the teacher interviewing Paul above did not immediately carry the sibling rivalry issue further, either through discussion, lecture, or any other technique. The emphasis was on Paul and his life.

Thus, unless there is a pressing general concern for an issue in the class, it is probably better to work at complex matters gradually. Sometimes a public interview will lead to readings for some students. And sometimes other value strategies are called for: discussions, thought sheets, value sheets, open-ended questions, and so on. A teacher has many available tools. There is almost always another day and another way for a teacher to deal with a topic.

Thus, public interviews are open dialogues usually built around a student's interests, activities, ideas, or feelings. Sometimes, however, they are built around a particular topic or issue. In both cases, they open up lives and share insights and perceptions. They inform, they illuminate alternatives, and they deepen understandings of one another.

The teacher with an accepting classroom climate need not fear, as may seem possible, that the public interview will get out of hand and lead to dangerous revelations. Students thirst to talk about deep, personal things in their lives if they can only do so without getting hurt. While there may be some danger that someone will say something that would be better left unsaid, there is much more danger, it seems to us, that the important things in life will go unsaid and unexamined, all too often to fester inside. If our experience is any guide, the teacher who considers using public interviews should be reassured. If the mood is right, students will enjoy them, ask for more, volunteer freely, and find the interviews educational and exciting.

10.　DECISION-MAKING INTERVIEW

. . . to assist students at solving their problems

Teachers engage in several kinds of interviews in their professional lives. What we call the *public interview* was discussed above. In chapter 5, in discussing the clarifying response, we described the use of brief exchanges initiated to stimulate students to clarify something they have said or done. We sometimes refer to such an exchange as a *one-legged conference.* Also, there is the familiar *data-gathering interview,* used to gain information from students about their lives; the *parent interview,* used to exchange information about a child; and the *instructional interview,* used to test or tutor a child in some subject area. These last three interview situations might well make use of some clarifying responses and techniques, but one additional interview form—the *decision-making interview*—is ideally suited to such an approach.

A student who has a decision to make and who comes to the teacher for help and advice enters a decision-making interview. Except for those rare circumstances when the decision to be made is beyond the abilities of the student, the consequences involved might be dangerous, *and* there is an alternative to the student personally making the decision, the value theory offers an ideal tactic for such interviews.

The theory outlines a role for the teacher that is characterized by the following.

1.　Unconditional acceptance of the student and the problem. Neither delight nor horror can be expressed at the issue or the student if the teacher is to help. Even when a young child talks about a decision that involves sexual activity that terrifies the teacher, the teacher must accept the issue, as calmly and seriously as possible, as something that is real and important to the student involved. Expressions of distaste or amazement— "You shouldn't be involved in things like that!"—only serve to disqualify the teacher as a helper. We may earnestly desire that the student not be faced with the existing circumstances, but if the facts of the matter are such that those circumstances *do* exist, all the teacher can do is help.

2.   Plenty of space for the student to think and clarifying questions to help her do so. The seven valuing processes suggest how to assist a person in thinking through a decision. Here are some examples:

- *Free choice:* Are there aspects of the situation that you are not free to change?

- *Searching for alternatives:* Could I help you brainstorm some other options?

- *Anticipating consequences:* Seems to me that X would probably happen. Have you thought of that?

- *Prizing and cherishing:* Which option would leave you with the best feelings afterwards, do you think?

- *Affirming choices:* Have you any feelings about others finding out about your decision?

- *Taking action:* Could I help you get started on that decision or, perhaps, ask how you are doing from time to time?

- *Building patterns in life:* How would this fit in with the rest of the things you are now doing?

The teacher must restrain himself from suggesting—however subtly—which alternative the student would be wise to select. The purpose of the decision-making interview is not to help a student make a perfect decision in one particular instance, but to teach a process for weighing such decisions in the future and to give the experience that can be obtained only from making the choice herself.

3.   No advice giving. Look at the issue from the vantage point of the student and not of the teacher. A student says, "I can't decide whether or not to go away for a long weekend, skipping school on Friday, or to stay home and study for Monday's big test." The temptation for the teacher to think and talk in terms of the importance of the schoolwork can be overwhelming, but must be contained. After all, it is very possible that, in a given circumstance and for a given student, the weekend away will be more valuable than the weekend of school and study.

Another student says, "The gang wants me to go stealing with them. What should I do?" Again, the teacher must refrain from voicing personal values against the issue, but must instead ask such questions as, "What are the alternatives? What might happen if you do this and then if you do that? Which choice will you be most proud of? What will you be least sorry for? Did you forget that so-and-so is a factor? It sometimes is difficult to decide in such issues, but you must do it; can I help further?"

If the relationship between the teacher and the student is honest enough that the student knows the teacher is not trying to manipulate matters, the teacher is justified in saying something like this, "I don't know what I would do if I were you, but if that happened to me, I would probably choose so-and-so because of so-and-so. I mention this to give you some idea of how one person might react, but you have to choose for yourself, based on your feelings and your values."

What kinds of decisions are suited to this approach? Here are some common ones.

1.   Whether to spend saved money on a model airplane or to wait longer and use it for a bicycle.

2.   Whether to drop out of high school or not.

3.   Whether or not to take on an after-school job.

4.   Which role to try out for in the class play.

5.   Whether to run for class office or not.

6.   Picking from among the various opportunities for a summer experience.

7.   Advantages and disadvantages of buying a car.

8.   What to do for a friend who is sick in the hospital.

9.   How to handle a situation in which the student has had a serious argument with a best friend.

10.   What to do when a student knows another student has not read the book for which he did a book report.

In summary, the decision-making interview grows out of the value-clarifying process. The teacher resists leaning toward one choice over another. Instead, he asks questions. He assists the student in thinking through the problem for herself. He gives no advice.

Such a procedure is consistent with the value theory, which stresses that ultimately all decisions, if they are truly to reflect values, must be made freely, after due reflection, and from an adequate exploration of all the available alternatives. It is such decisions which we are proud of, which we are apt to affirm, and which, certainly, we will act upon.

An interesting self-test for the teachers is to see how often students come in for help with personal decisions. Teachers who are quick to advise and judge, and who thereby restrict the opportunity students have to learn to think things through for themselves, would not—we would guess—have many students approaching them for help in decision-making situations. Teachers who listen respectfully, who ask questions designed to help students understand better, who respect students judgments even when they differ from their own, and who are reluctant to decide what is good for another person's life are likely to get many such invitations to help. Students seem to appreciate *help,* not dictation, when they face personal decisions, and to respect teachers who are willing to let them learn from mistakes, as well as from triumphs—as long as the teachers' knowledge of alternatives and consequences has been honestly and openly shared with them. In short, teachers have an obligation to point out what they consider an impending mistake, but an equal obligation to permit the student to learn from it.

Because of the large number of students in our schools who assert that they have no one with whom they can really share their problems—least of all busy school counselors—and in view of the many perplexing decisions which trouble today's children, the importance of the decision-making interview described here may well be substantial.

11. VOTING

. . . to open issues and quickly reveal a group to itself

The voting strategy refers not to the usual occasions in the classroom in which a vote is taken, but to a special technique, much like the public interview, that brings out issues and ideas that might otherwise be difficult to make public.

To use the voting strategy, the teacher poses a list of questions, similar to those used in the public interview, and students state a position by a show of hands. For example, the teacher might ask the following sequence of questions, pausing after each for a vote and for students to look around to see how others voted.

1. How many of you have ever been seriously burned?

2. Anyone here ever own a horse?

3. How many think sometimes of dying or what death might be like?

4. I'd like to see how much loneliness is in this group. Vote either that you feel lonely often, sometimes, or seldom. How many feel lonely often? Sometimes? Seldom?

5. How many have a favorite political party? How many have no clear political ideas?

6. How many feel strongly about some religion or religious beliefs?

7. Who here watches television more than four hours a day on the average?

8. How many would want to be told if they had bad breath that was annoying to others?

9. How many of you have no fathers living in your home?

The teacher may conclude such a voting session with something as innocuous as a "thank you, that was very interesting," and go on to a subject-matter lesson without fear that the time was wasted. If the voting is performed sensitively and paced evenly, the teacher can be assured that some students will for the first time understand how many of their peers have no fathers and perhaps think a bit about what it must be like to live in a fatherless home. Some students will note with relief that death is a topic that others think about and that it is possible to talk about it. Some will be reminded of the seriousness of playing with matches: serious burns might result. Some will consider how they feel about political matters, religious matters, how much time they want to use for television, and so on. A simple vote, with no one talking but the teacher, can lead to a lot of clarifying thinking.

Sometimes the teacher will ask three students to prepare a voting list for use at some future break in the proceedings. Sometimes the voting will lead to other value strategies, such as a discussion. Sometimes the teacher will merely say, "There were things to think about in today's vote. Anyone who wants to may write me a note sometime about things you thought about. I'd be happy to see that and maybe I'll make a little comment back, and you can reply to my comment, if you like. Do this anytime."

Sometimes the vote will lead to a subject-matter lesson and votes can be prepared, of course, with that in mind. One arithmetic teacher held such votes regularly and used the numbers that came out for all kinds of calculations and examples.

A vote must always be permissive and not mandatory; people may raise their hands for any position and may also abstain whenever they wish, with no questions asked.

Sometimes voting will be focused on a single issue. Here, for example, is a sequence used by a sixth-grade teacher:

1. How many people feel that a child in the sixth grade should get an allowance?

2. How many of you believe that there should be some work, some doing of chores, before a child gets an allowance?

3. How many of you believe that chores are something you should do anyhow, and that any money you get from your parents should come from special work, work beyond mere chores?

4. If you voted for allowances, how many think that a sixth grader should get more than one dollar a week?

How many say between fifty cents and one dollar a week?

How many vote for a number between twenty-five cents and fifty cents a week?

How many think the allowance should be less than twenty-five cents?

5. How many think that every child in the family should get the same allowance?

6. How many people would be willing to buy their own clothes if their allowance were doubled?

7. Do you think an allowance should be for:
- *Recreation*
- *Food*
- *Saving for big things, like an archery set.*
- *Whatever you want*
- *School supplies*

This voting technique is like the public interview in that it opens up issues and questions easily and efficiently. It is less personal and therefore less threatening, and therefore perhaps a good strategy to use before introducing the public interview to a group.

12.   FIVE-MINUTE QUOTE WITHOUT COMMENT

. . . to facilitate our speaking our minds and hearts

After a teacher has been working with value-clarifying techniques for some time, a climate grows in which the pursuit for clear values becomes more and more important. Students are taught the seven criteria for a value, how to recognize value indicators, and the questions which help to advance clarification. There is room, also, for a technique which we call the "five-minute quote without comment."

The teacher one day announces, "From now on whenever any of you has something you want to say to the group about something important to you, about our work together, about an outside issue that concerns you, about anything you like, ask me to schedule you a five-minute quote without comment. What that means is that the next time we have some free moments, I will let you come up front and tell us anything you want. Up to five-minutes' worth. I won't permit anyone to interrupt you or to comment after you have finished. We will just go on to our work. It will be your time to share, without fear of argument from me or the group, anything important to you."

What is sought is demonstrated free speech with brave talk removed, at least temporarily, from the need to defend itself. A statement should reach undisturbed to the four corners of the room. People need to state publicly what they believe in, if their values are to grow.

What often happens afterwards, if a student's statement has been particularly provocative, is that a rash of thought sheets will discuss the points raised. Students may well talk individually with the student who made the five-minute quote. There may be a movement to look at a values issue further, via a dittoed value sheet, a values continuum lesson, or whatever. A student who disagrees with a statement might ask for five minutes for himself. Naturally, we are not encouraging a debating society; the emphasis is upon affirmation of personal values, not upon finding holes in or taking pot shots at someone else's.

Occasionally, the five-minute quotes are read to the class by a student. This is acceptable, of course, and may provide a useful record in instances where review of the quote is helpful. Some teachers may record the quotes on audiotape, and these can be played back later in the term, used to lend importance to the statement, or used to play for absent students. A teacher may also ask a student to duplicate a statement so all may examine it more closely.

To summarize, the five-minute quote without comment is designed to help implement one criterion for a value: to affirm publicly what one values. Students are told that they may have, time permitting a maximum of five minutes to make a statement to the class. It is a chance for any student to have five minutes of control of the class' ears. It is his or her few moments to affirm something personally important. And, among its other benefits, it clearly demonstrates that the teacher respects students' ideas.

13. VALUE REPORTS

. . . to bring dreary student reports to life

Few classroom activities thirst for improvement more than the tired old student report, book report, research report, or term paper. They are dull enough to read, but to suffer through a session of oral reports can be devastating. When you consider how often writing a report is equivalent to copying from the encyclopedia or book jacket, the combined agony and the small educative value of the result becomes classical in its failure.

The value theory suggests a way to bring new life and real education to such student reports. The strategy is simply to base these reports on personal choosing, prizing, and acting. Using the book report for an example, compare the usual bland directions to summarize and evaluate a book with the following suggestive questions.

1. Which character is most like you? What did he or she do which you would like to do some day? What did the character need to do to get ready? What will you need to do?

2. What forces in life did the character attempt to shape? What help did he or she seek and how was it used?

3. In what ways would the character have made a good parent? A good teacher?

4. In what ways does the author's understanding of love (friendship, tenderness, etc.) differ from yours?

5. Describe how the major characters viewed money? Contrast and compare their views of money with your own.

6. Imagine that the hero of the story lived nowadays in this school (town, country). And imagine that he or she wrote a letter describing a personal view of things. Write such a letter. Then write a letter as you yourself would describe the same things. How are the two letters the same and different?

7. Who was the hero's most important human obstacle? How did she or he deal with this obstacle? Were there any other alternatives open? What would you have done? Are there any human obstacles in your life? How do you live with these?

8. Which of the clichés of our culture does the hero affirm or refute? Are there some clichés which you no longer believe in?

9. What things did the hero do for leisure which appeal to you? How can you get started in that activity?

10. What are some things which the hero might have done to make his or her life a richer and fuller one?

For the social studies, sense how the seventh-grade unit introduced through the sheet reproduced below differs in pertinence to life and thought from that of the more common assignment, "Pick a person and a country and report on them in six hundred words."

SOCIAL STUDIES

We are starting an important unit on South America. You will be asked to work on an individual as well as a group project. During the course of this unit, I hope to bring you into contact with the people of South America. You will be dealing with those people who are living, working, and struggling today as well as with those who lived and worked and struggled in the past.

You will be getting information from books, pamphlets, and articles which will enable you to answer the questions raised below. This should prove an interesting and rewarding experience if you will make it so.

Individual Report

For your individual report, choose one of the following people who fought to free South America from foreign rule: Jose De San Martin, Bernardo O'Higgins, Antonio Jose De Sucre, Francisco De Miranda, Simon Bolivar.

Your individual reports should consider the following: What was there in the life of the person you have chosen that interested you? Are there any things in your own life which are similar to this person's? For what things did you admire your choice most? Have you known any other adults who have these qualifications? What exactly did this person achieve? Were this person's goals or aims at all like any you have dreamed up for yourself? What difficulties did the person encounter in achieving those goals? In what ways was this person weak? How did this hurt him? How would this person fit in our world? Explain.

Where did his life seem less fulfilled or satisfying? Do most great people have large areas of their lives which are not fulfilled? Explain. What did friends feel about him? How important were their feelings to him? In what ways were friends' feelings influential? Where did he display his greatest courage? Where did he display his greatest wisdom? Where did he make his greatest contribution? Who benefited from this contribution? Are there any ways he lived which would be good for people to follow today?

Group Report

For your group report, choose one of the following countries that Bolivar helped to make free: Colombia, Venezuela, Peru, Bolivia, Equador.

Deal with the following questions as part of your group report: What do the farmers want in the country you have chosen? What stands in the way of getting it? How do farmers go about getting what they want? What help do they have? What hopes do their children have? What do they know of their own country? Of ours? What do they think and know about politics or their government? What is their day like? Where do they sleep? How many in a bed? What do they fear? When do they marry? What do they do for recreation? What part does religion play in their lives? What is their idea of a good life? How does it compare with yours? (Discuss this last question with your group and come up with some ideas.)

Answer these same questions for industrial workers and wealthy landowners. Are your answers the same for all of these people? If not, why not? Are any answers you have the same or similar to those of another group? Which ones? (Find this out by reading and discussing work of other groups.) If your answers are similar, why do you think this is so?

Finally, note the research report assignment given by a high-school English teacher in chart 3. The learning produced by that assignment was far different from the transporting of irrelevant information from a source book or magazine to some blank sheets of paper. Students were *educated* by that assignment. They better understood themselves and part of the world around them. And those reports were exciting to read!

No, student reports need not be dull and uninspiring. They can deepen insights into subjects being studied and exercise writing and research skills while at the same time being interesting and promoting clearer values. We can replace the hack work and the plagiarisms with creative and educative thinking if we make an effort to help students see reports as a chance to look searchingly at some alternatives for living and the consequences of those alternatives, all in the framework of the feelings and beliefs and actions of the student doing the report.

Chart 3   *Research Paper*

On May 1, you will all be required to hand in a research paper; papers will not be accepted after that date unless you have been absent. The paper should include an outline, footnotes, and a bibliography. You will be given more information on the format of the paper later. As for the content of the paper, choose one of the following types of people and answer the following kinds of questions about that type of person:

A.   What specific problems does this person have? What has caused these problems? Has the person caused some of these problems? Which of the problems have been caused by outside things or other people? Are any of the problems similar to yours? Is there anything in the person's life similar to yours? What is the average day of this person like? Where does this person usually sleep? What does he or she usually eat? What are the person's fears? Is anybody against this person? Why? Are the problems of this person unknown or misunderstood by most people? Why? What do this person's problems do to his or her body? What do they do to the mind or personality? What do you admire or hate in this person? Why? How is the persons family affected by the problems?

B. What can be done to help this person? Who is trying to help? How? What are the person's hopes and goals? How is this person better off today than a similar person would have been fifty years ago? Can the government change old laws or make new ones to help this person? Explain. Will changing people's attitudes toward this person help? Which attitudes? How can they be changed? What do your parents or friends think about this person and his or her problems? Do you agree with them? Why or why not? Can you do anything to help this person? What have you done or do you plan to do?

1. Alcoholic
2. Juvenile delinquent
3. Narcotics addict
4. Migrant worker
5. Cuban peasant
6. Cypriot Turk
7. Berlin citizen (East and West)
8. Southern black
9. New York tenement dweller
10. Sufferer of mental illness
11. Person in prison
12. Man or woman seeking divorce, before and after divorce
13. Hippy
14. Algerian
15. Gabonese
16. Indian untouchable
17. Compulsive gambler
18. Union person on strike for extended period of time
19. American soldier in Asia
20. Person facing capital punishment
21. Boxer getting too old to fight
22. Peasant in China
23. Coal miner
24. Unemployed person
25. Person over 70
26. Derelict
27. Pacifist
28. Physically disabled
29. Mentally retarded
30. Polio victim
31. Member of a mixed marriage
32. Orphan

---

14. ACTION PROJECTS

. . . to bring the students themselves to life

Occasionally, a teacher can talk about values too much. The words begin to sound hollow. Some highly verbal students become adept at talking a good game, but that's it. It may be time for an action project.

For example, students may have talked, complete with shocked and passionate reactions, of slaughter on the highways. One teacher challenged such a class to start a poster campaign about wearing seat belts. Safety was then closer to becoming a value than talk alone would permit.

Another class, after soul searching about race relations, arranged to work with a neighborhood group in a slum ghetto in an effort to make a filthy, rubble-piled empty lot into a children's playground. Students, teacher, neighborhood mothers and fathers, and children, kindergarteners to high-schoolers, worked side-by-side. The talk was about the work. It was a way of closing the gap between what students said and what they did. It was an action project with value implications.

Students have worked for the political party of their choice, in campaign headquarters during an election. They have organized and carried out letter-writing campaigns for causes they espoused. They have conducted surveys to gather and disseminate information. They have read to older and infirm citizens. They have worked together to produce a show which they have taken to the children's wards of public hospitals. The motivation is the same, to "put your money where your mouth is" and learn in the process.

If there is an injustice or some need, students can take action to help, individually or—if there is consensus—collectively. As they do, they learn and become clearer about what their values are.

It is important to note here that some students come back from an experience, such as working on a playground, with prejudices and stereotypes which are reinforced. This is a risk and is consistent with the value theory. We do not undertake an action project to have everyone come out with the same answer, but we go there in order to get more data—both on reality and on our own feelings—with which to make the decisions which we must make if we are to have values.

The form any action project takes is determined by particular situations, but three bits of advice may be helpful.

1. Encourage students to see that they have power. Children's collective and concentrated power—politically, physically, morally—can often be enough to make a real and lasting difference. Students often fail to see this and much too often become so accustomed to not seeing it that they slip into an adulthood that neither sees nor uses its potential power.

2. Permit the students to select or reject any action project. When teachers impose action upon a group, they leave themselves open to all sorts of criticism, especially when the value of field projects is not yet fully appreciated. Too many students, administrators, parents, and teachers see schools as places only to *talk* about things. Make certain that the students understand the kind of idea or understanding that needs more concrete representation or the kind of purpose they want to support, and explore with them, openly and creatively, possible alternatives to action. It is entirely possible, and not at all undesirable, for different action projects to work simultaneously at different and incompatible ends. Projects, of course, must be appropriate to the needs or values of the participating *individual,* not necessarily the class as a whole.

3. Finally, do not insist that every student participate in every action project. Some projects may contradict a student's values, may threaten his or her security, or otherwise result in more grief than education. Besides, permitting any student to abstain from action projects at any time provides a relief valve that forestalls much criticism, both from within and from outside the school.

15. ROLE PLAYING

. . . to heighten involvement in a topic

The delight most students take in playacting makes this an important value-eliciting strategy. Students seem to welcome the chance to take on a new identity in a temporary and protected situation. A flush of real feelings and penetrating insights—fuel for productive value thinking—often emerges.

Sometimes the teacher sets up role-playing situations with much structure, selecting the participants and outlining their initial stances. For example:

> "Bill, you play a counterman at a lunch counter in the South that has never served blacks. You be behind the counter attending to some washing. Chuck and Mary, you be black teenagers who have come to demand service." (After they have proceeded a bit.) "Fred, you be a white person who enters the lunch counter and helps with the argument on the side that seems to be getting the worst of it."

> "You three be students selected by your class to protest the lunchroom conditions in the school cafeteria. You want to be forthright but polite. Sally, you be the principal, who thinks the students have no right to complain." (After a while.) "Bert, you and Sally change places. You be the principal now and let Sally be the group leader."

> "Rick, you are the leader of a union. You walk up to Jim, who is a worker in the plant, and you tell him that you heard a rumor that he has been criticizing you for illegal use of union funds. After you have spoken for a while, either of you can call other members of the

class to join in the discussion. Simply say something like, 'Come over here Florence and tell him how we all know he's a crook, he's a liar, he's a nice guy, or something.' You can use others in any way you want. But, Jim and Rick, you two start by yourselves."

Situations need not be so carefully structured, and, after students get the hang of things, they can take off from the least bit of pre-planning. For example:

"Who will be three family members? One be the child and the other two be parents. The child comes with a request that the parents think is unreasonable. What might it be? Take it from there."

"Who will be three friends arguing on a street corner? OK. What do you three want to argue about?"

"Who wants to be a girl approaching her parents for advice on dating a boy of another religion?"

"You three want something badly, but he stands in the way. Plan the situation out in the hall. Let us know when you are ready to come in and act out the situation."

Any kind of potential or real conflict situation is useful for roleplaying, or any situation in which real feelings are often concealed. Consider situations in school, in the family, on the playground, at work, or in politics or government.

Start with a lot of structure and the most secure and outgoing students. Later use less structure and involve less outspoken students. Do not permit acts to drag; cut them short rather than let them become silly or boring. One way to liven things is to add characters while the play is in process ("Jean, you be the secretary that overhears the scheme and interrupts with a protest") or permit the actors to add characters as they see the need for it. The latter approach permits the scene to develop more in the control of the actors and is usually preferable. Or change roles in the middle of the play for an injection of life and a taste of what the other person feels ("Now the high-school dropout and the employer switch roles").

Following a role-playing situation, a discussion in large or small groups is valuable. Questions that often promote good discussion are:

1. How did you as actors feel?

2. How would you observers have done things differently?

3. Would things work out that way in real life?

4. What might we learn from this situation?

Of course, the teacher would make good use of clarifying responses, such as those in chapter 5's list of thirty, when a student expresses a belief, attitude, interest, aspiration, or feeling. The wise teacher also makes good use of passivity and often lets the discussion take care of itself.

16.   THE CONTRIVED INCIDENT

. . . to open minds to insights

Sometimes a teacher has to contrive a situation in order to get students to open their minds. Occasionally, we need to shock our students into an awareness of what they are for and against.

1.   Many teachers have used the experiment reported in Asch's *Social Psychology* (1952) involving the discrimination between two drawn lines. One by one students are asked to say aloud which line is longer. Almost all of the students are in on the ruse and say that the shorter line is the longer one. After hearing one after another of the conspirators say this, it takes a rare student to avoid twisting his or her visual perception. When the ruse is revealed, the teacher discusses with the students who mistrusted their own eyes the feelings and ideas that went into their decision. This then can be used to look at other "blind spots" we may have in our lives and to examine issues such as de facto segregation, conformity, success, organization people, and so on.

2.   A teacher found his class discussing rigged television quiz shows in a desultory manner. The class concluded that no one had really done anything wrong by giving some of the contestants the answers beforehand. Concocting a very difficult test, the teacher hinted to a few of the students that he wouldn't mind if they looked at the answers on his desk. After the quiz, in which the students who had the answers got perfect scores and everyone else in the class failed, the class was told what had happened. They all protested violently and complained bitterly about the unfairness of the situation. When the teacher reopened the discussion on the quiz scandals, the value indicators which emerged seemed to have been much more painfully considered.

3.   A teacher had a friend come into class billed as a famous expert on a topic the class had just studied. In order to draw out the value inclinations related to her topic, the speaker took a completely opposite view to the one which the class had come to understand. The confusion and doubt thus generated tended to foster clarification inquiry. Of course, they were let into the plot and also used this lesson for examining such things as the adoration of authority, definition of expertise, and the use of deception for educational purposes.

4.   Prior to studying the novel *1984*, the teacher came into class one day and said that she was sick and tired of the way the class had been behaving. She set up new rules, which were strikingly similar to the ones in the book, for controlling the class. The outrage this turned loose was handled via the clarifying operations and much insight into totalitarianism was gained through this direct, if contrived, experience.

5.   The students in one particular class became rather overimpressed with their academic superiority. It was a college-bound class and had in it some particularly gifted students. The rest of the school was often held in tacit contempt.

The teacher set up a field trip as part of a study of simple machines in their physics class. They went to a vocational high school. There each of the students from the so-called academically superior class was placed with a student from the vocational school. The vocational-school students had been asked to explain to the students assigned to them the most complex of their mechanical skills. The auto repair student proceeded to reassemble a carburetor, the sheet-metal student with deft skill completed a complicated soldering operation, and the machinist did a lathe set-up and machined a part to a special clamp she had devised.

When the students returned to their own school, the teacher opened up topics having important values implications: What is success? What is dependence and independence? Who is a leader and who is a follower?

What is the formula for a contrived incident? We doubt that there can be one, but a few general observations are possible. The contrived incident's purpose is to simulate as closely and as dramatically as possible something that will give students a real feeling or experience or understanding. It cuts through the easy level of words. It is like the difference between saying that war is hell and spending a few weeks in the middle of the stench, exhaustion, and desperation of a kill-or-be-killed situation. Since schools have a tendency to fill themselves with easy intellectualizations, it is often very useful for the teacher to identify the feelings or understandings involved and contrive something that will permit the student to taste them more directly than words permit. After the incident, an acknowledgment of the purpose of the incident and a discussion about what emerged from it are always in order.

Teachers who have used contrived incidents quickly recognize their importance. They produce learnings that are sharper and longer retained than those from almost any other strategy.

The next time a class is talking about fear, prejudice, fulfilment, tedious work, job insecurity, the importance of precise communication, or any number of other things that are easier to talk about than to understand and feel, try contriving a situation that will dramatize the topic being discussed. Then, of course, use clarifying responses to aid students in digesting that experience. Students usually are enthusiastic about learning from contrived incidents.

17. THE ZIGZAG LESSON

. . . for dramatizing an issue

What we call a *zigzag lesson* is less dramatic than a contrived incident, but it has a special flavor that adds life to discussions.

What the teacher does is identify a value area that she thinks the students have not clarified sufficiently, such as the idea in the first example below of what pride in work consists of. Then she prefaces an introduction of the idea with some innocuous questions which have the result of piquing students' interests and setting them to wondering what the lesson is all about. The subsequent confrontation with the central idea, then, is often startling as it contrasts with the very mild questions that preceded it.

The teacher asks some quick questions, not dwelling long on any of them: "How many of you can tell which shoe you put on first this morning? Do any of you tie double knots in your laces? How many have heels which wear out unevenly? How often do you look closely at a shoe, noting how it is stitched and cut?"

Then the teacher pauses and asks: "Did you ever think what it must be like to sit at a workbench and plan, cut, and sew a pair of shoes?" After that question settles and perhaps after some discussion, the teacher might continue to stimulate the valuing process with such questions as: "Can a person be proud of producing a good pair of shoes? Are you proud of the jobs you do? When is a job something to be proud of or something to get out of the way the easiest way possible?"

Charts 4 through 6 show three other lesson outlines that first zig along innocently enough and then abruptly zag to the heart of a value issue.

Chart 4   *Discrimination*

1. Make a list of all the persons who come to your house to visit or to eat. Make a second list of all those whose homes you visit on occasion.

2. Note how many in each list are relatives, how many are beyond walking distance, and how many you really are very happy to visit with.

3. Calculate the proportion of your lists made up of relatives, and other groups.

4. Look at your lists again. If you are, say, white, Protestant, and middle class, how many on your lists are white, Protestant, and middle class? If you are black and working class, how many on your list are black and working-class? If you are Irish, how many on your list are Irish? That is, how many on your lists are in much the same groups as you are in?

5. What is the difference between segregation and integration?

6. Would you like your lives to be more integrated? If so, what can you do about it?

7. Will you do anything? Can I help? Will you let us know?

Chart 5 *Migrant Workers*

1. How many had orange juice for breakfast this morning?

2. What other juices, if any, did any of you have?

3. Anybody squeeze juice this morning?

4. How heavy would you say one orange would be? How many would it take to make a pound?

5. Anyone think this morning how the oranges that produced juice for some of us got off the tree? How was it done? Who did it? (The teacher fills in information until the role of the migrant worker is clearly delineated.)

6. What do you think it is like to pick fruit and vegetables for a living? How would you like it?

7. We noted the working, living, and health conditions of migrant workers; what would be some of the important things to change in these conditions?

8. Where should the money come from to help migrant workers? Would *you* be willing to pay more for your fruit and vegetables? What would you be willing to give up if prices were to be raised for the benefit of migrant workers?

9. Is there anything any of us can do about this situation? Want to? Individually? As a group?

Chart 6 *Shoplifting*

1. Close your eyes. Imagine you loved some sport and decided you would love someday to own a sports store. People would come to your store and buy their equipment and you could give them advice. You could earn a living and stay close to what you love to do.

2.   What kind of a store would you choose? Would you want a large or small store? Would there be a place to practice associated with your store? How would you make it a happy store to work in and shop in? Would you want to put a snack bar in your store? What might you call your store?

3.   Imagine that your store did a good business, you were well-known, making money, and providing a good service. How do you feel?

4.   Keeping your eyes closed, now imagine that you began to do less well because some children from the neighborhood began to shoplift things from your store. How do you feel now? How might you treat a shoplifter?

5.   Imagine that things got so bad that you began to lose money, you couldn't pay the rent and other expenses because too much was stolen. Now imagine talking to a child caught taking stuff from your store.

6.   Open your eyes and let's discuss the situation. Start by sharing your reactions to this with your neighbor. Later we'll all get together and see if we can agree about what, if anything, might be done about shoplifting.

---

18.   DEVIL'S ADVOCATE

. . . for challenging mindlessness

Too many discussions in value-related areas suffer from having only two positions in the room: a consensus and a "don't care" position. Especially in certain political and social topics, dissension is often absent. What often is needed is persuasive argument *against* civil rights, *for* the use of profanity, *against* respect for elders, *for* revolution, *against* patriotism, and so on. At least, such dissension is needed if the alternatives to many issues are to be fairly treated. Since the value theory states clearly the need for examination of alternatives, the use of the devil's advocate is often a very productive strategy.

If someone has to advocate the unpopular side of issues, why not let it be a friend of the devil? The devil's advocate role lets the unconsidered alternative come in with full force. It helps prevent passive drift toward unconsidered consensus.

For example, observe how this fourth-grade teacher launched into a discussion of the first heroes of the space age:

> I want to play the devil with you. I'll screw on my horns and get ready to jab you with my pitchfork. Watch out.
> You know all of that stuff you've been reading about these heroes who go up in space ships? Well, this devil thinks they're not heroes at all. What's so

heroic about going up in a space ship? Why they have those things so carefully figured out that nothing can go wrong. With all of those movie cameras grinding and all of those TV cameras focused on them, you don't think our government could afford to have the bad publicity of anything going wrong do you?

This devil thinks that your walk to school every morning has about as much danger in it as the danger those so-called heroes had to risk. And to ride in a car without seat belts is twice as dangerous as that. But no one calls you a hero when you do that.

Anyhow, if there is such risk, what kind of person would leave a spouse and children to do something a monkey could have done? Finally, you foolish children, this devil wants to raise the question about all that money that goes into space projects. Did you know that we spend over a billion bucks a year, and that money could help wipe out slums, build new colleges, work productively on cancer and mental illness research?

So speaks this devil.

What a lively class session followed the devil's discourse. Few students take that kind of confrontation lying down, and the alternatives to consider filled the room. It was value clarifying on a high level, for students were forced to examine what they prized and cherished and consider affirming it in front of the entire class. There was no right answer with which even the devil wanted each student to agree. But the teacher, not the devil, wanted to make sure that students considered alternatives to the popular notions that are so easy to leave unexamined, thus encouraging misunderstandings and lazy thinking habits.

Teachers do well to announce to the class that, from time to time, they will play a role that is not their real one, that they will do it merely to present a position that has not otherwise arisen. It is often fun to label this role as that of the devil's advocate and to announce what you are doing when it is played, but usually that is unnecessary. The extreme and dogmatic statements that characterize the devil's advocate signal that something is afoot. Those statements also ignite interests, challenge thinking, and thereby help children move toward deeper understanding and clearer values.

19. THE VALUE CONTINUUM

. . . to reveal the full array of alternatives

We have observed that one of the most important elements of clear value thinking is a consideration of alternatives. The devil's advocate role is often useful for presenting one divergent viewpoint; but most issues are not a simple matter of black and white. Therefore, a method is needed to get at the full range of possibilities. In an era of centralization of news services, learning to search for the full range of alternatives in issues is perhaps particularly urgent. The value continuum suits this purpose.

It works like this: The class or the teacher identifies an issue to be discussed in class. It could be putting away supplies, federal control of education, interscholastic sports, religious tolerance, censorship, socialized medicine, birth control, or anything else. Then two extreme positions are identified— for example, someone failing to put away supplies is expelled from school versus someone failing to put away supplies is given a reward for showing independence. These two positions, sometimes captured in argument from two newspapers or magazines—one reactionary and one radical—are placed at opposite ends of a line on the board, and the continuum is born.

The task of the class, then, is to identify other positions in the issue and try to place them on the continuum both in relation to the poles and in relation to positions already placed. For example, a group might brainstorm and produce a continuum like that shown in Chart 7.

Chart 7　　*How Handle A Student Who Fails To Put Away Supplies*

Expel	Clean up after school	Note to parents	Chooses own punishment	Assign a monitor to him or her

(continuum continues)

Chooses own reminder method	Ignore it	Remind student	Reward student for being independent

---

Sometimes issues will be found which are multidimensional and therefore require more than one long line, but usually this is unnecessary. In any case, the importance of the value continuum is not in giving accurate visual representation to an issue but in showing the class that most issues have a wealth of possible alternatives, each of which has particular consequences.

The value continuum is especially useful in the initial stages of a discussion on a controversial issue, before the consequences of any one alternative are examined so thoroughly that students begin to take positions prematurely. It is, of course, best if minds remain open until the variety of possibilities that usually exist is developed.

One thing the value continuum, or "value line" as some younger children like to call it, does well is permit the teacher to introduce alternatives to an issue without having to appear to favor one or the other. There is some tendency for students to believe that, because Ms. Clark suggested that consideration be given a certain alternative, she favors that choice. This method affords an easy way to get alternatives opened up before heated discussion closes minds.

The method can also be used without discussion. An effective assignment is to state an issue—such as the extent to which one should conform to peers' pressure during a party—and then ask each student to identify as many positions as possible and to place them on a value continuum. Even without discussion or teacher comment, such an assignment pays high dividends. It forces students to think deeply and, to some extent, non-judgmentally.

Thus the value continuum demonstrates the complexity of thinking that most issues deserve and offers a method of simplifying the identification of alternatives. It helps overcome either-or thinking. Finally, it helps the teacher deal with the most controversial issues without appearing to be indoctrinating. It is a most useful value-clarifying tool.

four

PERSPECTIVES

Values and Thinking

All our dignity lies in thought. By thought we must elevate ourselves, not by space and time which we cannot fill. Let us endeavor then to think well; therein lies the principle of morality.

Blaise Pascal
(1623—1662)

Many of us are not aware of the close connection between the values we hold and much of the thinking we do. About 20 years ago, Louis Raths examined in translation a series of Russian elementary-school arithmetic books. After reading them very carefully, one day he realized that there was not one problem in all of the books which dealt with a person buying something for, say, 10¢ and selling it for 15¢. In the Soviet Union, where by definition everything was owned by the state, private profit being associated with capitalism and *enemy* countries, it was probably very reasonable that such problems should be excluded. This difference in books may not represent a Soviet value or a U.S. value, but it surely is a value indicator and possibly worth pursuing. We do not usually think of arithmetic as a political or economic statement. Nevertheless, it is in just such ways that our value indicators and judgments in these and other areas slip into our own books about mathematics without our being aware of it.

The same values assumptions are present in the history books we study, the science books, the geography books, and all other literature in the classroom. The values that we most take for granted do not provoke us into thought as we write these books or as we read them. Nevertheless, our thinking is greatly influenced by the value assumptions we encounter through study and other experiences. In fact, values and thinking are inextricably linked: to encourage development in one area is to encourage growth in the other.

Our approach to values education is to train students to think about values on their own—to train them in the process of valuing *and* thinking. We recognize that deprivation of certain kinds of experiences has behavioral consequences. Impulsiveness, for example, is generally associated with the function of thinking: People are impulsive when they do not stop to think. Another consequence of experiential deprivation is the failure to concentrate or pay attention to a task. The results of such inadequacies in thinking in our students are often repeated failures in their work.

We have taken the position in this and other books that if teachers provide a school life that is very rich in its opportunities for thinking and experiences for choosing, it is very probable that most children will reconstruct their own behavior to deal with these experiences. As we have observed before, teachers often say to children, "you should," "you ought," "you must," as ways of getting changes in behavior. Under these circumstances, students learn what the teacher wants and simply attempt to produce the appropriate response. In this book we have tried to show that where children have opportunities to think about and to choose their own responses, where these opportunities are so much a part of the curriculum that they are present day after day and week after week, the children mature. They are not told to grow or to mature, and they are not criticized for remaining the same. But in the overwhelming majority of cases, they do grow and change.

We believe that *experience* contributes most significantly to the process of maturing. Thus, teachers can and should guide children through a continuing process of developing problem situations rich in opportunities to think and to choose. Under these circumstances, children become more thoughtful, more aware of alternatives, and more aware of their consequences. We learn what we live. If, day by day, we live in a classroom where thinking and choosing are everyday practices, we are continually growing, and growth is maturation.

In this book, we conceive of thinking as processes associated with inquiry and decision making. Whenever decisions are made, value judgments are involved. Wherever inquiry goes on it is usually going on for some purpose. Such purposes are probable value indicators. When we set before children the task of comparing two or more entities, the thinking process is initiated in acquiring facts about similarity and difference. This is a step toward weighing similarities and differences in preparation for the step of *choosing;* and this act of choosing involves values. Where *summarizing* takes place, the thinking process involves analysis, abstraction, ordering, organization, and synthesis. Not only do these operations involve selections in the process of thinking, but also wherever decisions are made to include and exclude, values make themselves known.

While the emphasis in a classroom may be upon opportunities to think or to promote inquiry that emphasis also becomes a focus on decision making and therefore on valuing. If you are interested in a more detailed presentation of the greaty variety of thinking operations as these relate to subject-matter areas, we recommend the book *Teaching for Thinking: Theory, and Application* (Raths, Wassermann, Jonas, & Rothstein, 1967).

With an eye toward the thinking processes already mentioned, however, we will divide the materials for this chapter into the following categories: (1) comparing, (2) classifying, (3) observing and reporting, (4) summarizing, (5) interpreting, (6) analyzing assumptions, (7) problem solving (decision making), (8) criticizing and evaluating, (9) imagining and creating, (10) coding and reactions to coding.

COMPARING

Ordinarily we compare things with some purpose in mind. If we are planning to buy an automobile in a certain price range, we are very apt to look at several different makes of cars and compare them according to certain criteria. Ordinarily we ask for specifications and begin the process of comparing one with another until we have satisfied ourselves with a particular choice or have decided not to make a purchase. Comparing is not some time-wasting process! As we examine first one thing and then another we bring them into relationship with each other, noticing similarities and differences. As this process proceeds somewhere "in the back of our heads," a decision-making process is perhaps taking place in a guarded fashion. We may not actually make a final decision until we have done a good job of comparing, but such a decision or judgment is an inevitable part of the process of comparing, and it is forming even as the evidence is accumulating. We are of course much more ready to conclude the comparing process when we feel that we have had a large amount of data or at least enough data to make a conclusion.

Comparisons must take place on a much larger and less well defined scale also. Recently in the United States, the people and their representatives were faced with the choice of continuing with the system of weights and measures that had characterized our history or with choosing to change to a *metric* system that is already used by nearly all the countries of Europe and a number in Asia. After weighing the large-scale tangible and intangible consequences of the changeover, the country chose to make a gradual change to the new system. This decision will have very immediate personal effects on all people, including many who were content with the old system.

While adults must adjust somewhat abruptly to this change, our children will not have the opportunity to undertake the choosing and adapting the changeover requires. They will see only the results of the decision.

In this situation, the choice between alternatives was made for us. Many of us may not like to be told what we have to do, but in many situations that is probably the only way that we have to create a consensus without giving up any cherished value of our own. To help students understand the complexities of such decisions, it might be useful as comparative exercise to ask students to compare Celsius measurements with Fahrenheit measurements several times during a month. You might then ask them something about which system seems more convenient, whether they themselves would prefer one to the other, and perhaps what is good and what is bad about both systems. Value discussion might proceed from such comparisons toward, for example, establishing a consensus opinion (by voting) and discussing the merits of a single classroom system.

While we have used the proces of comparing in two specific examples so far, it is of course a process or set of processes that can be used in every conceivable subject-matter area. In the area of history, for example, students might be asked to read and compare two accounts of the causes of a certain war. As they notice that the substance of two accounts of the same thing are quite different, students begin to learn that mature adults differ in the positions that they take and that it may be possible to attribute some of that difference to the values that they hold. Of course we can not be sure that values are the cause of specific differences in books; but if the authors are still living, students might be encouraged to write to them and find out why they differ. They might reveal why they reject one or two arguments and why they accept one or two that other authors do not accept. Both the reasoning process this exposes and the act of responding to questions in the area of values are demonstrated to students in such an exchange.

In the field of science, students might be presented with rival explanations for the beginnings of the solar system and some rival predictions of its future. We all learn a great deal when sharply divergent views are brought into focus and we begin to see some of the possible value indicators which relate to their conclusions.

Political decisions are often good examples for exposing such value judgments—including those of an apparently scientific nature.

One such important decision had to be made by President Carter and Congress dealing with whether or not the United States should continue with the production of the B-1 bomber. According to reports, this bomber is a very expensive military machine. There were individuals and groups in our society who were very much opposed to spending the enormous sums of money required to develop such a plane, and they made their voices heard in Congress. As you might expect, it was not just a question of money that determined the final decision. Rather, it was a very complex matter of alternatives involving the safety and security of the country, and alternatives including spending the money for nonmilitary purposes. The proponents for the B-1 argued fiercely that to continue making the B-1 bomber would mean continued jobs for at least 50,000 people. This argument brings up the often-debated question of whether unemployment should be cured by making war materials and whether or not war materials should continue to be made in order to maintain levels of employment. Such questions obviously involve values in the decision-making process.

It is not just a matter of fact or of some scientific principle that decides which way problems such as the B-1 bomber decision are to be solved. As a matter of fact, in almost every problem of any significance, it probably is very good practice on our part to say shortly after we recognize the problem, "There may be many ways to solve this problem, but before we go at it what are some of the values we want to protect and that we shall defend in making the final choice of a solution?" In other words, it is not an academic, intellectual solution to a problem that we prize exclusively. We want to know all that is involved; we want to know who will profit and who will be hurt; we want to know what will probably happen in the future; we want to know what sacrifices are involved; and we would like to have all of these things made clear before we go into the process of decision making.

Pollution is another current area of decision making with scientific implications that would help introduce students to the complexities of comparison. This broad area includes pollution of the water, pollution of the air, pollution of the land (as in certain kinds of coal mining and also the making of dams), and pollution of foods and the food supply. Through reading newspapers alone, students will find information on the contamination of water that results in the poisoning of fish and the cases of illness which result from eating those fish. They will read about new drugs that are invented and used, sometimes without adequate trial on human beings under carefully controlled conditions, and the unfortunate human results of these actions. Many other examples of pollution could be offered here, but we believe that those who teach in the specialized subject-matter areas are sensitive enough to information in the daily press, on television and radio, and professional journals to be able to guide students to varied sources. Students might be encouraged to make comparisons between what is going on in different countries and what is going on within our own country. When students are faced with the problem of seeking relevant materials and then of comparing and contrasting the results of their research, they become deeply involved in serious study, learning a great deal about values and subject matter through the process.

There are many instances in different subject areas where such study can take place. Students might be asked to compare Lincoln's First Inaugural Address with his Emancipation Proclamation. They might compare one of the first books written by a famous author with one of the latest books. In a foreign language class, students may read two different translations of the same French, German, or Italian classic which they have read in the original language and see for themselves how different translators (including themselves) really produce different stories. In a literature class, we might ask students to record every adjective that is used to describe the hero or heroine in the first 50 pages of a book, and then ask them to record every adjective that is used to describe the same individual in the last fifty pages of the book. Students then compare the two lists of adjectives and come to some conclusion as to whether or not the hero or heroine is portrayed as having changed over the period of time represented in the book. Very often discoveries can be made of new values emerging in the life of a character.

It is possible to ask students to compare different sports, to analyze them and to say what they like or dislike about one or many. And it may be useful to ask children to compare some things which seem to be not at all comparable: perhaps a newborn calf and a newborn baby. We might ask them to point out the ways in which these two newborn creatures are alike, to list those ways on paper, and to indicate the ones that they enjoyed learning. Using a similar approach, we could ask children to compare cats and dogs, showing the ways they are alike and the ways they are different, and making some value judgments about what it is that they like and dislike about dogs and cats. Sometimes we ask children to make a comparison of two very different characters who are talked about in a book that is popular with the class. Or we might ask them to make comparisons of other things they ordinarily would not compare: a watch or a clock with a calendar perhaps. Through all these activities, we would expect to see the children trying to make connections. As a thinking and learning experience, this effort is very instructive, since it relies upon past experiences and present abilities, and also involves values or value indicators if we ask students to make some kind of judgment.

Perhaps we have given enough examples to show that even in an activity that seems almost wholly cognitive, there are many affective elements. Try as we will, we are unable to separate them completely. Our value indicators will often show up in our comparisons and in other thinking processes too.

CLASSIFYING

Whether we are asked to classify items or experiences or life forms or anything else, we are being asked to organize information or experiences. We should of course have some *purpose* in classifying, and in a classroom we may very well raise the question of purpose whenever classification is involved. The purpose may influence the way in which we will classify the materials.

Here again there are a great many different assignments that we can make for students. We might ask students to make a list of all the television programs that they watched during the week or that they regularly watch during the week. This assignment would involve making a list and then grouping the programs that have been listed. We would then ask the students to give each group a name. These names constitute the categories of classification.

New insights often come to students as the result of such processes. They may see that they are watching only crime programs or that their emphasis is on soap operas or sports. If these results are shared by students in the class, they begin to see again how values operate in the choices we all make.

The examples shown in Charts 1 through 4, present several columns of words with the direction that a classification should be made. In each case, the students might be asked to answer these questions: How did you happen to choose this way of classifying them? What is a second way of doing it? These two questions would be asked of each set in the charts.

Chart 1 *Classification*

Classify the following:*

guitar	harp	bass fiddle
French horn	oboe	tuba
flute	piccolo	viola
trombone	timpani	bass drum
piano	triangle	bassoon
saxophone	trumpet	gong
glockenspiel	cello	banjo
xylophone	violin	clarinet
castanet	English horn	celeste

Classify the following:

corn	peas	milk
dandelion greens	radish	carrots
lima beans	squash	cantaloupe
apple pie	eggs	rice
strawberries	fish	string beans
potatoes	orange	bacon
chocolate cake	ham	frankfurter
peanuts	oysters	pizza
bread	cheese	hamburger
lamb chops	walnuts	steak
honey	chicken	cauliflower
ice cream	waffle	lobster

Classify the following:

barometer	scale	model
telescope	electron microscope	mirror
test tube	prism	spectrogram
centrifuge	meter stick	sonar
periscope	clock	tracer

* From L. Raths and S. Wassermann, *Thinking Box #2*, (Westchester, Ill.: Benefic Press, 1971).

Chart 1   *Classification* (Cont.)

radar	magnet	rain gauge
microscope	Geiger counter	weather map
hand lens	camera	radiosonde
Bunsen burner	transistor	telemetry
tuning fork	X-ray machine	isobar
spectroscope	graph	sextant
thermometer	compass	ammeter

Classify the following:

peppers	cucumbers	blueberries
oranges	bananas	cabbage
cream	cauliflower	apples
peaches	grapes	spinach
watermelon	butter	lettuce
peas	radishes	strawberries
milk	rice	celery
onions	carrots	pineapples
eggs	cheese	eggplant
cherries	pears	flour

Chart 2   *Grouping*

Below are listed some foods. Group them in a way you believe to be proper.*

Applesauce, baked apple, biscuits, chocolate-cream pudding, cinnamon toast, cranberry sauce, creamed dried chipped beef, cream of tomato soup, custard, eggnog, fruit-jello mold, hot chocolate, leafy salad, macaroni-supreme salad, melon, muffins, omelet, oven-fried chicken, popcorn balls, steak, vegetable-oil pastry, waffles.

Sample Student Responses

1. Fruits, breads, meats, dairy, and vegetables.
2. Fruits, desserts, breads, meats, eggs, soups, salads.
3. Foods I like and foods I dislike.
4. Desserts, beverages, breads, proteins, and vegetables.
5. Fattening foods and nonfattening foods.
6. Breakfast, lunch, dinner, and snack foods.
7. Solids and liquids.
8. Foods that require cooking and foods that may be eaten uncooked.

* From L. Raths, S. Wassermann, A. Jonas, and A. Rothstein, *Teaching for Thinking: Theory and Application* (Columbus, Ohio: Charles E. Merrill Publishing, 1967).

   9. Foods cooked on top of the stove and foods cooked in the oven.
  10. Foods served cold and foods served hot.
  11. The basic four: breads and cereal, meat, dairy, and vegetables.

    1. Analyze each of the above groupings. Can you determine on what basis or principle the groups were selected?
    2. Look at the eleven groups themselves carefully. Do you see a way of grouping *them?*

Group the following in any way you see fit:
Connecticut, Delaware, Georgia, Maryland, Massachusetts, New Hamphire, New Jersey, New York, North Carolina, Pennsylvania, Rhode Island, South Carolina, Virginia.

Some Student Responses

    1. Middle states, New England states, southern states.
    2. Agricultural states—industrial states.
    3. Northern states—southern states.
    4. Union states—Confederate states.
    5. States with "new" in them and states without "new."
    6. Proprietary colonies—self-governing colonies—royal colonies.
    7. States named after a monarch and states named after a lord.
    8. States with Indian names and those named after a section in England.
    9. Types of settlers settling in each state.
  10. States may be grouped according to products produced.
  11. States may be grouped according to size or population.
  12. Number of rivers and number of mountains.
  13. States which produced the most leaders in government.

Additional assignments could include the actual listing of the states within the grouping system.

Chart 3   *Grouping Statements*

Below are twenty statements which reveal some attitudes. Group them according to the following scheme:*

    Which seem to make snap judgments? They reject the problem and introduce irrelevant material. Mark these *D* for dogmatic.
    Which delay making a judgment and ask questions which seem to be pertinent to the problem? Mark these *C* for critical.
    Which seem to accept the problem too readily? They show suggestibility or guillibility. Mark these *U* for uncritical.

* From L. Raths, S. Wasserman, A. Jonas, and A. Rothstein, *Teaching for Thinking: Theory and Application* (Columbus, Ohio: Charles E. Merrill Publishing, 1967).

Which sit on the fence? They will not even accept a temporary hypothesis. Mark these *H* for hypercritical.

———— **1.** You can not tamper with certain social institutions or you upset the applecart.

———— **2.** What type of experimental situation could we set up?

———— **3.** Is poverty a natural thing or is it created by human beings?

———— **4.** What would be necessary for the study of such a problem?

———— **5.** The causes of poverty are probably related to human behavior. What is there in that behavior that would shed light on the issue?

———— **6.** Poverty exists because of the greed of others.

———— **7.** Poverty exists because people are lazy.

———— **8.** To allow poverty is to be inhumane.

———— **9.** Justice, simple justice—and it will triumph in the end—demands that the problem be solved.

———— **10.** Human nature cannot be changed; it is a waste of time.

———— **11.** Might as well try to solve the problem of war.

———— **12.** This problem has no practical value.

———— **13.** Only poor people want this problem solved.

———— **14.** There will always be poor people.

———— **15.** Poverty is the easiest thing in the world to overcome if we only do something about it.

———— **16.** It would be important for us to determine what we mean by poverty.

———— **17.** We might have to study the causes of poverty.

———— **18.** The evidence would have to be pretty substantial before we could act on it.

———— **19.** How are we ever going to gather enough information to form any sort of hypothesis?

———— **20.** There's no getting around it; poverty is here to stay.

Charts 1 through 3 include exercises which were used by teachers and students in the operation of *classifying*. Chart 4 is a listing of suggestions which will indicate some further classifying possibilities.

Chart 4 *Classifying Suggestions**

1. Latvians, Dutch, Bulgarians, Portugese, Hungarians, Rumanians, Swiss, Spanish, Ukranians, French, Slovenians, Slovaks, Poles, Italians, Czechs, Serbs, Germans, Croats.

2. 1776, 1941, 1917, 1812, 1839, 1861, 1898.

3. Prokofiev, Beethoven, Tchaikovsky, Schubert, Verdi, Mendelsohn, Brahms, Schumann, Schuman Scarlatti, Rossini, Purcell, Haydn, Shostakovich, Mozart, Gounod, Vivaldi, Wagner, Smetana, Bach, Dvořak.

* From L. Raths, S. Wasserman, A. Jonas, and A. Rothstein, *Teaching for Thinking: Theory and Application* (Columbus, Ohio: Charles E. Merrill Publishing, 1967).

4. Tennis, pool, golf, hockey, jai alai, table tennis, volleyball, basketball, baseball, lacrosse, polo, football, soccer, badminton.

5. Matisse, Renoir, Picasso, Gainsborough, Dürer, Holbein, Vermeer, Rembrandt, Degas, Modigliani, Lautrec, Goya, Velasquez, Turner, Cezanne, Manet, Monet.

6. Meager, menial, mortify, demonic, domicile, needless, nocturnal, destitute, denounce, depredation, decry, mutual, mystify, negligent, nimble, monster.

7. Knox, Adams, Washington, Jackson, Lincoln, Marshall, Taney, Taft, Randolph, Tyler, Grant, Wm. Harrison, Taylor, Eisenhower, Jay, Seward, Jefferson, Hamilton.

8. Flute, violin, cymbals, tambourine, trumpet, harp, lute, clarinet, English horn, triangle, cello, viola, French horn, trombone.

9. Group the ways of earning a living.

10. Group the tools in a woodshop.

11. Group the parts of the body.

12. Group the countries of the world.

In almost every case when presented with a list, students will find a variety of ways of classifying the very same materials. This does not mean that there will not be similarities and even some identities in classification systems. Rather, we wish to emphasize that there *may* be differences and that, when we ask students to make classifications, and they present their own categories, we must remember that it is not our privilege to tell them that they are wrong. There is no one correct way to classify materials if the assignment allows students to make their own system. In other words, we must be sure that after giving students the freedom to do their own thinking we do not then bawl them out for doing their own thinking! At this point, some teachers will want to introduce students to several principles of classification.

Classifying is often associated with the concept of "higher mental processes." This label usually means that the activity is something that human beings do and that animals probably do not do. Many systems of classification are established for convenience. Children soon learn where the pans are kept in the kitchen, where the plates are, and so on. They come to learn that some rooms have a distinctive purpose: the bedrooms, the dining room, the bathroom, the furnace room, the garage. They learn that some of their clothes are for school, some for play, some for church, some for summer, some for winter, some for rain. They learn to classify time into morning, afternoon, evening, and night. As they grow up, they find that the games they play with other children have values-classification schemes associated with them, and they learn to make use of these systems for their own purposes. It is a valuable skill to be able to create classifications for our own purposes. Where there are purposes, there are value indicators. Thus, in classification thinking is again closely linked to values.

OBSERVING AND
REPORTING

Human beings are not mere intellects. We are often driven by impulse, passion, and routine, to obtain satisfaction for our physical needs. Sometimes we use our minds to further these ends. When this occurs, reasoning or thinking can become irrational.

Our ultimate contact with fact is through our senses. We touch, see, hear, smell, or taste elements of our world. The evidence from our senses we sometimes call *primary evidence* or *eyewitness evidence*. There are also times when we go beyond this source and accept evidence from other people's senses as they describe it. This may be gossip more than fact and we accept it at our peril. To be sure, we tend to put less faith in such evidence, because it is only a secondary account; but if the person has prestige, our faith in his or her evidence tends to reflect our faith in the person. This is often the way in which gossip becomes elevated to the realm of "truth."

Underlying this entire account is the acceptance of what our senses communicate to us as truth. It is not so much that other people are engaged in the task of distorting things, of purposefully recording what is untrue. They do indeed tell us what they feel and see and hear and smell or taste. But, on many occasions, different people exposed to what we call the same experience, report very different things, and they report them as having been perceived by their senses. This is not to say that we should immediately distrust what we ourselves see and hear, but we should be always ready to learn that someone else heard and saw something that was not altogether the same. In some very subtle way, our whole background of experience reaches into the present and influences what we see and what we hear and what we feel. Thus our perceptions may be viewed as value indicators. Whenever we are asked to undertake one or more observations and to report on them, we may indeed be reporting a mixture of fact and sense data and value indicators.

There have been some attempts to verify these characterizations of human beings. One of them is the so-called *serial reporting system*. One student is asked to read a report that contains many facts, some of them perhaps quite startling. The report might be something, for example, about the San Francisco earthquake and fire of 1906. After the student has read the report to a class, he is asked to write it out from memory. The teacher then takes this memory version and passes it on to a second student and she is asked to read it and then to repeat it from memory. This memory report in turn is passed on to a third student who is asked to read it and then to write it out from memory. This process is carried on by six different students before the final memory report is compared to the original printed report about the fire and earthquake. Sometimes this comparison provides a great deal of laughter and humor and many questions. Nearly everybody who is involved in this experience begins to sense that his memory contains much more than the facts of the case. Of course, his memory also contains his own past and the connections which a present experience makes with the past.

Another way of indicating how different we are in observing and reporting is to have a brief film shown to the entire class, and perhaps one in which there is some violence between individuals or between groups. Immediately after the film is over, the students are asked not to talk to each other at all about what they have seen or heard, but instead to write out a report of what seemed to them the most significant things which took place. Here again the differences in the reports are often amazing. What one person seems to see and emphasize another person may not see at all and hence does not emphasize. This is so much the case that sometimes the teacher has to rerun the film in order to convince some students that some occurrence really was on the film.

Showing films and asking for observations and reports is an excellent way to give students practice in comparing their perceptions with those of other people. They know what they themselves have seen and heard and they learn what other people have seen and heard: The comparison gives them a more realistic view of themselves and their own perceptions.

Another way we may put an emphasis upon seeing and reporting is through field trips. Sometimes we allow individuals or small groups to make a trip by themselves and to report on it. In an elementary or middle school, the children might go as a group with parents as aides. When the children return from such a trip it is very common to ask them to make notes and to write out their most important impressions of what they have seen and heard. Some students will be sensitive to the working conditions that prevail in a plant or factory. Other students will say nothing about such issues, noticing instead the machinery in use. Some students will comment on the kinds of work done by women and the kinds done by men and will make comparisons and judgments about it, while other students' reports will contain nothing about this matter.

What is it that directs one person's attention to certain things and makes her want to write about them when a person sitting right next to her does not even notice what she regards as important? We would argue that a person's background of experience helps to shape attitudes, purposes, interests, and activities and that these come into play when they are free to emerge. When no one is telling us what to see and what to write, our own background comes into play and is the source of what we want to write or what we want to talk about. Here, again, as we share these reactions with classmates, we begin to see ourselves more clearly. Furthermore, we begin to see that our "thinking" is not an intellectual machine; it is rather a function of our whole personality. What we have lived, what we have seen, what we have felt, and what we have suffered and thought about: all of these experiences in their interpenetrations come out in an atmosphere of freedom and encouragement. In other words, seeing and reporting may be generally considered thinking operations, but they almost always involve values. It is a major achievement when students learn that they need to be careful in phrasing their reports so that their own biases, their own prejudices, do not take over.

Observing and reporting can also be practiced in science laboratories where hypotheses are being tested. Students are asked to give precise accounts of what is done and what happens. Sometimes we ask students to go to a window in the classroom, look outside for a few moments, and then recall what they have observed. A variant of this procedure at a very simple level is to have a boy and a girl stand in front of the room for a few minutes and then step out into the hall. The other students are then asked to describe what they saw.

As an example of the importance of accurate observing and reporting, consider this situation. A man staggers into a drugstore gesturing unsteadily, his speech incoherent and his gait very irratic. A customer, in irate fashion, snaps at the clerk, "That man is drunk! You should throw him out of here!" As the clerk responds, leading the man outdoors, she notices that the man is pointing to a coat pocket. She puts her hand into the man's pocket and takes out some chocolate cubes, and puts one into the man's mouth. The man soon returns to the drugstore, his speech now coherent and his gait steady.

As you may have guessed, the man was ill and attributing drunkenness to him was an unjustified conclusion. If what the other customer had said about his condition had been repeated to five to six people, the sick man's reputation might have suffered significantly.

It is unfortunate that people often jump to conclusions supposedly supported by their senses but actually far beyond what their senses tell them. It is only as we have experiences of this kind, shared with our peers, that we learn the ways of caution. We begin to recognize that our background, our past, enters into judgments of the moment and sometimes corrupts them. In the instance of the irate customer, it was probably not a value of any kind nor a value indicator expressly stated as such which influenced the outburst as much as it was a disposition to be impulsive and not to consider alternatives. Considering alternatives is the very heart of the valuing process.

SUMMARIZING

There are many occasions when we find it advantageous to sum up what has taken place. To make a summary of past experiences is to try to winnow out the chaff and retain only the wheat. In making our summary we want to communicate what seems to us the most important elements of an experience. Like comparing, like classifying, like observing and reporting, summarizing is both a thinking process and a valuing process. We look back over what the experience included and we are faced with the problem of making selections: What is to be emphasized and what is to be excluded? Where such choices are being made, values are involved. What seems very important to one person and looms large in his or her summary may not even be mentioned by another person in the group. Some people remember a great many petty details; thus, instead of giving a summary, tend to repeat the entire experience and exclude or try to exclude nothing in their summary report. Still others mention only one or two things and a central meaning of the experience is overlooked. These different approaches can come to light in the classroom as summaries are shared by individuals in the class and as comments are made by students listening to each other. We sometimes hear such comments as, "I didn't notice that," "Did that really happen?" I don't see how that's important." In the process, students begin to see when and where people intrude more than their sense impressions, where they bring in judgments of one kind or another and perhaps their hopes and fears besides. It can be brought out by the students or by the teacher that there is nothing wrong with the inclusion of these things in the summary if the person who makes them sees clearly what they are and does not confuse them with sense impressions or with what we commonly call "facts" or "common sense."

As we have mentioned before, our thinking can at times easily mislead us when it is influenced by our fears, wishes, impulses, and prejudices. These influences are often all wrapped up together in a decision that is represented by value-type utterances. We turn now to still another example of a thinking operation that is imbedded in valuing operations in our everyday life.

INTERPRETING

Interpretation of anything from a dance to a menu is inevitably involved with values. To interpret something is to make an effort to get meaning from the experience or to put meaning into it, and we are not always sure which is the case. If we are asked to interpret a piece of modern art, what we see is a reflection of the meanings that we have been able to get from our study of or our preoccupation with the specimen of modern art. To interpret something is to look for meanings in that something, and these meanings are not always in the object being studied. Some meanings are indeed "in the eye of the beholder."

Aesthetic judgments frequently are very much influenced by the perceiver, as are the judgments we make of drama, fiction, poetry, scientific achievements, mathematical innovations, and just about everything there is in the world to interpret. We come to these experiences not with a past that is a blank slate but with a past alive with interactions of many kinds and learnings that have been derived from those interactions. All of this we bring to a new book, a new poem, a new opera. Consequently, it is probably true to say that each generation has the task of finding itself. In the process it tends to rewrite history, to reconceptualize art, and to re-create a great deal of the past. We should expect this change as the natural course of history and human development. The changes that have come over the world in this century alone seem to have been far greater than the changes that took place between the time of the Roman Empire and the beginning of the 20th century. Even so, these changes have become a part of our lives so gradually that many of us are largely unaware of them. One example of these far-reaching changes is the changes in race relations which have occurred in the United States just since about 1955. These changes have been immense and they have grown out of new and different interpretations of the Constitution. New justices in the Supreme Court, with new and different experiences, have been asked to make judgments about situations which involve people with new attitudes in new kinds of situations that have been precipitated by new industries, new products, new ways of working, and new ways of living. Interpretation in this case and others is a part of living that continues day after day, hour after hour, in all of us. Moreover as we seek meaning in life or seek the meaning of a single experience, we come to it not only with our thinking skills but also with our awarenesses of good and bad, beautiful and ugly, true and false, and other attitudes associated with honor, respect, and courtesy. Out of this amalgam, a new society is continually in the making.

We must help our young people to see clearly that their value indicators are almost always a part of their thinking and a part of their experience and that, if they are faced with making a decision, they should take time out to differentiate the "facts" of the situation from the value indicators involved, and anticipate first the consequences of one alternative and then those of another. The process of interpreting life and projecting it into the future is a human process. It is vitally linked to the process of survival and thus is a most valuable human behavior. We must do everything we can to preserve it as an asset and extend it as a resource.

ANALYZING ASSUMPTIONS

To end one of the processes of inquiry by actually assuming something is to take it for granted without further investigation. We may assume that something is true or probably true, we may assume that something is false or probably false, or we may assume that at the moment of inquiry there is no evidence either way. Regardless of the circumstances, the acceptance of an assumption is to take something for granted.

Assumptions play an important—often crucial—part in our everyday lives. It is, for example, common for us in our commercial dealings with various business people to assume that the product that we buy is of reasonably good quality and that if it should fail in use an adjustment will be made in our favor. We assume the integrity and the reliability of the people with whom we deal and we do this in such a matter-of-fact way that we are hardly aware of it.

We may also operate under such assumptions with people who think in terms of leases and contracts. We may assume in this situation also that we are dealing with people and not with leases and contracts, that the personal factor will take precedence over the small print. On many occasions in practice, we find that this is not the case at all, and that acquaintances and sometimes long-standing friends will hold us to the details of a contract we have signed even though the lapse from the contract requirements is more or less trivial and practically insignificant to us.

At a different level that also points to the importance of analyzing assumptions, we sometimes assume that advertisements in "quality" magazines are to be taken at face value, that the printed word is true. We sometimes support this belief by saying "They couldn't say that if it were false." Certainly this assumption is as naive as that which assumes that a written contract is less important than a personal relationship in all cases.

People sometimes make uninformed assumptions. A man may, for example, contemplate travel to a northern climate, to Vancouver for instance. If the stay is to be for several weeks he may make some assumptions about the weather in the region merely on the basis of its northern location. Following these assumptions he then packs heavy coats, thick socks, warm sweaters, and perhaps even snow boots, only to find that the weather is delightfully warm when he arrives, due to the city's warm coastal currents. When people do not investigate the accuracy of their assumptions before making a decision, they may end up carrying a heavy coat in 80-degree weather, very uncomfortable with their decision.

Other assumptions that can be misleading are those we make about the character of people whom we have just met. On the basis of a brief conversation, we may decide a person is intelligent, kind, and hard-working, all on the basis of some stereotypic observations. Where we recognize clearly that we are making shaky assumptions, we may go ahead anyway with the transaction, always aware of whatever risk is involved. Where we proceed without this realization, we may be dumbfounded when the truth reveals its consequences.

We sometimes make assumptions on the basis of quite small samplings of information. For example, we may read two or three issues of a weekly magazine and on that basis subscribe for a year or more. We may not even be aware that we are using such a slender base for a judgment that involves 25 times the amount of time in our experience! Another common oversight is to ignore the effect of time on our knowledge. At times we may find ourselves using facts that are anywhere from 5 to 15 (or more) years old. We may be quite unaware that conditions have changed radically in the particular field we claim knowledge in. Without realizing it, we make the assumption that the facts we have, though many years old, are current.

Ultimately, what leads us to these faulty assumptions is that we believe that our knowledge is always valid. We make assumptions about cause and effect. We make assumptions, when we use an either-or approach, that there are but two alternatives, and we do not stop to look for more than two. On other occasions we make a statement of the "if-then" kind, regardless of whether the sentence following the "if" statement is also true and follows from the stated assumption.

It is the case in these examples of misleading assumption that we make assumptions that very often deal with probable value indicators we are unaware of. As with all the other cognitive approaches we are faced again with the inroads of probable value indicators. We saw this component in the processes of comparing, classifying, observing, reporting, summarizing, and interpreting, and it is also present here in the assumptions we make. Values and thinking seem somehow so united that no clear-cut and total separation can be made. To protect the integrity of our thinking processes *we should be aware of both what we are doing and the consequences of what we are doing.* When we *know* about the critical assumptions that we are making, we can qualify our statements to students and other people in ways which will protect us and them. On other occasions, we may simply want to say to our listeners that we may be prejudiced in the particular instance in spite of ourselves and that, having warned them, we will go ahead with what we want to say. This is a much more intelligent way of operating than to proceed totally ignorant of what we are doing.

PROBLEM SOLVING (DECISION MAKING)

In our arrangement of the different thinking processes, we have more or less arbitrarily associated problem solving with decision making. Some examples should reveal the dimensions of this process. Consider the case of some neighbors near a street intersection who have had frequent opportunities to observe automobile accidents or narrow escapes at that intersection and have concerned themselves with efforts to remedy the situation. As they consider alternatives, they first discuss signs. They see the possibility of several large signs near the curbs which would inform passing motorists of the dangerous intersection. They also discuss erecting signs which require a great reduction of speed in that city block. Next they consider requesting that a traffic light be installed at the corner, so that safety will be maximized for children and adult pedestrians as well as motorists. Having observed a significant number of night accidents, the residents also suggest recommending more adequate street lighting. They further criticize the slippery type of pavement construction.

Throughout the discussion, any observer would be aware that the only consideration of the residents is not money. The shared problem solving produces an awareness of life-and-death values and an awareness of the priority of these values. The factors that come up for consideration in solving the problem tend to be value indicators. Some people will say publicly in such a meeting that no matter how that problem is solved or what it costs, they want life itself to be maintained and that they want fatalities to be reduced to zero. We begin to understand how much life means to those people as they stress its value in a problem-solving situation. The emotion associated with such discussions alone is an important value indicator.

Like public safety, visual pollution of public and private land is an area that arouses community action. As we bring specific instances of park and street pollution to the public's attention through an open meeting or through letters to the editor, we are inviting people to present possible solutions—solutions that may make a significant contribution to cleaning up this kind of pollution. Here again, problem solving is recognized as more or less a cognitive process, but it brings along many affective factors that are to be seen as probable value indicators.

Most local newspapers offer many editorial comments on spending planned by the local government. Often these discussions raise the question of alternative ways of spending the allocated money for a specific project, say a new building. Editorial comments, noting a local problem with water pollution, might suggest that instead of a new town building the community really needs new sewage-treatment facilities. Such questions of priorities are almost always a factor in problem solving, and values are the very essence of priorities. We can not escape them. They are there in all situations that involve thinking. (And not necessarily those, such as questions found at the ends of many textbook chapters, that involve finding the "right" answer.)

CRITICIZING AND EVALUATING

We use the word *criticizing* to include both the negative aspects usually associated with criticisms and the positive approach to what is being examined. We view the concept of evaluation in the same way. The latter term, *evaluation,* usually puts much more emphasis upon the criticisms which relate to purpose and to achievements which either relate or do not relate to purpose. Criticism, in its abstract sense, deals more with the qualities of what is being studied quite independently of any consideration of its original purpose.

Moreover, we believe that it is a reasonable expectation that people who want to criticize should really know what they are talking about. They should have examined the specific subject matter carefully, should know something about other related subject matter, and should be willing to have their criticisms challenged in print on radio or television, or in public discussion.

In our early days in school, we were told that the New England town meeting invited the community to speak what they believed on many issues. It was said that people who grew in this town-meeting atmosphere became accustomed to having other people differ with them and also to differing with them on clearly specified grounds. It often appears today that people no longer realize how to communicate differences with each other in this way, how to examine these differences in a temperate atmosphere, and how to sum up the pros and cons of many criticisms of many alternatives. It is often said that violence has taken the place of public communication. Many people have been frustrated in trying to produce certain changes in the community. They have received little regard for their efforts and practically no attention is given to their proposals. Disillusioned with local bureaucracies, such people organize movements which culminate in violence intended to bring about that change which they believe to be in the best interests of the community. All too often such violent behavior produces a great deal of damage, generates more differences than existed before, and lowers community morale for a time.

To help steer away from this violent mood, teachers must encourage open discussion and criticism among their students. Usually a well-chosen series of questions will get this started. A teacher might begin by asking students as a general question, "What are some of the things you like about comic books? What are some of the things you dislike about them? Please write your ideas on a separate sheet and let's have a discussion of our reactions to comic books." It seems fair to assume that many boys and girls know something about comic books and that some of them will have had a long experience with a few types of comic books, having read them week after week. With this experience behind them, they probably will feel some confidence in their ability to criticize comic books. If in the process they should learn that criticism involves both negative and positive aspects of a subject, if they should learn that people will ask them for the reasons for their judgments, then they may also learn that when they speak out for or against something they should know what they are talking about. Perhaps in the future when they criticize or evaluate some project, they will not feel insulted when someone asks them for their reasons. Rather, they will realize that the questioner may be trying to learn, may be using criticism and evaluation to discover reasons for the good and bad qualities of the subject under consideration.

A similar kind of group reaction may be encouraged from consideration of a new activity that has been proposed to a classroom. If, for example, an elementary-school or middle-school class has never put on a class play, we would expect questions to begin to fly almost at once when such a thing is suggested: questions about the content of the play or its author; questions about reasons for giving a play; questions about roles in the play and whether or not the class has people who can fill the roles; questions about costumes and time for rehearsals. These initial questions on many occasions may contain affective factors which should be dealt with as they come up. Further planning and criticism can follow this initial stage of reaction. It may be necessary to consult with authorities in school; it may be necessary to consult with parents and to raise questions about how the bussing situation will be modified and controlled. Here students will learn how leadership is expressed whenever genuinely relevant issues are proposed in a group discussion, whether the criticism is positive or negative.

To learn how to take criticism and how to give it is important to the valuing processes. We should learn how to be compassionate in our dealings with our fellow human beings. In the give and take of facing school groups everday, there is a wonderful opportunity for us to learn this important skill and important sensitivity. Here, of course, *feelings* often play a very important part. Sharp and negative criticism of something proposed by a shy classmate may be overwhelming and may cause that person to be even more of a nonparticipant than before.

Finally, we want to stress that criticizing and evaluating involve a point of view that involves both standards and knowledge. When we make criticisms, either positive or negative, those who listen to us assume that we have reasons for what we say. Very often these reasons will be based on a specific value, thus becoming value indicators. In such a public interchange, our values begin to gain public notice and we begin to gain confidence in sharing them with others.

IMAGINING AND CREATING

One of the mysteries of the advance of science is where and how new ideas originate in the fields of science. It is widely acknowledged that some specialized scientific method that produces or creates new ideas does not exist. Scientists say that many new ideas are "hunches" that appear suddenly and come from an unidentifiable source; ideas have come to some scientists in dreams and to others as they were getting on a street car; other scientists have found that new ideas have come to them on the basis of rather serious mistakes that they had made, once they became aware of what happened through the mistake.

By and large, however, we really do not know how new ideas come into being. We do recognize that all great scientists and also creative artists are people with active imaginations. In fact, many of us believe that without imagination and creativity, it is practically impossible to produce a unified theory of any kind. This does not mean that other cognitive factors are to be minimized or played down. Rather obviously, intelligence is a factor and the continual use of intelligence in problem-solving situations is an asset to the scientists who are in the process of creating. Even so, we find it hard to define creativity in a way that satisfies those who have been creative. We have taken the approach of observing people who have already become famous for their creations, hoping that through analyzing their lives for examples of their behavior under a variety of circumstances, to discover patterns which would explain their creativity. So far we have failed. We may agree on some aspects of the creative process, but we are not encouraged enough to believe that we can teach people to be highly imaginative or to be highly creative in advanced fields of knowledge. At the moment, it appears that some people have the capacity to create and that they represent a minority of the total population, while other people, the great majority, do not have these qualities.

In teaching, however, we must proceed on the assumption that there are exercises, like brainstorming and more direct assignments to promote imagining which will in time produce an effect that makes people more imaginative than they were before. We also hope to create an *atmosphere* conducive to creativity and to provide opportunities to write so that, whatever comes to mind, the student feels free to put it down on paper. Chart 5 offers a few examples of these exercises.

Chart 5   *Assignments to Promote Creativity**

1. How do you think people will look a million years from now? Draw or write about the ways people will look in the far, far future as you fantasize about it.

2. After identifying your favorite cartoon from the comic books or some cartoons from other sources, use your imagination to write to the character.

* From L. Raths and S. Wassermann, *Thinking Box #1* (Westchester, Ill.: Benefic Press, 1971).

3. Try to imagine that you are in a space ship visiting another planet. Make up a story about an adventure that you might have on that planet with the people who are there or animals who are there.

4. You have learned that in our past we have used oxen, camels, horses, wagons, chariots, bicycles, tricycles, planes, and trains to travel on. As you think about the far distant future, what do you see as possibilities for travel a thousand years from now? See if you can make a picture of what you think might be a method of transportation.

5. Invent a new toy and tell how it is to be used and draw a picture of it.

6. Pretend you are a famous scientist working on a new kind of invention. On a separate piece of paper write about your invention and tell how it will change our way of life.

7. Suppose you were an advisor to the President. What advice would you give to the President today? Write out your ideas and try to give some reasons for them.

8. You have just been given the opportunity to meet a character from one of your favorite books. Try to imagine what the meeting would be like. Describe the setting and write out the conversation between you and the character.

Wherever imagination is at work in the production of new things, new ideas, new arguments, new complaints, valuing is necessarily involved. The process of imagining and creating are almost inherently value-type activities. Although both are beyond ordinary processes of reasoning they are at the same time within the processes of valuing and do tend to produce probable value indicators.

CODING AND
REACTIONS TO CODING

Many of the exercises which relate thinking operations to valuing operations culminate either in discussions or in writings, with the emphasis on writings of many kinds. *Coding,* on the other hand, is a much simpler task. Chart 6 is a sample of this coding approach. The examples in this chart contain what we call *extreme* words. Once students have learned to code these words themselves, we can use the same process in coding their writing. In any writings produced by students, if we were coding the writing, we could put a large X right near the extreme word, as we ask students to do in this exercise. Some extreme words to beware of are "all," "never," "everything," "everyone," "always," "nothing," "nobody," and the superlative adjectives—

"best," "worst," "first," "most," and so on. Coding this kind of expression brings the phrases to the attention of those who use these words often and helps them to see whether or not this usage interferes with their achievement of values that they prize. Quite often, the very use of these words tends to stiffen the oppositions of other people and values relating to friendship are threatened along with values relating to cooperation. On many occasions, these extreme expressions do not represent what we really believe anyway. Thus, as Pascal said, "Let us endeavor then to think well; therein lies the principle of morality."

Chart 6　*Coding Exercises**

   1.　Each of the sentences below has an extreme word. Copy the sentence on another sheet of paper and put an *X* over each extreme word.

   a.　I have all the money I need.
   b.　He never believes me.
   c.　I never get what I want.
   d.　That store has everything.
   e.　Everyone likes milk.
   f.　Her team always wins.
   g.　There is nothing for me to do.
   h.　I always finish my homework.
   i.　Nobody understands how I feel.
   j.　Nobody heard a word I said.

   2.　On many occasions in talking and in writing we use adjectives which indicate our approval or disapproval of some of the things we are talking about. In this next exercise, you have an opportunity to examine some of your own writing to see if you are using value terms without quite realizing it.

   Make a list of the hobbies of the boys and girls in your class. Then write a short story about one of the hobbies on your list. The story should not be more than eight or nine sentences.
   Read the story you have written. Have you used any value words in your story? If so, mark these words with a *V* for value word.
   Have you used any extreme words in your story? If so, mark these words with an *X*.

Each sentence below has a value word. Copy the sentences on a piece of paper. Put a *V* over each value word.

   a.　That is good news.
   b.　The senator likes to make speeches.

* From L. Raths and S. Wassermann, *Thinking Box #1* (Westchester, Ill.: Benefic Press, 1971).

    c.   I will be glad when she comes home.
    d.   Spelling is useful.
    e.   I like my friends.
    f.   I hate spinach.
    g.   The play was bad.
    h.   This is an excellent book.
    i.   Chocolate cake is delicious.

Value words tend to show what you like or dislike. Coding these words can help you decide if you have said exactly what you mean.

3. Write a theme on the topic, "What Am I Like?" Then code your theme as follows:

    a.   Mark your extreme words with an *X*.
    b.   Underline and mark the *assumptions* with an *A*.*
    c.   Mark the *value words* with a *V*.

The purpose of coding is to help you write exactly what you mean. When you are coding your own paper, look for certain patterns of expression. Mark these patterns with the symbols *X*, *V*, and *A*. Now, reread your theme. Does it say exactly what you mean to say? Have you marked the patterns of expressions correctly? Are there any changes you wish to make?

4. Write a story titled, "Best Friends." Then code your story as follows:

    a.   Mark the *extreme* words with an X.
    b.   Underline and mark the *assumptions* with an A.
    c.   Mark the *value* words with a V.

5. When the astronauts landed on the moon, one news reporter made the following statement. Look for extreme words. Write down all the extreme words you can find.

Everyone here on earth is watching the astronauts as they walk on the moon. Some people thought it would never happen. But there were some people who always had hope.
Every country in the world has wanted to land on the surface of the moon. Now it has happened.
This is the biggest and the best space adventure in the history of our world.

This chapter offers many opportunities for students to express themselves in specific thinking operations. The students' responses can be used further as texts for coding exercises. As they learn to use the code, students will become sensitive to their frequent use of extreme words or to their frequent use of value-laden words.

* For many students, this assignment will prove difficult or even impossible.

Of course, there are many other possible coding factors that could be introduced for such exercises. For example, a teacher may become very sensitive to the word "or." Almost always when this word is used, it means that the writer saw the presence of two alternatives and no more than two. It is important to point out to a student such a tendency toward either/or thinking. Coding can bring this point home, especially once students recognize that there may be more alternatives and that they can alter their language to indicate that the two alternatives which are named in a composition are in reality two among many and not the only two.

A teacher may also want to use as a coding factor the qualifying words and phrases which students use, such as "it seems," "it appears," "I would guess," "probably," "perhaps," and "maybe." You may find that some students have one or two terms that they use over and over again. When this is brought to their attention by their own self-codings, they are apt to modify their behavior.

If the teacher introduces concepts related to grammar, she or he may also introduce a code letter for nouns, verbs, abverbs, prepositions, or infinities. Naturally, any large number of these should not be introduced. Nevertheless, over time many of them can be introduced and you may find that many students will be surprised to learn that they use verbs, adverbs, or pronouns.

Sometimes students have a tendency to generalize rather quickly on a very inadequate basis and to do this quite regularly in their writing. A teacher may want to use a *G* as a code word for this kind of communication.

Finally, it is a rather common practice among adults and children to make attributions to other people without realizing that it is being done. We sometimes say of persons whom we hardly know that they are friendly people, in this case attributing "friendliness" to them. In another context, we might say that the people in our class are not cooperative, thus attributing "uncooperativeness" to the group. Visiting another school we might say of the teacher of the class we observed that she did not like the children. We would be attributing to that teacher "not liking." We may believe that we have a solid basis for such attribution, but in most cases that would be doubtful.

Another common case is to say to a student, "You are not really trying." Since we really have very few ways of measuring effort, for us to say that no effort is being exerted is an attribution on our part and may be far from the mark. When we make attributions to other people and when they believe that these comments are unwarranted, we begin a process that may poison our relations not only with that particular person but also between ourselves and other members of the immediate group who may think that we are being unfair. Before we make attributions, we should make an effort first to find out more about what we want to say. We can ask more questions that we ordinarily would and have a better foundation for making a judgment. On the other hand, it may even be better for us not to make the judgment at all.

IN CONCLUSION

In this chapter we have discussed a number of the most common thinking operations which children and adults use. In every one of the ten operations we have shown that value judgments are often involved and that reason in isolation from these value components is practically nonexistent. We might even reverse the statement that thinking tends to be accompanied by value terms to say that valuing tends to be almost always accompanied by thinking. We come to the conclusion over and over again that other people do not always think exactly the way we think, that other people do not have the same values that we have; and we learn over and over again to listen to views that are different from our own and we learn how to express views that are different from others in the class. We also discover in the process of valuing that we cannot be absolutely sure of decisions because every decision is colored in part by whatever value judgments are involved. And so we learn that for every decision we make there may be evidence offered by someone, some place, somewhere that could perhaps influence us to alter our decision. This is not to say that we are unsure of everything and not sure of anything. But along with our confidence in some of our convictions, we do leave open a tiny hole of possibility that we may be wrong.

Living like this we find and our students will find that we tend to form many more friendships and many more friendly acquaintances than if we were dogmatic in our behavior. We not only learn how to live with people, but also learn how to solve problems with the free, willing help of those with whom we associate. We learn how to give and how to take and how to live in friendship with each other in this process. We do not believe that thinking solves every problem, nor that if your values are alright you will always find the best solutions to a problem. We try to use thinking and valuing operations in a contemplative manner to address ourselves to common problems. We find that we are able to work with people whose religions differ from ours, whose sex differs from ours, whose politics differ from ours, whose race differs from ours. These factors notwithstanding we can give and take and make progress on the issues that confront us.

Getting Started:
Some Questions and Answers

Many centuries ago Confucius noted that ideas have to be turned into action if they are to be of any worth. The purpose of this chapter is to help you turn the ideas of this book into action in the classroom, if you choose to do so, and to summarize some questions we have heard from teachers and some answers we have given to those questions. Many other questions—especially questions asked by those who would like to train teachers in values clarification—are discussed in *Values Clarification* (Kirschenbaum, 1977). This chapter is rather practical in focus. Questions with a more theoretical focus are discussed in chapter 14.

STARTING A
NEW APPROACH

Getting started with a new approach can be difficult. Even more difficult, perhaps, is persevering when the going gets tough, when the newness of the approach runs into the inevitable problems, confusion, and resistances. Our old ways are always more comfortable. Often we are not even expected to take new paths, so external motivation is missing. Sometimes we are even pressured *against* taking new paths, so why fight it? Why, indeed?

Because students will benefit? Well, yes, although we really cannot be certain of this until *after* we have suffered the trials of getting the new method to work.

Because it makes it easier for us to educate students who are so confused by values as to be apathetic, very uncertain, conforming, or irrational in the classroom? Again, yes, but we will not know about this until after we give it a try. Besides, it might be easier to suffer the apathetic, uncertain conformists and the others than to try to change teaching ways.

Because, if it does work, children will like us more and we all like to be liked? Perhaps.

Because, again assuming it works, parents and other teachers and school administrators will have more respect for our talents? Sure, why not?

But there is another reason: This method offers the opportunity to move to richer levels of satisfaction for the teacher too. It adds another, and, according to the evidence so far, very potent tool to the teacher's resource kit, and like the expert use of any effective tool, it gives immense satisfaction when it is well handled. To see children move from apathy or confusion toward positive, purposeful, proud living and learning and to know that you are partially responsible for this is to experience something deeply satisfying, both professionally and personally.

Why then do we emphasize the trouble of getting started? Because it *is* difficult. Few teachers appreciate how much of their professional behavior is a subconscious result of their past experiences, not the result of conscious decision. A number of us lecture because our experiences have associated lecturing with security or success or power or fame or something else personally meaningful. Some of us are lenient with students because *we* feel better when we are that way. Some history teachers are history teachers because *they* enjoyed history when they were in school—and they tend to teach it the way they remember that it provided enjoyment, even when it is quite clear that many of their students are not finding the same pleasure. And so it goes.

Similarly, there are foreign-language enthusiasts who are convinced that foreign languages are good for students. Teachers who found more satisfaction in the woodshop, however, will not easily be convinced that woodshop is not much more valuable than foreign languages. And the sad part is that, like many a political and religious discussion, we can consider these issues at great length without ever getting at the real reasons behind our support of certain subject matter and approaches. The "logic" behind arguments for foreign languages, woodshop, the lecture method, leniency, academic history, and so on is often a rationalization for the less understood need to defend a subconscious heritage.

Such predispositions help explain why education courses have not had much effect on teachers' behavior. It is not possible to argue away many teachers' needs to relive their past positive experiences. Thus, we run into the seemingly absurd difficulty of getting educational innovations that are demonstrably superior adopted by school people. Their satisfactions may just float in another sea.

There is a somewhat special obstacle for many teachers in a method such as the value theory that aims at developing the student's independence and self-responsibility. As Peck and Havighurst (1960, p. 193) put it:

> A good many Americans either do not really want children to become independently responsible beings, or they will not tolerate the frequent frustrations of selfish impulse which are required to treat a child in an ethical manner. This is true of a good many teachers and preachers, just as it is true of many millions of American parents. The millennium in human ethics will not come by wishing; it is a far-distant goal that must be arduously worked for, on a personal scale, day to day.

Of course, none of this is meant to imply that all teachers resist all change. Regarding children suffering from value confusion, many teachers are seriously concerned about the disinterested, conforming, and uncertain child and are not only willing but anxious to find some workable approach to such children. There are older teachers who see the unhappy results of moralizing—humans without the self-confidence and skills to guide their lives—and want to avoid that. Other teachers find pleasure in striking out and trying potentially more effective teaching approaches, sometimes because they recall with dismay and regret school days of their own that were frustrating or empty. Nevertheless, for all of us—the willing and the hesitant—developing new styles of behavior is not easy. Perhaps to be forewarned is indeed to be forearmed. For the hesitant, perhaps awareness of some of the common reasons that tie us to older practices will help overcome resistance.

GUIDELINES FOR GETTING STARTED

How, then, should you begin? What problems can we point to that might help a teacher minimize difficulties? Generally, we would suggest a two-stage approach. The first stage would have the teacher give some strategies of the value theory a preliminary test, with the object of perfecting them and getting subjective impressions of their effect. The second stage would involve a more systematic test of the theory and might follow several months of the more informal trial. (A way of systematically evaluating the value theory in classrooms is outlined in chapter 13.)

The following sections offer nine general guidelines.

Clarify Values Clarification for Yourself

The first step is to assure yourself that you have internalized the basic sense of the theory. You might try to review it for yourself, to see if you can outline its principles. Without such a grounding, it will be difficult to use the theory artistically or to improvise when, as sooner or later always happens in teaching, the delightful but unpredictable occurs.

Remind yourself especially that the values-clarification methodology has two elements: content and process. The content is some aspect of life that the students can connect to their own experiences. The process revolves around the seven valuing criteria: choice, alternatives, consequences, prizing, sharing, acting, and repeating. Chapter 4 details much of this.

Blend Freedom and Safety

Value growth flourishes in a schoolroom where students feel accepted, supported, relaxed, and generally unthreatened. Therefore, it is wise for teachers working for value development to work also for the proper classroom climate and, in particular, to try to have students feel safe and secure enough to think logically and express themselves honestly. To do this, students will have to perceive that the teacher basically likes and respects them and that they will not be punished in some way, overtly or covertly, if they make a mistake in judgment, look foolish as they search for clarity, or adopt a value that contradicts one of the teacher's or the school's.

This does *not* mean that the teacher must be extremely permissive, although it probably does rule out an arbitrary or autocratic climate. More important than permissiveness is respect and concern. Students must feel that, even though rules exist and there is teacher direction, the teacher respects the students' values and is concerned that the students work at those values in their own ways. Indeed, we have seen teachers develop an *unsafe* classroom climate by rapidly removing controls and direction in the mistaken belief that permissiveness is necessary for value development. As a result, the students' need for security was so threatened that neither values nor much of anything else was attended to.

This does not mean students should be denied freedom. Students need some freedom of choice if they are to practice directing their lives, and it is only through such practice that viable values develop. But freedom must be won gradually, usually, giving a whole class freedom quickly is giving more than can be handled. The problems of group decision making and group self-control are so complex even for many adults, that it is more likely to swamp than to support efforts at self-direction.

In short, try not to confuse a lack of controls with the climate necessary for value clarifying. The required climate is one of acceptance of and respect for students.

Stand Up for Your Values, But Encourage Thinking

Standing up for their own values while not standing in the way of students' thinking is very hard for many adults. Whether it is because we consider ourselves so wise or because we cannot easily entertain the idea that our values might not be ideal, or for whatever reason, the tendency to try to persuade children to accept *our* values is controlled only with great effort.

Most of us all too easily judge others, even other adults. We apply our standards to all sorts of actions for which those standards may not really apply. We assume that people who have not had our experiences should nevertheless have our understanding. We lecture about righteousness. We bribe and punish behavior to mold it to what we consider acceptable. We complain when children do not follow our excellent models. We preach, we nag, we cajole, we do many things to promote *our* values. We are delighted when students accept them, and we consider it a failure—sometimes a personally threatening failure—when they reject them.

However, as we discussed earlier, this moralizing—direct or indirect—has not worked very well. And it has robbed children of the privilege of thinking value-related issues out for themselves. This may in fact be contributing to the value confusion, apathy, conformity, uncertainty, and irrational behavior of so many children and adults today.

We must learn that we cannot foster the ability to think critically in value-related issues while demanding, however subtly, that the outcome of that thinking must conform to what we believe. If we attempt to inculcate values, we cannot expect that they will be thoughtfully adopted and freely lived. If we want children to really live what they believe and believe what they live, we must give them the opportunity to do so. When we restrict beliefs or actions, we restrict this opportunity.

This argument against "guiding" value decisions of children is strong even if the failure of that approach has not sobered us to the need for an alternative. The assertion here is that values, defined as freely and thought-fully chosen, prized, and acted upon, do not come from a process of adult manipulation. The definition of values says that they cannot come except by free, open, intelligent, informed choice.

This does not mean that teachers should accept any kind of behavior. Children have to be protected not from erroneous *beliefs*—those will be exploded in the process of free and thoughtful development of ideas—but from actions that will restrict their development in the future. Children are protected by various legal and social restrictions. Children, generally, may not quit school before a certain age; they may not contract to buy merchan-dise; they may not marry; they may not continually disrupt a classroom; and so on. But we assert that there is a difference between limiting children's behavior and respecting their right to their own opinions, beliefs, and values.

It might be a very healthy thing if every time an adult made a judgment that limited a child's actions or was in opposition to the child's ideas, that adult were to say something like, "But everyone may not agree," or "We have to do this for so-and-so reasons, but some people think that those and other reasons lead to different conclusions," or "You may campaign for your way, but for now . . ." or "Although my idea is so-and-so, you should have your own ideas, whether they agree or disagree," or in some similar way make clear that even while we limit behavior we want children to think and value thoughtfully and individually.

In terms of classroom behavior, this suggests that a teacher may readily limit behavior judged to be detrimental to students, explaining the reasons whenever possible, but teachers should not try to influence the values of students in any arbitrary, nonrational, or covert manner. They may argue for a particular value, but they should make certain that alternative arguments are presented, and that they respect the students' rights to adopt an alterna-tive. Value-oriented teachers are modest when it comes to their own values. They are proud of them, clear about them, and speak up for them, but they are also not certain that they are the last word for them or anyone else.

The following are six ideas to help in working toward the elimination of moralizing.

1. With values issues, avoid questions for which you already have an answer in mind, such as "Would you like me to do that to *you?*" after Jim socks Phyllis. Use open-ended questions, such as "What else might have been done?" (See the list of thirty clarifying responses in chapter 5.)

2. Avoid "why" questions, "yes-or-no" questions, "either-or" questions, or questions that tend to make students defensive, force them to rationalize their positions, or limit their choices.

3. Begin with written value lessons, such as value sheets and thought sheets, so that you can reread your responses before the student sees them and so that you can have time to think carefully before you respond.

4. Ask a friend to listen to your classroom responses or to read your written comments in value issues and to note moralizing tendencies.

5. Ask students if they feel as if you are unfairly loading the dice about issues and if you are accepting of alternatives values in cases in which you make your position clear.

6. Most importantly, consider beginning the use of value strategies with topics about which you have no strong feelings one way or the other, such as how children should spend leisure time or what occupation they should choose. When teachers have no position, they are less likely unconsciously to try to sway students' beliefs.

Start Slowly, but Not Too Slowly

Do not try the whole array of strategies suggested in this book the first week. It is probably wise to go slow at first, feeling your way and letting the students become accustomed to any departure from what they are accustomed to. Do not go so slow, however, that any method gets lost in the shuffle. It is probably wise to proceed fast enough that you do not forget the feeling of one technique by the time you get to the next and slow enough that each member of the class can assimilate each lesson at his own rate.

Of course, begin with the strategies that are most comfortable to you and the students. Value sheets and written comments on students papers are often an easy way to get going.

Many teachers have found it useful to make a list of the thirty clarifying responses in chapter 5 and to keep it on their desks or some place, as on a seating chart, where it can be glanced at during a class. This may be a helpful aid while learning to respond to students in a nonjudgmental, value-clarifying manner.

Keep Administrators and Other Teachers Informed

Some teachers have added to the difficulties of making innovations by waiting for a student or a parent to let administrators and other teachers know what is going on in the teacher's classroom, thus raising unnecessary envy and feelings of being slighted. Even though it is within the professional responsibility of teachers to use methods such as those of the value theory, it is wise to keep the lines of communication open between yourself and others on the school staff. It is often helpful to offer to explain what you are attempting to a parents association, a student assembly, or a faculty meeting. This is not to suggest that you need to ask permission to teach as you see fit, but rather that you may want to notify others of ideas that are new and interesting.

Talk About the Values Clarification in Tentative Terms

Until you have worked with this value theory enough to obtain the kind of results desired, it is probably wise to talk about it in tentative terms: "I'm *trying* this approach," not "I'm *adopting* this approach." This will help others understand that you are open-minded about it, and that you will need time to avoid the blunders that accompany all new ventures of this type. Then, when you do err or you work to perfect the methods, other teachers and administrators are less likely to judge you harshly. There will be enough difficulties while learning this or any new teaching approach to make the addition of harsh judgment unnecessary.

It is perhaps wisest, in fact, to label your venture "an experiment" and, until you have become somewhat skillful with the valuing strategies, to use the experimental approach, recommended in chapter 13. Certainly do not insist that other teachers use your methods. You may champion them and help others understand their advantages, but you will only increase resistance by moralizing about value clarifying, to say nothing about inviting questions about the consistency between what you say and the theory itself.

Prepare for Some Conflict

Some teachers think that they can always avoid antagonism and conflict with others. It is perhaps possible, but often only by doing nothing. Anything as "different" as many of the suggestions in this book will threaten some teachers. They will not want to see those suggestions working successfully in their schools. Prepare to defend your right to try those suggestions, but be careful to speak only for yourself. Do not insist that others do as you do. And do not wilt under the first conflict, or you forego your chance of doing much beyond the ordinary.

Make the Ideas Fit You

Do not try the ideas of this book without adapting them to your personality and situation. You may find that you will have to revise some of the techniques and discard others. Some things just do not work well for some people and in some situations. There should be enough information in this book to provide most teachers with a great variety of workable methods, however, and the teacher who gets the "feel" of this approach will doubtless create more.

Encourage Several Colleagues to Join You

Without insisting, try to get at least one or two others to join you in your experiment. This will give you added support and will provide for some exchange of experience and opinion. It might be possible, if there is enough interest in one school system, to invite someone who has worked successfully with the value theory to consult with you. It may even be possible, of course, for one or more who have used this approach in a school system to act as resource people for others who might want to learn it, as in an in-service workshop. It is not only extremely helpful to work with other teachers, but it is a professional responsibility that is often not fully recognized.

SOME QUESTIONS TEACHERS OFTEN ASK

As we have spoken to others about our value theory, many teachers and teachers-to-be have reacted with an anxiety born of conflict between attraction to the ideas and real hesitations. These hesitations often come out in the form of questions: Should we not moralize about some things? What if I lose control of the class? How can I do some of this without adding to my already overloaded schedule? We conclude this chapter by looking at several such questions. You may notice that some of these questions have been discussed briefly in the preceding pages and that many of the questions and our answers overlap.

1. What about classes that have to be tightly controlled to avoid discipline problems?

Many teachers see value approaches as implying so much permissiveness that it raises discipline and perhaps safety problems. This implication is not intended. As was discussed earlier in this chapter, the requirements for value clarifying are not lack of control or permissiveness. Teachers may limit behavior in any reasonable way, it seems to us, and still maintain an atmosphere conducive to value clarifying. What is needed, however, is *intellectual* permissiveness backed by an honest respect for the experiences, thought processes, and values of students. Teachers can limit classroom behavior and be consistent with this value theory as long as they do not limit thought.

It is important to remember also that discipline represents behavior that is consistent with the purpose that guides the work. Discipline, in the majority of cases, is not some "outside" problem; it represents the teacher's success or failure in concentrating her or his own and the students' behavior on the issues being discussed.

2.   How can I do this with my already overworked schedule?

This is a common problem. The reality is that many teachers *do* have more than they can now handle, and it is unfair to ask them to do more. It is even more unfair to make them feel guilty as they struggle with a task that is too large with too little support.

We humbly suggest that each of us should do the best we can. Do just a bit, if that is all that is reasonable. Some strategies, of course, take less time than others and are easier to get started. Teachers may be heartened to know, however, that in many cases the value approaches of this book, once mastered, make teaching easier, more enjoyable, and more effective. Values clarification often brings a class together, increases mutual appreciation, leads to more supportive teaching-learning relationships, and generally makes a classroom a more happy place. Squeezing value approaches into a crowded schedule may be the large investment that has even larger dividends.

There is still another benefit, and it may deserve an entire volume some day. As teachers work with value-clarifying techniques and become more or less dedicated to them, some very significant changes begin to take place in *the teacher.* Their own lives and purposes, aspirations, attitudes, feelings, thinking, beliefs, and activities begin to be a focus of self-examination. They begin to know themselves better, becoming secure with those selves and secure as people.

3.   I already use these approaches. What's so new about them?

The goals of values clarification are shared by many other programs and theories, of course, and many educational practices overlap those this book recommends. For many teachers, the value theory will be nothing more than a confirmation and an extension of what they already know and do. Such teachers, and we hope there are many of them, may only use this book to identify some new ideas and techniques and to learn a framework for focusing their clarifying work on students who need it most. Such teachers may also find the book useful in interpreting to others what it is that they have been doing.

4. It's too complicated. I don't know where to begin.

For teachers who have not worked in ways similar to these approaches, it may seem as if the recommended strategies are forbiddingly different. For such teachers we would recommend an easy, slow start, perhaps with value sheets adapted from those in this book, and occasional clarifying responses in the margins of students' papers. Also, consider some other strategies easy to get going: thought sheets, weekly reaction sheets, open-ended questions, coded student papers, time diaries, and student reports. The major recommendation here is to take it slow without dismissing the ideas entirely. Choose a few techniques and work with them. The more formidable ideas and commitment may come later, especially—as is very possible—if the initial trials prove rewarding to the students and the teacher. Few teachers, and we hope this is reassuring, fall flat on their faces with the value theory. About the worst that can happen is that there will be no visible change in the students' behavior. (But be cautious in attributing no change to the theory or to your use of of it; it may simply be insufficient dosage.)

5. What will people say if I start raising unusual and controversial issues in my classroom?

Some will say how delighted they are that someone is finally helping children think through these complex and important ideas. Some may recognize the degree of conformity and passivity that surrounds most of us and will compliment you on the courage it takes to face these ideas. Some may complain indirectly that you are permitting students to think about ideas that they would prefer to try to indoctrinate. Some may wonder why you try to do such difficult things and why you do not stick with the routine subject matter, so easy to drill and test.

What you might tell people who inquire is:

• You only raise issues about which you believe students are old enough and wise enough to make at least preliminary judgments, and you start with the worries, attitudes, feelings, and goals of the students themselves.

• You insist that consideration of all ideas—those raised by you or students—be thoughtful, informed, and deliberate. You consider that an important goal of a person's education is to learn to think critically about complex and controversial ideas.

• You do not permit students to indoctrinate one another nor will you do this. You are not trying to change the ideas of students but to help them learn a process of thinking and valuing, so that they are less likely in the future to follow any persuasive leader blindly, to settle important ideas only on the basis of emotional preference, or to confuse thought with irrational approaches to vital issues.

• Children are never *required* to consider a value issue. The option of "passing" is always offered.

• Children are exposed to most of these ideas regardless. Your job is to insure that the exposure is intelligent and balanced.

• One of the reasons such ideas are considered touchy or controversial is that many persons avoid them, do not deal with them squarely and forthrightly.

• Such issues are too important to avoid.

You might find interesting the arguments of Hunt and Metcalf (1955) for helping students explore six areas of culture that remain largely closed to intelligent consideration and thus prey to all forms of myths and fears and irrational beliefs: economics (capitalism, socialism, colonialism), minority-group relations (Jews, blacks, American Indians, de facto segregation), social class (success and failure in a class society), sex, courtship, and marriage; religion and morality; and nationalism and patriotism (local allegiance versus world allegiance.)

6. Can a teacher get *too* personal?

One of the authors of this book knew a teacher who embarrassed some of his students with his questions. The issues raised or the way they were raised somehow seemed intrusive and even vulgar, at least to several of the students. And something happened which brought that teacher into open conflict with some of the parents. One of his students, a junior high school girl, fell in love with the teacher. The teacher apparently encouraged this and, when asked about the situation, went so far as to insist that it was desirable for the student to transfer her affections from her "unsympathetic" parents to her "understanding" teacher. To make matters worse, at least for us, the teacher claimed support from values clarification for what he was doing. He seemed to interpret our suggestions as supporting his behavior.

Let us make clear that we offer no such support. First of all, we do not recommend raising issues that students feel to be intrusive or vulgar. There are plenty of issues in life on which to exercise value thinking. It is not necessary to include those that violate good taste. Students can learn to think for themselves on issues that do not cross those boundaries.

Secondly, we recommend that a teacher immediately stop value-clarifying activities whenever students show signs of being embarrassed or becoming anxious. Very few teachers are trained to deal with strong emotional disturbances, and we believe that it is their professional responsibility to avoid what they cannot competently handle. Whatever is your intention, a strong emotional reaction is probably a signal that something is wrong. It is a signal to stop. In such a case, you may want to get help from other professionals to determine what remedies, if any, need to be taken. It is certainly a signal not to resume that course of action again without careful reconsideration. By all means, whatever you do, do the least harm.

Most fundamentally, we urge teachers to make sure that their own emotional selves are in some minimum state of order before they go charging close to the emotional selves of students. The teacher in our story above appears to us to have entangled his personal self and his professional life in very undesirable ways. It seems possible to us that the teacher permanently damaged the relationship between that student and her parents.

In a way, of course, all activities carry with them some dangers. In the past, we have usually been in the position of urging teachers to open up *more* of life to student deliberation. We have long been dismayed at how many teachers disallow discussions of issues outside the bounds of narrow academic definitions. Our push therefore has been towards openness and the recognition that especially in these shifting times students need to learn how to think deliberately about important nonacademic questions. But we do feel obliged to emphasize that there are limits to this openness and study of life. Good taste, persistent sensitivity to the impact you are having on students, and awareness of your own limitations and emotional needs are among the ways to mark those limits.

Above all, we urge teachers to keep alert to emotional tones in the classroom and to be very conservative when in doubt. We urge teachers to consult with some of their peers, administrators, or mental health specialists when uncertain. And we urge all professionals to speak up when they have reason to suspect that a colleague might be engaging in questionable activities.

A final note to keep all of this in perspective: notwithstanding all these cautions, after hearing of thousands of teachers who have opened the classroom to more consideration of students' current interests, concerns, attitudes, worries, aspirations, beliefs, feelings, and goals, we have heard of very few cases indeed that we would judge to have been harmful. Most teachers clearly act with what might be called common-sense prudence.

7. Will this value theory work with all children?

This theory will probably not help children suffering from some fundamental problems, such as physical or emotional illnesses. It may even add to the difficulties of some emotionally disturbed children. Some emotionally disturbed children already have more in their heads to think about than they can comfortably handle. It would be counterproductive to add new questions or issues about life for them to ponder. (See chapter 15 for more on this topic.)

But values clarification is applicable to most children. It is especially useful for students who are difficult to motivate and are sometimes called "slow learners." As reported below, the value strategies have been found effective in moving underachievers to normal work levels.

We would generally not recommend dismissing these approaches for a student without a trial. After a fair chance, those situations in which the value theory does not work will clearly show themselves. As with any other educational approaches that have not worked in certain cases, teachers will know when that is happening.

8. Can very young children work on values?

We are not certain about this, but what evidence there is suggests that values work with young children has some benefits and few drawbacks. Teachers of young children have been successful in setting up clarifying climates that students have carried with them to the playground and later grades, and some simple issues can, of course, be dealt with even by preschool children. We would recommend caution in choosing issues. If students can make reasonably intelligent choices in an area, clarifying efforts seem warranted. And certainly a nonmoralizing value approach can show children at an early age that they are expected to think for themselves, be proud of themselves, and use their intelligence to guide their own behavior.

9. I don't have any clear values myself. How can I help others?

A confused teacher can help confused students in the same way that a physician with a heart condition can help patients with heart trouble: by doing what has to be done. There are some advantages, of course, for children in dealing with teachers who have clear values, but a teacher who can operate in the style of this value theory can help children. We see no reason why teachers with less than clear values cannot do this. The crux of the issue is whether or not such teachers can control their behavior enough to focus on students' actual needs, and not what the teachers think the students need or the teachers would like to offer. This ability is a function of understanding and self-control, functions that can be performed even by someone whose own values are still being clarified.

10. Can teachers express personal values in the classroom or must they remain forever neutral?

Our position is that ideally teachers should be able to be quite candid about their points of view and values. By being so, and by being accepting and respectful of students, teachers reassure students that honest talk is permissible. Another advantage is that students then have a real position to look at, to cross-examine, and to measure against their own ideas. Teachers, of course, should make it very clear that an expression of their position is not an indication of what would be desirable for others. We all have different experiences and outlooks, and we should all select values that are individually suitable.

Sometimes, however, we find it desirable to compromise with the ideal. Sometimes, for example, children are too accustomed to following what an adult says, even when the adult cautions them not to do so. And sometimes a teacher may want to keep his values hidden for more personal reasons. Further, sometimes a teacher will purposely play a devil's advocate role to bring a special point of view into the classroom in a dramatic fashion.

Consequently, although we generally find it advisable for teachers to be as honest and open as they hope students will be, for immature students, whatever their ages, and for other special reasons, we sometimes recommend that teachers be wary about revealing their positions. Of course, even with immature students, once the difference between revealing our own position and proselytizing is understood, candor can replace concealment.

Incidentally, it is useful for those same reasons for teachers to reveal their *lack* of clear values. This shows students how difficult it is sometimes to be certain about some issues, and it also underlines the importance of candor and honesty on all sides.

11.   Should we not moralize about anything? Even about such vital issues as love, patriotism, and the role of values themselves?

Let's start by making some distinctions. First, teachers can speak up for personal values without discouraging students' thinking. For example, a teacher could say, "It's very important to me that we be kind to one another and not do anything that hurts others. I know that others do not value kindness so highly, and some think it is just plain sentimental. But I want you to know where I stand. Please take a few moments to share your thoughts about this with one or two others sitting near you. How important to you is kindness or not hurting others? Or is it important at all?" The tone of that teacher does not seem moralizing to us. The teacher seems to us to be trying to state a value and stimulate thinking, not merely selling a point of view to passive consumers.

There can be no law or no rule that we have to like each other. Liking each other cannot be legislated. We do hope that by observing some very ordinary routines of decency in human relations—such as being kind to each other—we will as we work together, grow to like each other.

A teacher can, on the other hand, communicate that we should be kind to each other without any qualification: "There is really no question about this in most people's minds. No thinking is required, no decent person would disagree. It is a truth we would be foolish not to accept." *That* teacher seems to us to be moralizing, and we would predict that such an approach would not contribute very much to a student's purposefulness, positiveness, pride, and enthusiasm. In that sense, we would not recommend moralizing, even about kindness.

Imagine another teacher insisting that students take turns speaking, not interrupt each other, and listen carefully to one another, and going so far as to punish those students who persist in violating those rules. Further imagine the teacher justifying those rules by saying that he values courtesy because it makes us all feel better and gets more and better work done. Here too there seems to us to be a moralizing and nonmoralizing way to do this. The moralizing way would be to discourage students from critically examining the teacher's position and the class rules in some way. Such an approach would tend to emphasize the *absolute and general* truth of the teacher's position.

The nonmoralizing way would instead communicate, explicitly or implicitly, that students can appreciate those rules for themselves if they *think* about them: "It's not a matter of 'because I say so.'" The teacher might simply make a statement to that effect ("Think about this for yourself."), which might be sufficient, especially if the teacher honestly believed students could make reasonable judgments and the students intuitively knew it. The nonmoralizing teacher also would emphasize the relative and specific truth of her position by somehow communicating, again explicitly or implicitly, that taking turns works best in this situation and for now and that in other situations and at other times we might want to change priorities. Again, the teacher might simply put that statement into words the students could understand: "If an emergency arose, we might *welcome* important interruptions, of course."

Thus we have tried to distinguish three kinds of acts: a teacher standing up for values without moralizing, a teacher setting classroom rules without moralizing, and a teacher moralizing. To us, moralizing is the act of trying to get others to accept a general value position without thinking for themselves. Our experience tells us that that does not do much good for one thing. Moreover, it does breed some problems, in part by communicating to others that we do not trust them to make their own judgments and that we believe reality is so simple that it can be managed by abstract and absolute principles.

We believe that standing up and championing one's values is important, but it is also important to communicate to others that they must learn to think things through for themselves and that we are ready to assist them in doing so. Likewise, identifying general principles is important, but it is also important to learn how to apply principles in life's multidimensional realities.

This is not to say that we are against teachers leading the way toward moral thought and enforcing humane rules of behavior. We merely wish to distinguish that kind of behavior from efforts to get people to accept someone else's values unthinkingly or to view value issues as separate from everyday life.

As for us, we do not intend to moralize about our values theory—that is, we do not mean for others to accept it uncritically or thoughtlessly. We mean to present it, together with our reasoning, and then to invite others to consider it, apply it to their own situations, and then see if it does anything that they would judge to be useful for them.

In short, we believe that if we want citizens who are able to thoughtfully choose, prize and act in the complex present and the unknown future, we defeat ourselves by moralizing about anything.

12. Somehow I do not feel as if I am making progress when I attempt to work with values. Is there something wrong?

With value clarifying there is a different feeling of progress than there is with more fact-oriented subject matter areas. It is less tangible, less testable, less quick. It is more like the progress that comes with teaching a very complex skill. The sense of progress comes from identifying behavioral change, and it is sometimes as difficult to see this as to be aware of the changes in a child's height. As a consequence, several teachers have complained that in teaching values there is no feeling of accomplishment. Nothing seems to change. For this reason, we recommend the collecting of behavior profiles from time to time, much like a parent marks the height of a child on the back of a door. Occasional checking of such profiles, perhaps using the forms presented in chapter 13, will provide not only evidence for others but evidence for your own sense of accomplishment.

13. Is it "bad" not to have values?

The answer to this question depends upon what "bad" means. For a person in a period of great change, as in adolescence or in the midst of a major life readjustment, few values may exist. For those in a more stable portion of life, we might expect some patterns of life to have been worked out based on choice, understanding, and pride. If this has not happened, we would suspect that this person is operating at a lower level of life than need be.

Especially for children, the crucial question to us is not how many values they have or what those values are, but what *processes* they use when faced with value-related decisions. Do they acquiesce readily? Do they act impulsively? Do they choose things they are not proud of? Do they do one thing and say another?

We would be inclined to say that, from *our* set of values, it is "bad" not to be able to use the valuing process. More precisely, we would predict that a person who cannot use that process is likely to live a less satisfying life than a person who does. Such people will certainly make less use of their human capacity for intelligent self-direction, which is something we personally would regret. Others, of course, might appraise this situation differently.

14.   How do I find issues to introduce for clarification?

Listen to students. That is the first guideline. Listen especially for their attitudes, beliefs, interests, worries, activities, aspirations, goals, and feelings.

Then consider searching for a question students can apprehend in one of our culture's value-rich topics: family, friends, love and sex, marriage, work, leisure, segregation, politics, money, war and peace, religion, television, the movies, government, unemployment, and inflation.

Here are some further general guidelines that may be helpful:

a.   Things most worth clarifying are of *concern to the individual.* In short, personal meaning must exist for the students.
Examples: Things the student worries about.

b.   Things most worth clarifying involve a *variety of alternatives.* In other words, there should be no universal agreement about the issues, otherwise there would be little room for choice. On the other hand, there may seem to be agreement when in reality there are unconsidered or suppressed alternatives.
Examples: In the first group, issues about urban renewal, about teen-age marriages. In the second group, comments on the equality of all people, the right of the government to tax income.

c.   Things most worth clarifying are *significant for many lives,* for substantial groups of people, as opposed to issues which touch upon just a very few lives.
Example: The issue in a particular court trial is less important than the principle underlying the trial.

d.   Things most worth clarifying affect *large areas of life.*
Example: Choosing friends has a more pervasive influence than choosing a pair of shoes.

e.   To be most worthy of clarifying, an area must be *open to control.* There must be something that can be done about the issue.

Examples: War, not seasonal changes. For young children, what should be done to make school better, not whether or not one should go to school.

f.   Things most worth clarifying are *related or joined to other issues.* It is most useful to work on issues that help illuminate other issues.
Examples: The role of women in society touches upon marriage, working women and working mothers, dating behavior, and so on.

g.   Things most worth clarifying *recur* as opposed to being transient.
Example: Sensational topical issues are less useful than persistent issues, such as independence and dependence, courage, appropriate male and female role behavior, and graft.

Another point is germane here. Oftentimes a "small" value issue will grow from the interests or attitudes of students but can be extended to more profitable issues by the alert teacher. So, for example, a consideration of the wisdom of purchasing bicycle safety lights can lead to considerations of which of life's risks are worth controlling, what is the role of one person (such as a bicycle manufacturer) regarding the safety of another (such as the purchaser), and the uses to which we put our money in general.

Of course, even consideration of "small" issues is useful to the extent that it sharpens the skills of the valuing process and makes those skills more accessible when other issues arise.

Nevertheless, beware of merely flitting from topic to topic, touching a number of issues briefly but never pursuing any. Remember that students need to learn how to apply their human capacity for intelligent thought to the rich, complex questions of life and that this often requires persistence.

15.   I tried a few things, but then what? Where does it go from here?

Often a teacher will try some values activities in the classroom and then wonder, "So what? It was interesting, but it doesn't seem to *lead* anyplace." We finally realized, after hearing many reports like that, that some teachers equated values clarification with the occasional use of values activities. Completing unfinished sentences, sharing opinions, putting preferences in rank order, and so on—the kinds of activities listed in chapter 9—that was how values clarification was defined by many teachers. And those activities do indeed seem to go nowhere.

When we began teaching others about values clarification some years ago, we had great difficulty explaining how teachers could actively help students to think about values without imposing their own values on the process. To solve that problem we found ourselves inventing many little values activities and using them on our audiences, to communicate our style. This worked fine: audiences liked the activities and liked us for abandoning lecture-discussions for something more engaging. But all too often audiences remembered only the activities and carried with them the belief that that was the sum and substance of values clarification. That teachers could add values clarification to informal dialogues, as in chapter 5's clarifying responses, or use it to enrich the curriculum, as in chapter 10's subject-matter options, was not clear at all. And so teachers used some of those values activities and it seemed little more than an interesting interlude.

Actually it was probably more than that. There is evidence that the use of occasional value activities unconnected to anything else, used simply as interludes or change-of-pace activities, does serve positive purposes. A number of research projects reported in chapter 12 used values clarification in that way. Used in this way, it is like a daily ten-minute exercise program for an office worker. Such an exercise program is not a substitute for a more physically active life, but it is likely to be better than nothing. And like morning exercises, values activities do not have to go somewhere. There is no immediate and direct connection to anything else. We just do them and expect gradual improvement.

Obviously, we would prefer that not all teachers restricted values clarification to occasional values activities. In our own teaching, we make use of the clarifying response, the value sheet, and an integration of values into our subject matter, for example, much more than we ever make use of the unconnected value activity. We view the values clarification methodology as much more than occasional fun and games. It is a way of assisting others to move toward value-directed living and it can take many forms. The adult who appreciates those forms can best integrate clarifying experiences into ongoing activities naturally.

Research Findings

Values clarification presents an empirical theory, not a series of concepts to be taken on faith. More than that, it is a teaching theory, a theory formulated to guide practicing professionals, not only a guide for researchers. The theory says that if we occasionally focus students' attention on issues in their lives, and if we then stimulate students to consider their choices, their prizings, and their actions, then the students will change behavior, demonstrating more purposeful, proud, positive, and enthusiastic behavior patterns.

Thus it is a change in behavior, not a change in values, that we watch for. To be more specific, we have suggested that the following eight behavior patterns, in the absence of severe emotional disturbance, can especially be assumed to reflect unclear values: (1) apathy, listlessness, disinterest, (2) flightiness, (3) a general uncertainty, (4) inconsistency, (5) a tendency to drift, (6) overconformity, (7) overdissention, and (8) posing or role playing. The validity of the theory thus might be tested by seeing if the procedures of values clarification reduce the incidence of any of those behavior patterns.

We could, of course, use the value-clarifying methodology with individual young people who, by demonstrating some of those eight behavior patterns, give evidence that they need special help in values clarification. Or we could use the methodology on whole groups, to assist groups in moving further from those patterns and, more generally, in developing skills that will presumably help them avoid those patterns in the future.

That, broadly speaking, is the theory. That theory has been tested by a variety of research projects since its first publication, and although no one of those projects can be judged definitive, the accumulated evidence seems to support the validity of the theory.

Furthermore, the research has *extended* the theory. Several creative researchers have wondered whether the values methodology would produce effects other than changes in the eight behavior patterns originally postulated as associated with unclear values. They have confirmed several such effects. For example, Arno and Gorsuch (1974) found that values clarification accelerated the maturation of children's value preferences, so that they more nearly resembled the value preferences of adults. Clarke (1975) found that values clarification reduced drug use among groups of teenagers. And several studies have shown that the learning climate in the classroom improves after the addition of the values methodology.

Since the first edition of this book, we have come to the point where we can list with some certainty some things a teacher can expect if he or she uses the values methodology. Part of our certainty comes not from the formal research, which is summarized in more detail at the end of this chapter, but from a consistency in the informal reports we have received from the many teachers who have tried values clarification over the past two decades.

248

Combining what we have learned from those informal reports with the research project reports, we have some confidence that values clarification, properly used, can be expected to make a contribution to these purposes:

- A reduction in the intensity and/or frequency of the eight unclear behavior patterns.

- A reduction in some forms of deviant or disruptive behavior (such as drug use and uncooperative classroom acts).

- An increase in self-direction and trust in oneself (including more self-acceptance).

- A maturation of expressed values (a shift away from values generally judged immature and toward these generally judged more mature).

- An improvement in the learning climate (more participation, more responsibility for what happens, more interest in learning).

- An improvement in social relationships (more friends, greater group cohesion, more empathy for others).

- An improvement in learning outcomes (especially in reading and in learnings on the level of life applications).

- A venting of personal pressures (expressing problems, venting fears).

- An increase in hope and faith (more confidence that problems can be solved, progress is possible, personal power can be marshaled).

- An improvement in student-teacher relations (more feeling on the part of students that teachers are helpful and kind; more feeling on the part of teachers that students are worthy of respect and affection).

We hasten to add that not all those outcomes will hold true in all situations. In fact, it has been our experience that some teachers will find no changes at all. Values clarification, like many other teaching methodologies, does not work in all situations and for all teachers. But the outcome listed above are common and—perhaps this is reassuring—outcomes likely to be judged negatively by educators are rarely reported, while those that are—such as an increase in student confusion over what is expected from them—tend to exist only temporarily. In sum, we are confident that values clarification, used in the style communicated by the preceding chapters, is very unlikely to do any harm and is very likely to promote the results listed above.

That summary statement, however, general as it is, is best treated simply as an invitation to do your own research. The most pertinent question for most teachers is what, if anything, it will do for them. What worked in another situation at another time can only be encouragement to try it, not proof that it will work that way for you. Education is much too variable and too complex for absolute proofs. The next chapter discusses ways you might monitor your own results if you choose to see what values clarification can do for you.

We conclude this chapter with sketches of a good deal of the research that has been completed to date.* The reports are divided into four sections: work with children of elementary school age, work with adolescents, work with adults, and training or methodological studies.

RESEARCH WITH ELEMENTARY SCHOOL CHILDREN

Brown's Study with Elementary Teachers

Georgia Brown did a study that paralleled Simon's study (1958) with high-school teachers. (See page 259 below.) She asked a group of sixteen elementary teachers (K—6) who were taking a college education course to respond with value-clarifying questions to a child who seemed to have unclear values and to keep records of what happened. Each teacher also identified a second child in each class that was similarly a value "case" to act as a control. Control students received no special attention.

The experiment continued for fifteen weeks and included children who were overconformers, dissenters, apathetic, underachievers, indecisive, flighty, and poseurs.

Unlike Simon's high-school teachers, all but one of these elementary-school teachers did master techniques of responding to students in a value-clarifying way. Excluding the teacher who did not learn the techniques, *all* experimental children were reported to have improved markedly while *none* of the control children changed. A teacher typically wrote that whereas a student was not purposefully and constructively involved in schoolwork before the experiment, he or she was very much more involved afterwards.

An incidental finding of this study was that teachers and children enjoyed the process, and teachers themselves seemed to become much clearer about their personal values and, in many cases, became more dedicated teachers. Brown says that teachers with whom she had been in contact after the experiment continued to use the techniques.

---

* We are indebted to Howard Kirschenbaum for many of these reports. He collected research on values clarification and would welcome receiving additional reports. Address him at the National Humanistic Education Center, 110 Spring St., Saratoga Springs, N.Y. 12866.

Three Elementary-School Experiments

A series of studies with the value theory was carried out in one suburban elementary school. Three investigators who taught in the school, one each in grades three, four, and five, carried out identical designs to test the value theory and two other teaching theories developed by Louis E. Raths, theories dealing with emotional needs and thinking. These studies are reported by Jonas (1960), Machnits (1960), and Martin (1960). Only the portion of the studies dealing with values is discussed here.

Each investigator identified children in the class who fell into the categories that we suggest are likely to be related to a lack of value clarity. In the third-grade class there was a child who was a nagging dissenter and very flighty. In the fourth-grade class there was a very flighty child and one who regularly took on "artificial" roles to play. In the fifth-grade class there was a child who was extremely overconforming and a child who was very apathetic.

Value-related behavioral types were similarly identified in different third-, fourth-, and fifth-grade classes that were not taught by the investigators and that were not part of the experiment. These children were used as a comparison group. They were not matched to the experimental children in any way other than representing the same types of behavior patterns and received no treatment other than that usually provided in the classroom.

These children, both in the experimental and comparison classes, were rated as showing the behavior patterns for which they were chosen *very frequently* and *very acutely* and were judged to be children who would be unlikely to change those patterns in the normal course of school instruction. These ratings were made not by the classroom teachers involved in these experiments but by teachers of music, art, library, and physical education and by previous teachers of those children, none of whom were told the nature of the experiment.

After initial measures were made of these children's behavior using the ratings noted above, the investigators began to try to clarify the values of the six in the experimental classes. They worked from October to February, carefully recording and reporting what they did for each child. An attempt was made to have one brief encounter that would be of a value-clarifying nature with each child each day. Because these were teachers of self-contained classes who had substantial flexibility in their programs, they managed to do this on most days.

The process they used was that of encouraging the children to look at themselves and their behavior, examine alternatives in their lives, consider what they prized and what was important to them, and make choices for themselves. This was done persistently, but gently. The details of the encounters are instructive, and three sample encounters are reported in their entirety from the work of Jonas (1960), pp. 162, 164, 167:

Teacher: As I see it, you have done a lot of thinking about hamsters and you really like them.

Student: Yes, I love Alvin.

Teacher: Do you think more people should own hamsters?

Student: Yes. They're wonderful pets.

Teacher: Would you like to be in a play?

Student: Yes, I guess so.

Teacher: What can we do to get you into a play?

Student: I don't know.

Student: (Says that she planned to go swimming at the "Y" after school.)

Teacher: Is that something you like to do?

Student: Yes.

Teacher: Would you recommend swimming as a sport?

Student: I sure would.

Teacher: Do you swim often?

Student: I hope to once a week.

The findings of the three studies were similar: the behavior patterns of the children in the experimental groups were reported by the art, music, and other teachers—and often spontaneously by parents as well—to have improved significantly. No such change was reported for the comparison group.

One exception was the third-grade child who was a chronic dissenter. He improved somewhat, but not enough to be included as a "success" case. The investigator (Martin) suggests that his limited success with the dissenting boy may have resulted from the difficulty he had in developing enough rapport with him to communicate effectively. Martin wonders if the value theory can work as easily with students who typically reject teachers.

A Study at a Campus Elementary School

James Raths (1962) reported on a study at the Campus Elementary School of the University of Wisconsin (Milwaukee). At that school, the four teachers of grades five through eight were concerned with the frivolous and superficial way with which students approached their learning and the low ranking of school activities in the hierarchy of student interests. The assumption was made that because the students were confused about their own purposes, beliefs, attitudes, goals and interests, they failed to identify with the purposes of the school. Accordingly, a program was initiated to help students become clearer about their own purposes. The hypothesis was that they would, in turn, become more active and purposeful learners.

All 100 students in the four grades were placed in the study. First, a beginning evaluation of each student was made by the teachers of art, music, library, and physical education. Each of those teachers evaluated each student on a seven-point scale *(very often to* almost never) along the following dimensions:

- Raising of questions and alternatives
- Initiation and self-direction of classroom activity
- Perseverance
- Active participation
- Attitudes toward learning

Then the four classroom teachers initiated a program that contained three essential elements: (1) an atmosphere in which students could express their real feelings without fear of harsh judgments or ridicule by others, (2) efforts to elicit attitudinal statements from students, and (3) the raising of questions with students that would help them think about their attitudes. To elicit student attitudes, teachers used free writings, writings in response to provocative issues, and role playing in which students had to make choices about issues, such as breaking in on a lunchroom line.

At the end of the year, a final rating on the same five dimensions was made of each student by the art, music, physical education, and library teachers, who had no access to the original ratings and who did not know the nature of the study in progress.

Raths reports that 88 of the 100 students made gains on all five rating dimensions. Of the twelve that did not, *all* were found to suffer from patterns of unmet emotional needs.

Weintraub's Study on Proud Behavior

Herbert Weintraub carried out a small (and unpublished) but interesting study. Reminded that many students do not behave in ways they are proud of and that being proud of personal behavior is a criteria for a value, Weintraub wondered what would happen if he encouraged children to consider just that one aspect of life: being proud of personal behavior.

The experimenter randomly selected a fifth-grade class and had the teacher of that class instruct the students to write on a sheet of paper "those things that they said or did in the last twenty-four hours of which they were proud or happy." Students were asked to do this anonymously, with no identifying material on the papers, and were told that the papers would not be read by the teacher (unless they were marked with a large "R"). The directions were generally accepted by the students and they wrote rather freely.

Students were also asked to write, on the back of the sheet, those things that they did or said in the preceding twenty-four hours of which they were not proud. (This part of the exercise was later questioned as being potentially guilt-arousing and unnecessary for the purposes of the experiment and the value theory.)

This procedure, writing what one was proud of or not proud of, was repeated the first ten minutes of every day, for six weeks.

There was also a control group of five similar classes. For all six classes, teachers who were unaware of the nature of the experiment rated each student on eight scales that were presumed to be related to value clarity (from "always" to "never"):

1. Interested and involved in classroom work.

2. Independent—willing to act without detailed directions.

3. Assumes responsibility for his own actions.

4. Listens and shows respect for the ideas and experiences of others.

5. Sticks to activities, shows persistence.

6. Gets enjoyment from his own activities.

7. Interested and involved in nonschool activities.

8. Works well by himself.

Teachers also rated each student on two scales that were embedded in the rating sheet but that were presumed unrelated (at least directly) to value clarity:

1. Participates and shows enthusiasm for music-related activities.

2. Participates and shows enthusiasm for art-related activities.

These latter two dimensions were called "placebo" scales.

All teachers completed a rating sheet on each student before the six-week experimental variable was used and after it. Comparison was made of the growth of the experimental students and the control students.

Weintraub found that on all eight value-related scales the experimental group was superior to the control group. There was no difference between the groups on the first nonvalue or placebo scale, suggesting that the growth in the experimental group was not caused by any bias in the completion of the rating sheets. The second placebo scale (art) did show a significant difference favoring the experimental group, raising the above interpretation into question. The fact that the experimental group had an art teacher that was not shared by the other groups might account for this finding, however.

In an analysis of the writings themselves, Weintraub found that students tended to write less toward the end of the experiment, supporting the observation that boredom set in and that once or twice a week (for a greater number of weeks) might have been better than every day for this kind of an exercise. Even more preferable, Weintraub feels, is a variety of questions, with a different one posed each day. (See the section on weekly reaction sheets in chapter 9.)

He also found that what students were *not* proud of could often be classified as things that they considered their duty.

In a parallel study, however, Weintraub found no growth difference between another fifth-grade class and the five control classes. The two studies were identical, except that in this latter study students were given a sheet headed on one side, "My Last Twenty-four Hours. What I did that made me feel proud, happy," and on the other side, "My Last Twenty-four Hours. What I did that made me feel sorry, ashamed, sad." Also, each sheet had printed on it, spaced along the side, the phrases "In school," "At home," "At play," and "Other places and times." These phrases were to stimulate thinking, which they did. The former study merely had students write "proud" on one side of a sheet and "not proud" on the other and obtained somewhat fewer responses. No explanation for the differences in the findings was offered.

Blokker, Glaser, and Kirschenbaum's Elementary School Study (1976)

In this project, 22 fourth- through sixth-grade teachers from several buildings in one district attended a four-day values-clarification training workshop. They reported that the training program prepared them adequately for the use of values clarification in the classroom "very much so," 44 percent; "yes," 52 percent; and "somewhat," 4 percent.

Teachers then worked one hour a day for five weeks with their students, in the form of a unit called "All About Me," modified by each teacher to suit particular situations. The teachers felt that they were either very successful in implementing the unit (16 percent), successful (36 percent), or moderately successful (44 percent). About 250 boys and 250 girls participated.

Significant changes, lasting four weeks after the unit ended, were demonstrated in the students' improved decision-making abilities, as measured by

Ojemann's Social Causality Test (1961), in their increased belief in their personal control over their own lives, as measured by the Nowicki and Strickland Internal-External Control Scale (1973), and in their increased overt self-reliant behavior, as measured by the revised Devereux Elementary School Behavior Rating Scale (Swift & Spivack, 1974). All these measures have been shown to correlate with low drug abuse. The five-week program produced no significant changes in self-esteem, as measured by the Cutick Self-Evaluation Form (1962).

Because problems in the assignment of teachers to control groups rendered control-group data unusable, it is impossible to attribute any changes to values clarification alone, however.

Wenker-Konner, Hammond, and Egner on Disruptive Behavior

Ronnie Wenker-Konner, Eileen Hammond, and Ann Egner (1973) employed a strict behavioral design to study the effect of values-clarification strategies on the participation rate of fifth graders.

First, Raths' eight unclear value behavior patterns, apathy, flightiness, etc., were translated into 55 discrete classroom behaviors. These, in turn, were grouped under five major headings: active participation, alternative behavior, inappropriate verbal behavior, refusal to participate, and none of the above. A test of interrater reliability indicated an average of 99.7 percent agreement between the experimenter and an independent observer when both observers rated the same children at ten-second intervals.

Ten children, unknown to the teacher, were selected for their lack of participation and their disruptive behavior and were observed for ten days to obtain a baseline score for their behaviors. Then for 15 days, the teacher introduced values-clarification strategies for part of the day, ceased using them for two days, and finally recontinued their use for two more days. The ten students were observed throughout the entire period.

Analysis of the results indicated that during the period of the values-clarification activities, the students' active participation increased, their alternative behavior, inappropriate verbal behavior and refusal to participate decreased (the change in all four categories was extreme), and—as predicted—there was no significant change in the random "none of these" category.

Covault's Fifth-Grade Study

Thomas Covault (1973) measured the effect of values-clarification strategies on fifth-grade students' self-concepts and "related classroom coping and interacting behaviors."

He found that two classes of students who experienced 11 one-hour sessions of values clarification, as compared to the controls who received the same amount of time in physical education with the investigator, (1) improved in self-concept, as measured by the Sears Self-Concept Scale (Sears & Sherman, 1964); (2) improved in initiation and self-direction in classroom activities; (3) improved in positive attitude toward learning; and (4) reduced the amount of behaviors that were apathetic, flighty, uncertain, inconsistent, drifting, overconforming, overdissenting, and role-playing.

Guziak Replication of Covault's Study

John Guziak (1974) replicated the Covault study, cited above, and produced essentially the same findings. Some differences in the studies were: (1) Guziak used only eight sessions, compared to Covault's eleven; (2) Guziak's control groups experienced a "well-organized music class," compared to Covault's physical education class controls; and (3) while Covault taught both experimental groups, Guziak taught one and had another school psychologist teach the other.

Gray's Sixth-Grade Study

Russell Gray (1975) taught a one-hour values-clarification session, once a week for 11 weeks, in four sixth-grade, Catholic-school classrooms. He spent an equal amount of time in three control classrooms, teaching two groups creative writing and tutoring mathematics in the other with small groups.

Gray found no significant differences between the experimental groups and control groups on the Piers-Harris Children's Self-Concept Scale (Piers & Harris, 1969) or on six of the seven items on a standard sociometric questionnaire. On the seventh item ("number of rejectees"), the control groups did better than the experimental groups.

Kelly's Study on Elementary Students

Felonese Kelly (1976) compared the growth of two groups of upper-grade elementary students. One group of students had six teachers who were trained in values clarification. The second group had six teachers who were not trained. Kelly found that the students with the value-trained teachers improved significantly on measures of self-concept and sentiment toward school and showed no difference in reading improvement.

We note that the comparison-group teachers did not receive any training, and thus it is difficult to rule out the possibility that special attention alone was responsible for the results.

Frigerio's Sixth-Grade Math Class Study

Frigerio, in an unpublished study, compared two academically superior, sixth-grade math classes. One class was given values-clarification experiences once a week for 40 minutes and every other day for 15 minutes. The other, a control class, used equivalent time in a seminar on drug education. The experiment lasted one term.

Pre- and posttests were completed on competence in mathematics and on values awareness (employing a test devised by Hopp, 1974). Both groups grew significantly in mathematics competence, with the experimental group showing the most improvement. The experimental group also showed significant growth on the values-awareness test.

Frigerio concludes that the effect of the values-clarification experiences on academic growth was—if anything—positive, and the effect on values growth was clearly positive. Moreover, the students grew in other ways that were evident: "As the values-clarification program progressed, I also noticed a more positive general attitude in the experimental class. They were more enthusiastic and zestful. In addition, our teacher-student relationship grew much closer. They were warmer, friendlier, more inclined to the sharing of confidences." At the end of the program, the students responded to a questionnaire which showed that all those experiencing the Values Program enjoyed it. Thirty-nine of the forty-one students favored making it a permanent part of the school program. Thirty-four students said the program helped them feel better about themselves and thirty-eight said the program helped them to work better.

Gorsuch, Arno and Bachelder's Study of Boys in Grades 4–6

Gorsuch, Arno, and Bachelder (1976) conducted a sophisticated study of the effects of a values-clarification program on fourth-, fifth-, and sixth-grade boys who were in YMCA programs in several different cities. Some boys experienced the values program in brief summer camp programs and others experienced it in clubs that met regularly throughout the year. The values program "focused upon techniques for clarifying values, making decisions, and linking values to action." Values discussions of 20 to 40 minutes were integrated into the regular sessions of existing YMCA clubs and summer camps.

The program strategies were meant to be fun, fast-moving, and geared to the children's level of thinking. Leaders encouraged the children to identify and discuss issues of relevance to them. The most often used strategy and the one which was felt to have helped the children the most was the "trigger story." These were short, unfinished problem situations which children were asked to finish by exploring alternative solutions, considering consequences, and finally making personal decision about the best action. Role-playing the decision enabled children to practice linking a decision to actual behavior.

The experimental groups showed three major changes, significantly more than the boys in matched control groups. First, the expressed values of the boys seemed to "mature"—that is, the values shifted significantly away from initial values toward those that boys generally saw as "desirable" and more likely for adults to hold. Second, those behaviors that are typically defined by the culture as being deviant, such as the excessive use of alcohol, came to be increasingly defined by the boys themselves as being deviant. This finding emerged even though the norm is for children to become increasingly tolerant of deviant acts as they grow older. And third, the boys became significantly more concerned with internalized values as an influence on their decisions and less ready to base decisions solely on external circumstances.

These changes, moreover, increased as exposure to the values program increased. Boys who were in brief summer camp programs changed less than boys who were in clubs that met throughout the year and boys who experienced only one year of the ongoing meetings changed less than boys who experienced two years of it. The authors conclude:

> Although there are several areas which would warrant further study and research, the evidence gathered to date . . . indicates clearly that the program is effective and can be used in typical program situations. The leadership training procedures have been tried in several locations and the positive results achieved with the youth participants have been achieved in both the club and camp setting . . . The best results [were] achieved with regular, consistent use of the educational program and over a period of more than one year, even though positive results were also found in the one-year span.

RESEARCH WITH ADOLESCENTS

Simon's Study Using Trained High-School Teachers

Simon (1958) reported a study in which ten high-school teachers were taught to use the value-clarifying processes. Each teacher was asked to choose a student who seemed to have a pattern of "nonvalue-based" behavior—specifically, one who was apathetic, flighty, indecisive, inconsistent, overconforming, nagging and dissenting, or posing in various roles. Through an in-service program, teachers were to learn the techniques and apply them to the selected child.

The report indicated that most teachers did not seem to use the techniques effectively and consistently and that most children did not change their behavior. For a number of reasons, some teachers did not master the theory. Among those that did, some did not implement it.

One of the most interesting aspects of the report deals with the difficulties high-school teachers had in learning and using the theory. The subject-matter orientation of those secondary teachers seemed to be a substantial block to the development of interest in values. Simon recommended and has since completed the development of special strategies so that the study of values would more clearly enhance academic study.

James Raths on Underachievers

James Raths (1960) reported on a study of the effect of the value-clarification techniques on high-school underachievers. Underachievers were defined as students with high measured scholastic potential but low scholastic performance. In this study, 13 matched pairs of underachievers were formed on the basis of grade level in school, sex, IQ, socioeconomic class, and rank in class. From these matched pairs, six were randomly chosen to be in the experiment. From each of the six pairs, one was randomly chosen to be in the experiment and one was left as a control.

J. Raths met with each of the six students in the experimental group during study period or before or after school once a week for 15 weeks in private conversations of approximately 20 minutes. Each student was asked to meet with the investigator to help the investigator "understand the thinking and values of teenagers nowadays." All agreed to do so, apparently without understanding that the study was focused on something quite different. In fact, what J. Raths attempted to do was to clarify the values of the students to test the hypothesis that this would help them find more purpose in their lives and thus make their schoolwork more effective.

The research report includes details of Raths' procedures. In effect what he did was ask questions and occasionally get student reaction to written paragraphs of one sort or another that elicited statements of students' beliefs, attitudes, interests, problems, and aspirations. In some instances he was able to have students give him written work they had done that contained such personal statements. Then he responded to those statements with clarifying techniques. For example, he would ask students how they had chosen something, if they were *glad* they had chosen it, if they had considered alternatives, and so on. Sometimes he would merely repeat back what the student had said.

Throughout, the mood seemed to be permissive and accepting. The investigator's goal was to prod six students to think about their beliefs, attitudes, and so on, without threatening them or promoting any values of his own. From the sample conversations in the study reports, it would seem that this was accomplished. That the students continued to attend the conferences willingly attests to the satisfaction that students seemed to find in the process.

J. Raths found that during the one semester of the experiment five of the six experimental students did better than their matched controls, as measured by improvement in grades and rank in the class. As Martin had (1960), Raths also found it difficult to develop rapport with one student. This was the one student who failed to do better than his control in grades and rank in the class.

In discussing the findings, Raths noted that a few chance occurrences had disrupted the experiment and said that an experiment with a larger sample would provide a better test of his hypothesis. A more significant weakness is probably the failure to give the control group special attention, thus allowing criticism of the study on the grounds-that it might have been the *amount* of attention, not the *kind* of attention, that made the difference.

Lang on Underachievers, Dissenters, and Apathetic Students

Lang (1961) designed a study that faced the issue that Raths' (1960) study left unresolved. His study took place at the college level and included along with underachievers some apathetic students and some nagging dissenters. Like J. Raths, he used matched pairs, with one of each pair receiving the value-clarification approach in private conferences. But Lang took the precaution of having each of the control students receive an equivalent amount of attention. In this case, each had meetings with college faculty members who used, compared to the value-clarification approach that Lang used, relatively directive counseling techniques.

Lang had 16 meetings of approximately 15 minutes with each student in the experimental group. His sample included seven underachievers with seven controls matched for age, sex, residency (on or off campus), marital status, IQ, and cumulative grade average. A few underachievers who were found to have unusual physical or emotional problems were excluded from the samples on the grounds that their problems were more deep-seated than values problems and that therefore they would not be expected to respond to value-clarification techniques. Also in the experimental sample were five apathetic students and one dissenting student, with matched controls. None of the students or faculty members who worked with the control students knew of the hypotheses under study.

Before-and-after measures were taken on experimental and control students. For the underachievers, grade-point averages were collected. For the apathetic and dissenting students, ratings on the severity of the identified behavior were collected from each of the four or five instructors teaching the students during the semester of the experiment.

Lang's findings were mixed. The clarification techniques worked well with the underachievers but not so well with the apathetic or dissenting students. For the underachievers, six out of seven experimental students improved more than their controls did. For the apathetic and dissenting students, only four of six experimental students did better than their controls.

Lang did a follow-up study after two years. He found that the advantage shown by the experimental underachievers in grade-point average had evaporated. He concluded that more than 16 exposures to the value strategies are necessary for long-term effect.

Clarke's Study on Drug Usage

A large and complex study took place in Visalia, California, under the sponsorship of Operation Future, with Jay Clarke as director (1974). The population included 851 fifth through tenth graders, two groups of pregnant minors, two church groups, and 65 young people on probation.

Individuals were surveyed and rated according to (1) their use of various nonprescribed drugs, (2) their perceptions of themselves in reference to the eight behavior patterns associated with a lack of value clarity (apathy, flightiness, and so on) and (3) their school behaviors. These initial data showed a high correlation between drug use and unclear value behavior patterns.

The population was then divided into experimental and control sections. The experimental sections were provided with value-clarifying experiences.

The effects of those experiences on behavior patterns was mixed. Some of the experimental groups reported no change, some reported regression, and some reported gains—that is, *less* apathy, flightiness, and so on. Some of the reported gains were extremely large.

When it came to drug use, the findings were unmistakably significant. All groups reduced their intake of drugs. Almost all groups reduced their intake of alcohol as well. Some of the gains were again extremely large.

Another set of findings indicated that in the control groups, *without* the use of values clarification, there was a significant decline in the students' social adjustment.

Josephson's Study of Eighth Graders

Josephson (1970) conducted value-clarifying activities with a class of above-average eighth graders and compared their growth with that of a similar class that had no special program. Josephson met with the experimental class one period a week for 12 weeks.

He found that the experimental group improved significantly in terms of self-ratings on social adjustment, as measured by the Binkley Social Desirability Scale of School Behavior, and did not change in terms of personality characteristics, as measured by the Cattel High School Personality Questionnaire. Both of these findings were predicted. Unpredicted was an intriguing but tentative finding that the experimental students shifted their self-ratings so that they became more like the ratings they were receiving from peers and teachers.

Barman's Study on Biology Achievement

Charles Barman (1974b) and two colleagues each taught one experimental and one control class of high-school biology students. The experimental groups had value-clarifying lessons once a week for 18 weeks. Except for that, both groups received the same Biological Sciences Curriculum Study (BSCS) Yellow Version biology course.

The values-clarification groups increased significantly, compared to the control groups, on cognitive achievement, measured both by the objective BSCS final exam and by student self-evaluation on behavioral objective for the course. There was no significant difference between experimentals and controls on attitudes toward biology.

Rutkowski on Attitudes Toward Chemistry

David Rutkowski (1975) found that values-clarification strategies and a "values level" treatment of subject matter tended to increase his high-school chemistry students' positive attitudes toward science. Using the students as their own controls, he administered an attitude test four times before beginning the experimental treatment and four times during it. The increase reached statistical significance only during the values-clarification period, but it lost its statistical significance the last time the test was administered.

Pracejus' Reading Study

Eleanor Pracejus (1975) compared two reading programs with eighth graders. One group read a series of stories and had discussions based on the publisher's recommended approach, which was not value-oriented. The second group read the same stories, but had discussions based on the values-clarification approach. Each treatment lasted 12 sessions. The values-clarification group improved significantly more in reading comprehension.

Little on Driver Education

A study by James Little (1975) showed a values-clarification approach to driver education more successful than a lecture approach in terms of students' attitudes toward the course, attendance, and grades. The values-clarification class was taught by the experimenter, the other by a colleague committed to the lecture approach. The same text and testing procedures were used.

Olson's Study of the Valuing Process of Ninth Graders

Olson, working with ninth-grade students, seemed to find evidence that values-clarification experiences did not brainwash students into concluding that there is no other way to approach values. Although we have not seen the complete study, we found three quotations from it (Loggins, 1976, p. 3):

> The longer one participates in values clarification, the more [the student] expresses an autonomous view regarding the ordering (sequence) of the presented valuing processes.

> Actually, the longer they were involved in the valuing process, the less likely they were to agree on the valuing method prescribed (the seven valuing processes).

> Treatment [experience with values clarification] produces an awareness that students may arrive at values differently rather than by the prescribed method.

RESEARCH WITH ADULTS

Klevan's College Study

Klevan (1957) studied the effects of the value-clarifying techniques on a group of college students (mostly sophomores) taking a course in education. He was particularly concerned with (1) changes in consistency of attitudes, (2) expressions of purposefulness, and (3) expressions of friendliness among class members.

The instructor of the course focused on a series of issues in education, selected by himself and the students, and stimulated thinking on those issues. There was a systematic attempt to help students see the importance of such things as defining terms clearly, identifying assumptions in thinking, searching for alternatives, and keeping an open mind. In general, the instructor used the value-clarifying method of discussion. Paramount was the desire to keep the atmosphere permissive and accepting while stimulating individual thought. One clever way the instructor stimulated thought was by having each student write opinions, by filing those writings, and by later returning them to the student if conflicts and inconsistencies arose among a student's papers.

There were two comparison groups, taught by a different instructor and *not* matched in any substantial way with the experimental group. These were given the same before-and-after measures as was the experimental group.

Klevan found that during the experimental period (one term) students in the experimental class did develop significantly more consistent attitudes and did express more personal purposes than the students in the comparison classes. He found, however, that growth in friendliness was not different among the groups.

Because of the many uncontrolled factors, it is not possible to attribute any of these results to the experimental method alone. Nevertheless, Klevan's personal observations were that many students in the experimental group became much clearer about what they believed and showed substantial increases in educational commitment and personal spirit.

Shields' Philosophy Class

Harry A. Shields carried out an unpublished study in a philosophy of education course at a Catholic college. He undertook to give his group of 28 students a variety of value-clarifying experiences over a ten-week period. His class met twice a week during that period, giving him twenty 90-minute sessions. He used class discussion to ask clarifying questions, assigned value sheets such as those in chapter 6, and wrote clarifying responses in the margins of student reports that were returned to students. As a control, he used another class he taught in methods of teaching. He did not emphasize values-clarification in this group.

To measure his results, Shields used two approaches. First, he had each student in the experimental and control classes complete in two successive weeks, before the ten-week experiment was begun, a rating of themselves along eight variables, five associated with value clarity (interested and involved in classroom work, independent, persistent, responsible, and enjoyment of learning) and three as control or placebo scales (enjoyment of music, participation in athletics, and being friendly). An average of the two pretests (whose scores were similar) provided beginning scores. The same self-rating sheets were used after the experiment and provided ending scores.

As a second measure, Shields assigned—both before and after the experiment and to both experimental and control students—papers that expressed attitudes. These papers were unstructured. The pairs of papers (a pre- and a postpaper for each student) were given to three independent judges who judged the change in the papers (improved, same, worse). Judges did not know whether papers came from the experiment or the control groups. They used the following criteria: quality, clarity, and depth of thinking; organization and logic; and quality of the response to the questions the experimenter wrote in the margins.

The findings of the students' self-ratings were inconclusive. The growth of the experimental group was perhaps slightly greater than that of the control group, but the unreliability of the instrument prevented any possibility of the difference reaching statistical significance for a sample of that size.

The judges' ratings of the student papers, however, favored the experimental group at the .01 level. All three judges saw much more growth in the papers written by the experimental students. Inasmuch as the two courses differed in many ways—especially in subject matter—it is impossible to be certain that the growth in the experimental papers can be attributed along (or at all) to the value experiences.

Dee's Value Sheets in a Technical Course

Frank P. Dee conducted an unpublished study in an adult-education class at Rutgers University that showed that adults studying a technical subject (business organization and management) would enjoy and find "helpful" brief but regular interludes of value discussions.

Dee asked the instructor of the course to distribute value sheets (as in chapter 6) at the end of each of five successive weekly sessions for students to consider at home as an optional assignment. These sheets dealt with some aspect of business ethics, financial policy, or sales practices. Students were then given the first ten minutes of each session to discuss, in small groups, their ideas and feelings about the sheet distributed at the end of the preceding week's session. The instructor used this time to prepare his lesson or to counsel individual students. The instructor took no part in the value-sheet discussions.

A comparison class had similar discussions, sparked by similar sheets. Their sheets, however, did *not* contain such value-clarifying questions as "What would *you* choose," "What would make *you* proud," and "What have *you* done."

A simple questionnaire completed by both groups indicated that the value sheets were seen as a helpful and enjoyable experience—probably more so than were the similar nonvalue sheets—and not as an unwelcome intrusion into the technical aspects of the course. Dee suggests that most subject-matter specialists can probably find value sheets that would more than justify the time they take from the regular class content.

Gordon's Study of Student Teachers

John Gordon (1965a, b) worked with white student teachers assigned to predominantly black urban schools. He wished to discover whether values clarification could be a means of improving the understanding and empathy of those middle-class white teachers for the students.

Gordon divided the student teachers into three groups. In one group each teacher worked individually with five students using the style of values clarifications. In a second group each teacher worked individually with five students using the style of a subject-matter tutor. The third group of student teachers acted as a control.

Gordon found that both groups of teachers who worked with students individually grew more than did the controls in understanding the children in their classes. He also found that the teachers who interacted in the style of values clarification reduced their "feelings of social distance" from black students more than did either the tutoring teachers or the control teachers.

Curwin's Evaluation of a Training Program for English Teachers

Curwin (1972) conducted a values-clarification program for 28 student teachers of English or preservice English teachers and wanted to know relatively precisely what benefits, if any, flowed from that program. He made a detailed study of the participants' self-reports and concluded that participants became clearer about several issues in the field of teaching and English teaching, had a somewhat greater awareness of the alternatives open to them as English teachers, would use many of the values-clarification activities they had experienced with their students, and believed that the course was very useful to them.

Smith's Study of Two Styles of Drug Education

Bryn Smith (1973), in a study sponsored by the Florida State Department of Education, measured the relative effectiveness of two ways of presenting drug information to preservice elementary teachers. One was the traditional, teacher-as-authority method. The second was an open, value-clarifying discussion method.

The values-clarification group "was found to be superior in all ways measured." Namely, members of this group did more independent reading, scored higher on various effective and cognitive tests and developed a greater sense of community enabling them to solve problems together more effectively.

Problems in the assignment of teachers to groups, however, raised the possibility that teachers assigned to the teacher-centered group and to a control group might have resented such placement, thereby biasing the results.

Wilgoren Comparing Two Value Approaches

Wilgoren (1973) compared this book's values-clarification approach with Donald Oliver's approach, which uses more of a cognitive-confrontational values model. Fifty undergraduate teachers in training who signed up for the experience were divided randomly into two experimental groups and two control groups. One experimental group had a six-week program of value-clarifying strategies twice a week, each for 75 minutes. The other experimental group spent the same amount of time using Oliver's strategies.

Both groups showed a positive change in self-concept, compared to the control groups, as shown by the Berger Self-Acceptance Scale (protest) and the Phillips Self Questionnaire (posttest). There was no difference between the two approaches.

Osman's Study on Teachers

Jack Osman (1974) used 15 value-clarifying strategies with 88 future teachers in his college-level health education classes. He found a significant difference between their scores on a pre- and posttest of self-actualization, as measured by Shostrom's Personal Orientation Inventory. The lack of a control group prevents the conclusion that this finding was attributable to the values clarification.

However, using self-reports of the students, Osman found that almost 50 percent rated themselves as having become more involved in the valuing process since the course began. More than 80 percent expressed a greater awareness of their values. Almost half stated that their speech had become more consistent with their actions as a result of their experiences in the course.

RESEARCH ON TRAINING AND METHODOLOGY

Kirschenbaum Evaluation of a Training Program

Kirschenbaum (1977) measured the outcomes of a two and a half-hour in-service meeting he conducted with 80 elementary and junior-high teachers. They had had no formal exposure to values clarification previously. Using a group of students from the district, Kirschenbaum demonstrated the strategies of voting, rank orders, the continuum, the proud whip, and the public interview and then gave the teachers a chance to practice creating and experiencing the first four of the strategies in small groups.

One month later, the teachers filled out an anonymous questionnaire, indicating which of the strategies they had used in their classrooms during that month and whether they planned to continue using them. Of the 80 teachers, 75 percent indicated they had used one strategy, 50 percent had used two, 30 percent had used three, 12 percent had used four, and 8 percent had used all five. Wherever a teacher had used a particular strategy, 82 percent indicated they planned to continue using it.

Redman's Evaluation of Training Program

George Redman (1975) conducted an exploratory study with teachers volunteering for values-clarification training in which he found that, after the training when the teachers responded to a nine-minute conflict film, they showed significantly greater "openness," defined as (1) an identification with and/or support of the needs and interests of students as individuals and (2) a recognition that their assessments of the film were subjectively held. The method of selecting the sample as well as the lack of a control group make it especially difficult to generalize from these findings, however.

Betof's Evaluation of a Training Program

Edward Betof (1976) evaluated the impact of a 36-hour training program in values clarification. He sent a questionnaire to 226 teachers who had completed that training, and 80 percent responded.

How, if at all, had the training program helped them? More than 60 percent said that it helped them (1) to aid students with personal growth, (2) to clarify their own teaching philosophy and expand teaching skills, (3) to facilitate teacher-student interaction, and (4) to facilitate teacher-staff interaction. From 50 to 60 percent said that the training program helped them (5) to use values clarification within the school curriculum and (6) to aid students' academic growth.

Did the training program help some teachers more than others? Betof found no differences. Teachers were able to improve their teaching regardless of sex, class size, subject matter taught, grade level, years of teaching experience, age, or number of graduate credits accumulated.

Pozdol's Evaluation of a Training Program

Marvin Pozdol (Kirschenbaum, 1977) also evaluated the results of teacher-training in values clarification. He sent an anonymous questionnaire to 200 former graduate students who had taken his "Introduction to Values Clarification" course. Seventy-five percent responded.

Some sample data: "The requirement of tape recording some of my values-clarification sessions was worthwhile" (Strongly Agree—35%, Agree—46%, Disagree—11%, Strongly Disagree—1%), "I use at least one values-clarification strategy each day" (SA—4%, A—33%, D—53%, SD—5%), "I use at least one v.c. strategy each week" (SA—30%, A—50%, D—13%, SD—1%), "Since completing the v.c. course I have searched for and read books, articles, etc., related to v.c." (SA—21%, A—53%, D—20%, SD—1%).

The overall results indicated that the course had been successful, that teachers were using values clarification, that they felt it had helped them personally and professionally, and that they wished to pursue their learnings in this and related areas.

Raduns' Assessment of Ecology Values

Linda Raduns (1973) developed an instrument to measure how fully college students hold clarified values in the area of ecology. A fully clarified value was defined as one that met the seven criteria of the values-clarification theory.

After administering her instrument to 94 college students taking an elective health education course emphasizing values clarification, the following hypotheses were confirmed: (1) the subjects did not hold many clarified values in the area of ecology, and (2) there is a difference in the value held depending on whether it concerned what "others" should do or the action the person is actually willing to take in behalf of the value.

Sklare Comparing Massed and Spaced Values Experiences

Gerald Sklare (1974) compared the effects of massed and spaced values-clarification experiences. Four high-school psychology classes were involved. One class had ten values-clarification lessons on ten consecutive days. Another class had such lessons once a week for ten weeks. Two control classes had the ordinary psychology curriculum.

There were no significant differences found between the experimental groups and the control groups on the Rokeach Value Survey (measuring student value priorities), on the Prince Differential Values Inventory (measuring value orientation from "traditional" to "emergent"), or on a Dogmatism Scale.

In general, the experimental group with values clarification spaced over ten weeks showed greater changes than the experimental group with the ten consecutive sessions, although these differences were not always statistically significant.

Conducting Your Own Research

We view values clarification as a theory for teachers to use and test, not merely a theory of explanation. Values clarification postulates a relationship between certain student behaviors and the clarifying methodology. To give students an opportunity to change these behaviors, teachers may want to call on the theory's methodology.

Louis Raths has long advocated such teaching theories. (See chapter 15 for comments about two of Raths' other theories, on thinking and emotional needs.) A teaching theory gives power to the teacher who must make decisions. It informs decisions by telling the teacher how to create opportunities for students to change their own behavior if he or she wants to test the theory. A teaching theory has the additional advantage of being personally valid. Thus, although in chapter 12 we spoke of the general validity of the theory, it is more pertinent to speak of the validity for one teacher. It might work for you and not for me. It might work here and now, but not there and then. This chapter suggests how any teacher can test the theory to determine the extent to which it is personally valid.

Our first recommendation is to review the research studies that have already been completed. Reading through even the brief summaries of the research reports in chapter 12 is likely to suggest some ways to go about personally testing the theory.

As you review the studies, note the short time periods used in most of those reported projects. Often exposure to the methodology was brief and follow-up measurements were taken immediately after that exposure. We would recommend extending both of those time periods whenever possible. We need to know more about the effects of long-term exposure to values clarification and how long afterwards any changes persist.

If the completed research does not give you sufficient guidance on how to proceed or before you decide how to proceed, consider designing for yourself some variation of this three-step procedure:

1. Measure the degree of value-related behavior among students.

2. Use the value-clarifying process.

3. Again measure the degree of value-related behavior.

The hypothesis is that, as students have opportunities to become clearer about their values, they will behave differently: more purposefully, positively, proudly, and enthusiastically.

Of course, this is likely to be so for students who are *already* purposeful, positive, proud, and enthusiastic, Thus, it is suggested that whenever possible, teachers focus their experiments and their value-clarifying experiences on those who need them most. Some student types that seem especially in need of valuing experiences, what we call value-related behavioral types, are discussed in more detail below. These types of behavior, of course are occasionally exhibited by most students, but some students seem to be almost chronically typified by them. This latter group, we believe, might well be provided special help in clarifying their values.

VALUE-RELATED BEHAVIORAL TYPES

The Apathetic, Listless, Disinterested Child

These children lack interest in almost everything. They often go through the motions expected of them, but they just do not care. They are passive and indifferent. They look out windows, fool with things in their pockets, day-dream frequently, and get excited about almost nothing. They are difficult to motivate and often become school dropouts. The words "apathetic" and "disinterested" suit them well.

The Flighty Child

These children are interested in almost everything, but just for a fleeting moment. Flighty children are characterized by quickly shifting interests. They want to be stars in the play, soon change to painting scenery, but before work is begun ask for the jobs in publicity or make-up. They flit from this to that. They seem to have no stable interests. Their attention span is short, and they rarely follow through with something begun.

The Very Uncertain Child

Some children seem unable to make up their minds, not sometimes, but almost always. Simple choices throw such children into a quandary. They take a long time with decisions. They seem to be in doubt about what they want and what they like. They often prefer that others make decisions for them and almost always are reluctant to be involved in decision-making situations.

The Very Inconsistent Child

These children support one thing today and support just the opposite tomorrow. Now they are for integration; later they will likely be for segregation. Or they talk for peace in this context and war in that context. They blow hot and cold. They seem regularly and persistently to take positions and engage in behavior that is inconsistent. Sometimes they say this but do that. Sometimes it is just that nothing is repeated.

The Drifting Child

Some children seem to drift through life. No purposes seem to guide them. They seem not even bothered by worries. Nothing seems very important. They take what comes without trying to change things or themselves. They respond, but not with gusto. They almost never get deeply involved. They do not seem to expect much and they do not seem to give much. Their manner is typically lackadaisical and it seems appropriate to refer to them as "drifters."

The Overconforming Child

These children will expend great efforts in trying to conform to what they perceive to be the norm or the power position. Sometimes they will say or write what the teacher or other grownups want them to say or write, but sometimes they do just the opposite when the peer group is perceived as dominant. Overconforming children seem to have no positions or ideas of their own. They take their cues from others. Left alone, they often feel lost and anxious. They need to get direction from others.

The Overdissenting Child

Most children dissent sometimes, but some children seem to be persistent, nagging dissenters, finding fault whenever they can, picking and complaining at all but invisible stimuli. These children do not seem to be rational dissenters, although they will oftentimes be very skillful at making up arguments when they need them. The dissension seems irrational. It almost seems as if they like to be different and thrive on contention. It seems as if, not having value patterns of their own, they get their identity by opposing others, especially those in authority. This kind of nagging dissenter is not a very pleasant person to deal with.

The Role-playing Child

Finally we note the poseurs, the children who search for their identities by pretending to be someone else. They may be class fools, stoics, or romantic lovers, or they may use an ever-changing variety of roles. They often seem to be acting, and in an unreal and immature way. The roles seem contrived, not really the child at all. We call this type of child a poseur or a role-player.

Now we do not assert that these are the only types of behavior patterns that identify children with very unclear sets of values. We have reason to believe, for example, that the chronic underachieving child is often in this category, although underachievement can also result from other causes. Nor do we assert that the types we have listed *necessarily* represent value confusion. Each case would have to be studied to see if there were physical or emotional factors that were motivating the behavior pattern. But, lacking such other causal factors, we would say that a diagnosis of value confusion is at least preliminarily warranted. Our experience further confirms that the majority of students whom teachers would classify as apathetic, flighty, very uncertain, very inconsistent, drifters, overconformers, overdissenters, or role players respond very positively to a program of value-clarifying experiences.

MEASURING
VALUE-RELATED BEHAVIOR

The hypothesis of a teacher's experiment can now be restated more precisely as follows: As students who demonstrate those value-related problem behaviors are provided value-clarifying opportunities, those behavior patterns will become less frequent and/or acute.

What the teacher or group of teachers does is measure the degree of value-related behavior problems (apathy, flightiness, and so on) before applying the value theory and afterwards and compare the two measurements to see if there has been any change. It is very useful when doing this to include measurements of a group of children who are not exposed to the value theory, as a control, to see if any changes might have occurred even with no special value experiences, perhaps just because of maturation.

There are several ways to go about measuring the degree of value-related behavior. The simplest way is for the teacher to identify those children in the class who have problems in their value-related behaviors, as in the list presented earlier, and to make some informal notes for each student on the extent and the acuteness of that behavior over the period of perhaps, one week. Chart 1 shows a sample form that might be used to record this data. If this is done early in the year and again after the value experiences have been provided, a comparison of the before and after notes will give evidence as to whether the value experiences were effective. If there are other students, either in the experimental teacher's class or in other classes, who have been typed as value-related problem cases and who have not been provided value-clarifying experiences, data collected before and after the experiment on these students can be used to indicate whether any change can really be attributed to the value experiences, for less of a positive change would be expected in this group than in the experimental group.

Chart 1   *Form for Measuring the Degree of Value-Related Behavior Problems*

Student's name————————————————————————————

DIRECTIONS: Please rate the above students on the frequency and acuteness with which he or she exhibits each of the eight types of behaviors listed below. Use the scale provided for your ratings. An elaboration of the meaning of each type of behavior is available if you would like.

Apathy   frequency this student exhibits this trait————
                acuteness of this behavior for this student————

Flightiness: frequency————   *Frequency Scale*
                 acuteness————   0—Never
                                   1—Almost never
Uncertainty: frequency————   2—Perhaps every few months
                 acuteness————   3—Monthly, on the average
                                   4—Several times monthly
Inconsistency: frequency————   5—Weekly
                 acuteness————   6—Several times weekly
                                   7—Daily
                                   8—Several times daily
                                   9—Hourly
                                   10—Constantly

Drifting: frequency————   *Acuteness Scale*
                 acuteness————
                                   0—Not at all
Conformity: frequency————   1—Extremely mild
                 acuteness————   2—Mild
                                   3—Medium
Dissension: frequency————   4—Relatively acute
                 acuteness————   5—Acute
                                   6—Extremely acute
Role playing: frequency————
                 acuteness————

We need not rely upon such informal measures, however. Indeed, it is recommended that whenever possible more precise and systematic measures of value-related behaviors be made. One way to do this is through a simple sociometric device. Duplicate a sheet that lists all the value-related behavior types, as in Chart 2. After students have been together long enough to know one another, each student is then given a copy of that list, together with a name list of all those in the class. Students are then asked to fill in the form with whatever names apply.

Chart 2 includes two non-value-related types—good-looking and well-coordinated—as control items and to disguise the nature of the instrument somewhat. You could use such an instrument before and after the experiment and then compare results, seeing how many names were left off the sheets that were originally on them. Of course, we would expect less change in the two non-value-related types—good-looking and well-coordinated—than in the other eight types. If the instrument was given to other classes as well, further controls would be available with which to compare experimental results. And if value experiences were focused on only some of the value-related types in the experimental classroom, we would expect them to change more than their counterparts not so treated. (Some teachers have used clarifying responses with only a part of their students to test the effectiveness of the theory.)

Chart 2   *Who is Like This?*

1. I do not seem to be interested in anything. I sit quietly, dully, passively, bored much of the time in school and out of school. I don't care one way or the other. I am apathetic, *disinterested.*
  a.   What students are VERY MUCH like this?
  b.   What students are SOMEWHAT like this?

2. I am *flighty.* I am interested in a lot of things, but only for fleeting moments, then I get interested in something entirely different. I can get started, but I don't seem to follow through. I am attracted to a million things, but I don't stick with anything long enough to do something about it. I fly rapidly from this to that.
  a.   What students are VERY MUCH like this?
  b.   What students are SOMEWHAT like this?

3. I am considered *good-looking.* I look like people in movies or in pictures. Some people might call me handsome or beautiful.
  a.   What students are VERY MUCH like this?
  b.   What students are SOMEWHAT like this?

4. It's hard for me to make up my mind. I take a long time to make decisions. I am full of doubts. I am often *very uncertain.*
  a.   What students are VERY MUCH like this?
  b.   What students are SOMEWHAT like this?

5. I am *very inconsistent.* Today I may be for something, but tomorrow I may be against it. It's hard to tell what side I will be on. I say this, but I do that. Or sometimes I say one thing and then, later, say just the opposite.
   a.   What students are VERY MUCH like this?
   b.   What students are SOMEWHAT like this?

6. I just seem to drift. I go from here to there without having much to do with it. And I don't care much. I go the way events take me. I don't struggle. Some people might call me a *drifter.*
   a.   What students are VERY MUCH like this?
   b.   What students are SOMEWHAT like this?

7. I am *well-coordinated.* I may not be strong, but I can control my motions and can play sports very well. Some people say I am graceful. I am not at all clumsy.
   a.   What students are VERY MUCH like this?
   b.   What students are SOMEWHAT like this?

8. I like to *conform* to what is expected of me. I may conform to what a grown-up wants. I may conform to what other kids want. I may have one person to follow and I do whatever that person wants. But I don't much want to be independent. I like to follow someone else's lead.
   a.   What students are VERY MUCH like this?
   b.   What students are SOMEWHAT like this?

9. I am just the opposite of a conformer—I like to dissent, to argue with anyone and everyone, to take the opposite point of view. I seem to be against most everything. I like to argue, complain, *dissent.*
   a.   What students are VERY MUCH like this?
   b.   What students are SOMEWHAT like this?

10. I like to make believe that I am somebody else. I often *play roles,* pretending that I am somebody different, right in the classroom or outside. I like to act, even when there is no play.
   a.   What students are VERY MUCH like this?
   b.   What students are SOMEWHAT like this?

See Chart 3 for another example of a form that asks students to rate each other. That form, designed by Arlene Zuiker, includes many non-value-related items. The value items are indicated with an asterisk.

Chart 3   *"Who is this"* . . . *Completion Sheet*

   1.   Who always keeps his or her place in line?
   2.   Who always runs to the head of the line?
   3.   Who always enters the room quietly?
   *4.   Who does not seem interested in anything?

5. Who does his or her work with self-direction?

6. Who always likes to play alone?

7. Who is usually the leader in a group?

*8. Who sits quietly in class and appears bored in and out of school?

9. Who likes to play basketball?

10. Who would rather just take care of equipment?

*11. Who appears interested in many things, but never completes an assigned task once started?

12. Who is willing to listen to the ideas of others?

*13. Who likes to start one thing and then quickly flits to another?

14. Who usually asks for help during a reading assignment?

15. Who enjoys being in math?

16. Who do you consider good-looking?

*17. Who do you think has a hard time making up his or her mind?

*18. Who do you feel is very often uncertain about himself and his work? (or herself and her work?)

19. Who usually works hard during art?

*20. Who is for one thing one day and against it the next day? Who is it difficult to tell which side they are on? Who says one thing one minute and another thing opposite to the first the next minute?

21. Who wastes time in class?

22. Who is "popular" with all of his or her classmates?

*23. Who would you call a "drifter?" Who goes along with things without ever voicing an opinion and just seems to go along with the crowd?

24. Who is well-coordinated? Not strong, but controls motions and can play sports without being clumsy?

*25. Who likes to do everything grown-ups expect? Who likes to do everything the kids in the group want her or him to do?

26. Who usually tells on children who break the class or school rules?

27. Who usually seems concerned about the "person" of all her or his classmates?

28. Who usually shares thoughts during class discussions?

29. Who usually talks out of turn?

30. Who is someone you respect and might like to have personality qualities like?

*31. Who always likes to be different from the group?

*32. Who likes to "dissent"—to argue with anyone—and complains a lot?

33. Who seldom forgets a room job?

*34. Who likes to make believe they are somebody else? Who likes to "act" even when there is no play?

It is also often possible to have other teachers contribute to measures of the kinds of behavior noted above. You might start by making a tentative list. You might, then, watch those children for a week or so, revising the original list if necessary. Then you could gather data from others to see if those students are chronically and generally representative of value types. Former teachers could be asked how they saw those students on the list. (To do this, it is better not to ask if the child is like this or that, but to ask an open-ended question, "What were some outstanding characteristics of this child last year?" And it is better, too, to add a few extra names to the list, to conceal a bit what is sought.) Students who are currently apathetic, for example, but who were not at all apathetic the previous spring might well be excluded from the value list. Their apathy may be too situational or temporary to qualify them for categorization as a value "case." Something other than value confusion might well be causing that apathy.

You could also go to school records and see if related data are available. And you could go to other teachers who currently come into contact with the children being studied. In a departmentalized curriculum there will be several such teachers; but even with a self-contained classroom, often there is an art teacher, a music teacher, a physical-education teacher, or an administrator who will know some of the children well enough to venture a judgment. A form, such as in Chart 1 or Chart 2, may facilitate the gathering of these data. Be sure to add some extra names to the list, so that respondents do not get the idea that all children deserve extreme ratings on the scale.

Some teachers have even gathered information from parents, and a form for that purpose could easily be devised. It is even possible to ask students to rate themselves. To do this, a sheet might be developed that described the eight characteristics in a paragraph or so and asked each student how much he or she is like each of those descriptions. The child could also be asked to rank the eight paragraphs and perhaps a few extra ones in order of their accuracy as a self-description. Parent information and student self-ratings would not be the only data available, but it could provide an interesting bit of supplementary information.

Of course, not all of these sources of data need be used. Generally, the more the better, but teachers need strive for no more completeness than they need.

It is important, regardless of what measuring system is used, to eliminate from the list of value-related behavioral problem cases all those who suffer from physical or emotional disturbances, for those disturbances need treatment other than values clarification. The school nurse, the student personnel services staff, parents, and the students' permanent record folders offer sources for finding such information. Children in need of physical or emotional treatment should be helped to get those first. Until a child feels emotionally secure, for instance, value-clarifying experiences are probably of little benefit and may even add to his or her disturbances.

The above procedures are for identifying children whose behavior classifies them as suffering from rather extreme value confusion. You could, after identifying them, work mainly with those children, for example, by focusing value responses such as those in chapter 5 on them. In addition you could work with the class as a whole, using any number of the value strategies.

You could also take measures on all class members on behavior associated with value confusion and then test for change in every student. This is usually unnecessary, because students who show no tendency toward being flighty, for example, have little room to grow in that dimension. They cannot be significantly less flighty at the end of the experiment. It is certain that not all students suffer from value confusion. Many homes and situations that students find themselves in have been helpful for them in the area of values. Therefore, general class measures of value growth are as inappropriate as general class measures of improvement in physical health, for example. For some children, there is not much room for improvement.

However, it is possible to measure not changes away from apathy, flightiness, and so on, but changes in general patterns of behavior. For example, J. Raths (1962a) reports an experiment in which all children were exposed to value-clarifying experiences and changes on all children were measured in terms of: (1) positiveness of attitudes toward learning, (2) activity in raising questions and alternatives, (3) initiation and self-direction in classroom activity, (4) perseverance, and (5) active participation. In this experiment, several auxiliary teachers (art, music, library, and so on) completed a form for each student at the beginning and at the end of the year, and comparisons were made between pre- and postscores. If there were classes not exposed to the value processes, comparisons could also be made with such groups. The assumption in this type of measurement is that the clarifying experiences have a positive effect on the kind of learning behavior for which most teachers strive.

Some teachers who instead of measurements of value-related behavior problems, wanted to obtain general classroom measurements, in positive characteristics associated with clear values—such as degree of enthusiasm, positiveness, pride, and purposefulness—have measured those dimensions. Charts 4 and 5 show forms prepared for four characteristics: interest and involvement, independence, enjoyment of learning, and perseverance. Note that those forms, one for teachers and one for parents, include two control characteristics not believed to be particularly responsive to value experiences: neatness and cleanliness, contentment and stability. These control items would be expected to change *less* than the value-related items in response to a value-clarifying experience.

Chart 4   *Letter to Parents*

Dear Parent:

A small but important research project is underway in your child's school. The project is seeking more effective ways of helping children.

It would be very helpful for this project if we could have some idea of how some parents in this community see their children. For this, we ask your help.

Would you be kind enough to complete the form below for your child _____. You need only put a check on each line at the point that shows how you see the child (outside of school) and fill the dotted line below.

Then seal this sheet in the envelope provided and have your child return it to school. It will be sent directly to the research staff for analysis with other sheets. No one in the school system sees these sheets.

Thank you for your valuable cooperation.

always active	*Interested and involved in nonschool activities*	always passive
always	*Neat and clean in appearance*	never
always	*Independent–Willing to act without detailed directions*	never
always	*Seems content and pleased*	never
always	*Seems to enjoy school*	never
extremely persistent	*Sticks to activities*	gives up extremely easily

How are you related to the child?_____

(father, mother, older brother, etc.)

Chart 5   *Teacher Form*

Student_____

We need some confidential information about some students, for a research project underway here. Please make a check (✔) on each of the lines at a point that best describes the above student.

| always | Interested and involved in classroom work | never |

| always | Neat and clean in appearance | never |

| always | Independent–Willing to act without detailed directions | never |

| always | Appears stable and secure | never |

| always | Enjoys learning | never |

| extremely persistent | Sticks to activities | gives up extremely easily |

Rater: _____   Date: _____

Coordinating Teacher: _____

Perspectives on the Theory

There has been a burst of interest in values and moral education since the first edition of this book appeared in the 1960s. The card catalogue in the library and the periodical indexes will give the most dedicated scholar more than enough leads to current developments. Yet, with it all and with sharp criticism from some quarters (see, for example, Cochrane, 1975; Lockwood, 1975; Olmstead, 1975; Rokeach, 1975; and Stewart, 1975), we find more need to refine our theory and to improve our communication of it than to change it. To us the basic tenets still seem sound and the methodology still appears helpful. This chapter will discuss our current evaluation of the theory.

LOOKING BACK

We started, of course, with the thinking of Dewey, and his belief that humans can reflect about values issues as well as other issues, and that they gain the most from their value-related experiences when they do so. Dewey was after a greater integration "of sense, need, impulse, and action" and reflection on current experiences was the route to that integration (Dewey, 1934).

For us, the word *clarification* has come to possess some of the characteristics of the way in which we use the word *truth*. The search for truth seems to be never-ending. We seek it and never quite reach it. So it is, we believe, with respect to clarification. We make attempts to see ourselves more clearly, to see the ramifications and the implications of an issue more clearly. But to see them with *absolute* clarity is quite probably a goal never to be reached.

In earlier chapters, we emphasized that the *activities* in which we engage are not necessarily values; they must be looked at as probable indicators of values, and in the process of clarification they may or they may not turn out to be values. This process is similar with respect to attitudes, interests, beliefs, feelings, and so on. In values clarification, we are trying to clarify *value indicators* to see if they were indeed values or if we wished to raise them to the value level.

There is an analogy here with an idea from Dewey. He looked at principles or generalizations not as assertions of truth, but as invitations to inquiry. In other words, the validity of a principle was continually being inquired into by examination of some application of that principle. We see value indicators in this same light, as starting points for inquiry into their value status.

We took over the criteria for the definition of value almost wholly from Dewey, as it is set forth in his book *Theory of Valuation* (1939). Our additions to it were not fundamental. They were intended as a step toward further clarification, an effort to make more explicit what was meant by value in the context of a teaching theory.

As one of the starting points, we took another idea from Dewey. Dewey said that character was the interpenetration of habits. We took this definition more or less as an axiom and asked what habits most closely related to values constituted a significant concept of character in terms of their interpenetration. Our list originally included habits that dealt with purposes, habits that dealt with attitudes, habits that dealt with aspirations, habits that dealt with actions, habits that dealt with thinking, and habits that dealt with interests. We assumed that as these habits interpenetrate and become more integrated by thinking and feeling people, they would be better able to live principled lives. They would be better able to make sounder decisions for themselves and grow in ways that they valued.

The object then became to try to clarify any of a person's expressions that seemed to be related to those habits, which in their interpenetration might indicate character. Essentially, the clarification processes consisted of questions. These were formulated in such a way that *only* the students had the answers to them. They were about the students' purposes, their aspirations, their attitudes, their interests, their feelings, their beliefs, and their activities. We suggested that teachers could use the questions in such a way as to help the students integrate these habits for themselves and in doing so would make a contribution to the development of character.

It did seem and still does seem that not all people would achieve this status through classroom clarification methods. We realized that some would achieve it in large measure and some would have great difficulty and would perhaps fail to integrate more of themselves in any significant way.

In an effort to propose a rationale which could be tested by classroom teachers, we asked what behaviors children might reveal which were indicators of an *absence* of this kind of integration. In other words, we were looking for how children behave when values are very muddy. At this point, we assumed that values tended to give direction to life, that values tended to invite us to do something, and that values were things that made a difference in choice situations. We received many suggestions from cooperating teachers and finally set up as factors for further inquiry the following behaviors: apathy, flightiness, overconformity, overdissention, uncertainty, inconsistency, role playing, and chronic drifting. Those were the starting points for inquiry into possible value-related behavior. In other words, we made a beginning by trying to locate children with one or more of these behavior patterns and using them as experimental subjects in an attempt to test the clarifying procedures.

This implied an assumption, although when it was involved in an experimental design we thought of it more as an hypothesis: By applying the suggested clarifying procedures, teachers could assist students in acquiring the interpenetration of habits which in turn would constitute character development. We did not have techniques for appraising character. Instead, we sought evidence as to whether children began to develop purpose, whether they became less flighty, whether they became more independent in their thinking rather than overconforming and overdissenting, and so on. In our preliminary trials, there was some evidence which indicated that such changes were occasionally taking place and, quite naturally, there were other instances where no change took place. Yet we felt as though we were on the right track and we continued.

You will notice that there is a departure from routine educational experimentation here. Ordinarily, where the emphasis is on reading, we test to see whether or not reading scores have changed. It is the same with arithmetic or spelling or science. We thought, however, that it was much more significant to test for changes in behaviors, such as changes in apathy, flightiness, overconformity, and so on. This meant an almost complete neglect of whether our attempts to clarify actually clarified anything. We still know little about this side of the whole theory.

SEVEN CRITERIA

The seven criteria for a value grew from a notion of what would characterize people who were fully using their intelligence to guide their lives. The value-clarifying process rests on those criteria. For example, one of the criteria for a value is that it be something that penetrates a person's life, that it uses some of a person's limited energy and resources, that it really shows up in the person's behavioral decisions. And, therefore, the clarification process uses such questions as "Do you intend to do something about that idea you expressed?" "Can I help you do something about that?" and "Are there some examples in your life that show how you lived in this way?"

Now it is interesting to ask if all seven criteria are necessary. Can a person be helped to live an intelligently self-directed life without some of those seven? Some people seem to believe that the criterion about incorporating choices into behavior is not vital. Others question the necessity of sharing personal values with others, especially when there is a risk in speaking out. "Can't I value something and keep it to myself?"

It would not be too difficult to design research that would omit various combinations of the criteria and see if the results indicate that some are unnecessary. It would be a somewhat more creative task to see if *other* criteria, when translated into clarifying operations, augment the seven we have already identified, thus suggesting that we should reserve the term *value* for something that satisfies more than seven criteria. We believe the decision should be made on the basis of which processes help people become more purposeful, alive, and intelligent in their relationship with their environments and, if it can be measured, more integrated and harmonious within themselves.

Incidentally, for some purposes it may be useful to describe the valuing methodology in more psychological terms. In that case, the seven criteria may emerge as different factors. For example, we might call one factor *thought provocation*. Perhaps there is the tendency to *encourage the use of personal power*, to encourage persons to assert themselves, to put their ideas into practice. Perhaps *pressure for independence* is significant for those unaccustomed to the decision-making process. There may be other or different factors, perhaps something to do with *pride*. It is possible that such a recasting of the valuing process will aid understanding and facilitate study and communication of the ideas.

ETHICAL RELATIVISM

Some people have charged us with being ethical relativists. By that they seem to mean that we accept one value as being as good as another. That is far from our position. We believe in *clarifying* values, helping people better integrate their beliefs, feelings, activities, purposes, and so on, through awareness and reflection.

Encyclopedia Britannica (1963, vol. 17, p. 761) speaks of the role of clarification this way: "Like all other branches of philosophy, ethics is in fact a theoretical study in which we try to clarify concepts. If it has more immediate practical importance than any of the others, that is because muddles about the fundamental notions about morality can have serious consequences in human action."

Encyclopedia Britannica (1963, vol. 8, p. 778) also discusses pragmatism—especially the contribution of John Dewey—and concludes with this statement: "Similarly there are for Dewey no self-evident or universally valid rules of conduct: moral rules are hypotheses which have been found to work in many cases and hence offer helpful suggestions; they offer nothing more." Now that is very close to our position. We are concerned with the continual, reflective search for clearer values.

This is not our focus because we believe that such a search will uncover a set of eternal, universal values. If such values do exist, we believe clarification will help reveal them, but clarification need not lead to universals to be useful. Clarification can offer us guides to behavior that, as they get clearer, work better and better in the life we now lead. We want to help people do better with the lives they experience. Dewey said, "A moral law, like in physics, is not something to swear by and stick to at all hazards; it is a formula of the way to respond when specific conditions present themselves. Its soundness and pertinence are tested by what happens when it is acted upon."

Whitehead (1958, p. 53) says something similar: "In scientific investigations the question, True or False?, is usually irrelevant. The important question is, in what circumstances is this formula true, and in what circumstances is it false? If the circumstance of truth be infrequent or trivial or unknown, we can say, with sufficient accuracy for daily use, that the formula is false."

We share that disinterest in universal absolutes. This is not to say that we accept the idea that standards cannot exist or that "anything is as good as anything else." We agree with Whitehead and Dewey that there is a qualitative difference in ideas and activities and that that quality is to be judged by the thinking that has been involved in it, the connections made between it and our existence—past, present, and future. Clarification is a process for refining that thinking and improving that quality. That judgment about quality is to be made in particular contexts, when "specific conditions present themselves," not in any final abstract way.

In a sense, the values that we carry exist as in a bag on our back. Meeting a new situation, we might reach into the bag for some bit of our past and try to see whether or not it is appropriate to the new occasion. Much more often than not, it does not fit exactly. Time, circumstances, the individuals and groups involved, our own growth, perhaps our physical condition, and our most recent experiences often reveal a necessary modification in the application of a past wisdom. So we adjust and this new adjustment to life then also goes into the bag and becomes available for possible application in future situations. Thus, past value clarity *serves*, not controls, the present; and present value experiences serve, not limit, the future.

We might note that some values seem to us clearly better than others. We align ourselves with the values of thoughtfulness, respect for others, the right of others to interpret their own experiences, and gentleness, to give some examples, and our book hopefully reflects such values. We have certainly not tried to conceal that those are among our values. But we also insist on the right to change our values as the world evolves and we continue to learn. It is not that we necessarily will change, of course, but that we and all others must be afforded the right to keep open to life. To us one value does not seem as good as another.

One final point, somewhat redundant but perhaps worth noting: There is a disadvantage in talking about values as if they were abstractions, as we did in the preceding paragraph, for that may encourage the view that values are entities that exist independently of our experiences and that somehow we are not fully responsible for our values. We hope our position on this matter is clear. We define values as evolving directly from our experiences and existing only as our experiences reflect them: we clarify our values from our life experiences and our real-life behavior provides the evidence of what we have come to value. To us, values are not best viewed as abstractions. And value issues are not, for most of us, philosophical issues. Value issues are imbedded in the complex pushes and pulls of everyday life. A value issue is seldom even as "simple" as should I marry a person I do not fully love." It is more likely to be "should I marry a person I am not sure I love, but who likes my body, while I'm not sure I'll get another chance, I'm getting older, I have a fairly good job, the person drinks too much, etc." In short, it makes little sense to us to talk about a values issue out of the context in which it rests or to talk about values outside of the lives of the people who carry them.

CLARIFYING AND INDOCTRINATING

Values, as we define them, cannot result from indoctrination; they require free choice, among other things. But beliefs, attitudes, or purposes are not defined by this theory. Does that suggest, some ask, that we can indoctrinate something if we simply call it a belief? Take courtesy, for example. Most parents would probably be happy if their children were courteous. Some parents might even call that a prime goal of child rearing. Is that not to be trained, rewarded, exhorted, indoctrinated, or otherwise "taught" to the child?

Here adults seem to have a choice. They can leave it to the value level—that is, really give children alternatives, free choice, and freedom to act upon their choices—and trust that the wisdom of courtesy will prevail. If courtesy does prevail, it is likely, of course, to prevail in a deep and satisfying way. But courtesy may not prevail, and then the consequences are as obvious as they are uncomfortable.

The other choice is to remove courtesy from the area in which children are left free to decide things for themselves. Following this road, adults acknowledge that they are unwilling to take the risk of children's decisions, and so they do not let children choose. They *teach* (or indoctrinate) courtesy; they do not *clarify* the issue. The risk here is that they may in return get courtesy only when someone is looking, or when the rewards are high enough, or at the expense of personal pride and satisfaction, or in other unwanted circumstances.

There is another danger. If too many decisions, like courtesy, honesty, cleanliness, and so on, are removed from children, will there be enough left to give them practice in valuing and the sense of worth that we believe comes with valuing? This is the real danger, as we see it. It does not seem very serious to us what is done with courtesy or almost any other individual issue. The pattern, however, is of greatest moment. What seems to us of paramount importance is that children be given a measure of freedom to exercise intelligence and individuality, and in increasingly large amounts as they mature.

In general, we would say that the issues that should be left to the child are (1) those that contain alternatives the consequences of which the child is able to grasp to a reasonable extent and (2) those whose alternatives are neither very distasteful nor dangerous so that any choice can be tolerated.

A TENDENCY TOWARD TRIVIA

We sometimes think that we do not stress adequately the difficulty and importance of carrying on clarifying operations upon the most vital issues, problems, and concerns of individuals and society. As the history of this entire movement has revealed, it is very possible to trivialize the whole matter of values clarification. For example, teachers may use a half dozen problematic situations within one classroom hour. They may flit from the hydrogen bomb, to whether or not people should kiss on the first date, to a television program, to the drinking of too much cola, and perhaps, to whether it is alright to show up late when you have an engagement with your best friend. Of course, the multiplication of examples is not a bad thing, but when variety is offered exclusively and in profusion, there is a temptation for teachers to use it without generating much reflection or clarification.

Examples might focus upon those issues, problems, or concerns which the teacher believes represent serious and significant matters in the lives of individuals and in the life of our society. And a variety of questions may serve to open up issues and create an atmosphere that later can be used for serious reflection. But we believe that the content we use for clarifying should be consistent with the ends we have in view. Excessive use of trivial, almost inconsequential problem situations does a disservice to the important goals we have. Jumping about may titillate students, may excite them for a few moments, but the question may well be asked whether it makes any kind of lasting contribution to the major purposes of value development of which we have spoken.

ASSESSING
THE BENEFITS

Should all people get the same value-clarifying treatment? We are not sure of the answer to this question. Many teachers apply value-clarifying strategies to whole classes while, we hope, allowing students who find it uncomfortable to "pass" or to participate only superficially. We have no evidence that such an approach causes any ill effects and we have much evidence that it is beneficial, which leads us to conclude that a general treatment for all is defensible.

Yet there are many unanswered questions. Is there an age before which the clarification process is useless? What are the most critical years for valuing of various kinds, if there are any? Can someone be too old or too psychologically rigid to develop clearer values?

This raises a question about the relationship between the effect of the clarification process and personality variables. Are there variations that work best when matched with particular personalities or particular behavioral patterns? Should the apathetic child be worked with the same way as the dissenting child? Should the apathetic ten-year-old child experience the same clarifying processes as the apathetic twenty-year-old boy, with adjustments only for the level of cognitive abilities?

The finding reported by J. Raths (1962) that all of the students who did not profit from the value experiences were found to have marked unmet emotional needs raises the questions of the relationship between emotional problems and value problems. Can a person whose life is devoid of affection, for example, profit from a values-clarification process? If so, under what conditions? Our original hypothesis is that emotional needs must be satisfied before much progress can be made with the development of clear values. Indeed, we suspect that it may be harmful to confront children who have insufficient ego strength with many decisions, as the values-clarification strategies tend to do.

Do *all* children profit from the values-clarification procedures, no matter how much impetus they get to clarify their personal thinking (as opposed to indoctrination) from home or other sources?

Is there any harm in getting too much? Or is it, as we suspect is true, that values clarification is much like most vitamins, an overabundance of which (within obvious limits) simply washes through harmlessly?

Martin (1960) suggests that some children have more difficulty getting clearer values through a teacher's efforts than do other children. His research suggests that dissenting children and perhaps flighty children are hardest for a teacher to work with because they present special difficulties in the development of an accepting and open teacher-student relationship. Indecisive and posing children are next to difficulty. Martin hypothesizes, with apathetic and overconforming children the easiest. Is this true? And, if so, does this suggest a technique that emphasizes the development of easy communication *before* the implementation of the value techniques? Or is there some way that bypasses the need for direct communication and still permits the clarification processes to work? The value sheets discussed in chapter 6 may provide a possibility.

TEACHERS OF PROBLEM STUDENTS

Some schools, in urban slums for example, contain a high proportion of "problem" students. This is especially likely if the school has a high proportion of minority students. As we see it, much of the resentment and hostility and alienation of such students stems from their lack of personal power or hope for the future. At some level of awareness, they are angry at what life has already done, seems to be doing, and probably will continue to do to them and their families.

One thing that values clarification can do is to help people clarify what power they do have and how to use it productively, especially without medium-term consequences that negate short-term gains. Values clarification can do this in small ways, when it comes to solving particular personal problems, and in more general ways, as in cooperatively solving community problems. The net effect of this process on people, from our experience, is that their personal power becomes more available to them. We would expect, then, that negative behaviors based on a feeling of powerlessness or hopelessness would diminish.

Thus, perhaps for more than for any other group, value-clarifying experiences—chances to think through what their lives are for in some accepting, aware, and realistic fashion—are needed by alienated students. We do not believe that the value-clarifying methodology by itself will solve the problems of such children. We would add a heavy dose of emotional-need satisfaction. These students usually need to taste much more success, for example. And they need to see the objective reality of space existing for them in the future—in jobs, in families, and in communities. But we do believe that the value methodology can be a vital part of any program for the disadvantaged. It may, in fact, be the crucial element in releasing their personal and social productivity.

Also in need of research, and in the same vein, are the possible uses of this methodology with delinquent children, institutionalized children, adult prison inmates, and others who consider themselves outcasts from society. There is some reason to believe that the effects here, too, might be worthwhile.

TWO SETS OF PROBLEMS

Two sets of problems continue to frustrate us as we talk to teachers about values clarification. One set revolves around a tendency of teachers to ask values clarification to do more than it can do. This tendency arises in part because values clarification does make a contribution to a variety of teacher purposes It can, for example, motivate bored students to get more involved in school. It can improve the classroom climate. It can also help students to appreciate each other's individuality and their own individuality as well. It can help a teacher find ways to deal responsibly with sensitive issues. And it can help humanize an otherwise cool institution. This leads some educators to believe that values clarification *by itself* can do those things, which may be true for a while but seldom for long. Values clarification can support such purposes. It may even build a momentum that allows other improvements to be made. But values clarification is not designed to do those things by itself.

So we caution teachers who expect values clarification by itself to repair a sterile curriculum, change a punitive atmosphere, or eliminate the anger of students. That is asking too much. Values clarification's purpose is to assist students in becoming more aware of their choices, prizings, and actions and ways in which those might be integrated. As such, it is a useful addition to an otherwise nourishing school environment. It is not meant to be a whole diet.

These comments lead us to the second set of problems we still face. Values clarification requires an artistic touch. Teachers must learn to sense when to raise an issue and when to let an issue pass without comment, when to speak up in defense of their values and when to approach students gingerly. The nuances of such decisions seem to us too complex for strict prescriptions.

In weak moments we are tempted to try to offer such guidelines to teachers. But the temptation fades quickly. Even learning to diagnose cognitive levels, as Kohlberg's moral development group recommends (see, for instance, Kohlberg, 1969, 1973, 1975a), has turned out to be a formidable task for teachers. So we retreat closer to the level of art and hope that teachers catch the sense of values clarification and use it with flexibility and taste, naturally and appropriately. It is not an entirely satisfactory solution to us, for we suspect that many teachers seek additional guidelines, but we do feel good about reminding teachers that the sensitivity of the artist serves them well in the classroom.

COMPARING
MORAL DEVELOPMENT AND
VALUES CLARIFICATION

Some people have asked how our work in values clarification compares with the moral development research of Lawrence Kohlberg and his associates (see Kohlberg, 1973 & 1976). The two approaches seem to us different in some ways. For example, moral development is rooted in the work of Jean Piaget and research psychology. Values clarification comes more directly from John Dewey and the work of educators.

The goals are also distinct. As we understand it, moral development builds on the observation that people at different ages tend to reason differently when making judgments about topics like stealing and lying. Younger people, for example, are more likely to concern themselves with punishment and the approval of authority figures while older people are more likely to think about what is best for all concerned. Proponents of moral development believe that there are predictable stages through which this kind of reasoning develops and that people move upward most readily when they are assisted in moving through those stages one at a time, without skipping any of them. To us, the key goal of moral education seems to be to get more people reasoning at the higher levels. Explicit is the judgment that higher is better. (Kohlberg, 1975a).

In comparison, values clarification builds on the observation that, regardless of their level of moral thinking, some people are better at integrating their lives than are others. While some people have difficulty escaping being fractured, inconsistent, and confused, others are able to move toward integration, consistency, and purposefulness, and thus toward a condition where they can more readily lead value-directed lives. Values clarification takes the position that we assist people in moving toward integration when we invite them to reflect on personal choices, prizings, and actions when considering (1) aspects of their own lives (interests, attitudes, beliefs, feelings, and so on) and (2) personal or social issues (such as stealing, jealousy, tidiness, and rule making). The goal of values clarification may be said to be to assist people in integrating their current lives and in learning skills that will serve them similarly in the future. Explicit is the judgment that, given the complex nature of current society, many individuals and groups can use that kind of assistance.

Although the goals of moral development and values clarification seem to us distinct, they are certainly not incompatible. The push of moral development seems vertical, upward toward new levels of moral thinking. The push of values clarification is in part horizontal, toward a better fit of current thinking, feeling, and acting. We see no objection to a teacher providing experiences that might lead students to shift the level of their moral thinking toward a more mature stage and also providing experiences that might lead students to integrate their current lives better. In some cases, the same experiences might serve both purposes, and we suspect without much evidence to support it, serving either purpose will tend to support the other. Values clarification certainly seems to promote more reasoned, comprehensive thinking, and as we noted in chapter 8, we believe we can make use of the Kohlberg findings to do even better with that goal.

Actually we believe that values clarification serves vertical or developmental purposes as well as horizontal or integration purposes. For one thing, values clarification seems to increase people's confidence that they can deal productively with life's confusions; we would guess that that helps some people to reach out into life to develop themselves further. They consciously seek alternatives and project them into the future. Values clarification often raises new topics to student awareness and stimulates thought that expands appreciations and understandings. Also, with its emphasis on acting on personal beliefs and purposes, values clarification sometimes leads to experimental behaviors and the evaluation of behaviors, which is often particularly growth-producing. Then, with its emphasis on speaking up and openly sharing thoughts in a group, values clarification often exposes different levels of thinking to students. When teachers openly share their thinking as well, some of the highest thought levels are exposed. This naturally challenges and provides models for those who are ready to advance to more mature thought levels. Thus values clarification not only assists students in integrating their lives on current levels, but very likely introduces development-stimulating dissonance. It is partly because of that dissonance that we recommend caution when applying values clarification to emotionally disturbed students; such students may well already suffer more dissonance than they can productively handle.

To use an analogy, values clarification seems more to us like natural food containing many nutrients, from which different people will take different things according to their current needs. Moral development seems more like a specific vitamin supplement, which serves a specific purpose (a certain kind of cognitive development), useful for those who need it at the time.

On the issue of development, we would prefer that the moral development posture was more open regarding the benefits of the higher levels. We can see no way of being certain that higher is better for all people at all times. We would even speculate that it is not so, that there are reasons for life being the way it is even though those reasons are not always apparent to us. If some people reason one way and other people reason another way, more may be lost than gained by eliminating that difference, assuming we could do so. People best make judgments about what life should be very tentatively and temporarily, we believe, for we may one day want to change our minds and we may never understand it all.

But such speculation aside, there appears to us clear disadvantages in assuming that students would be better off reasoning at a higher level than they currently reason at. The disadvantages are similar to those accompanying an assumption that students would be better off taller, brighter, or younger. First, when a teacher feels students are not as good as they might be, the teacher would be hard pressed to avoid communicating that judgment, to avoid making students feel deficient or inadequate. If higher is better, lower is worse, and that is a message not comforting to anyone's self-esteem.

Second, the judgment that higher is better obscures the need for teacher judgments about what one student or one class might need at any particular time. If a teacher were to assume that higher is *sometimes* better for *some* people, we believe the teacher would be more likely to view a person or class diagnostically and pick up many more urgent needs, and especially pick up cases where higher might even be disadvantageous, if such cases should ever emerge.

Third, we fear that the posture that higher is better might encourage teachers toward authoritarian relationships with students, for the teacher's job would be to make students into something different than they now are. Students would become objects to work on. Students may even become adversaries—as when they fail to change and thus frustrate the teachers' best intentions.

Compare the certainty of the moral development judgment about what is good and bad with the more open posture that we recommend for values clarification. Rather than saying that being value-directed is good in any absolute way, we say that some people have difficulty becoming as value-directed as they would like and that when value-clarifying assistance is offered many will take advantage of it. Rather than saying that it is better for teachers to offer assistance than not to, we advise teachers to try to do so if they prefer the kinds of behaviors that have been associated with value direction: more purposefulness and less apathy, for example. And rather than saying that values clarification has identified a permanent truth, we prefer to say that it seems to serve many people in our present society and that we should use it only if it continues to show that service.

This difference suggests an experiment. On the one hand would be teachers who were certain that students would be better off if they had clearer values. On the other hand would be teachers who were open about the issue of "betterness" but who believed that students might be able to take advantage of value-clarifying opportunities. The test would be to see which teachers produced greater desired change. Our hypotheses would be that the more open teachers would do so.

Other comparisons could be made of moral development and values clarification. For example, values clarification currently ranges much more broadly into affective domains. Clarifying feelings—especially feelings of prizing and cherishing—are central to its methodology. Values clarification similarly touches action or behavior more directly; moral development more thoroughly considers general questions of moral justification.

Values clarification is much more concerned with everyday issues, such as what to do with leisure time and personal relationships with friends. Similarly, values clarification involves fewer hypothetical issues ("Should a person break a law to free a slave?" "Should a poor man steal a drug to save a wife?"). It involves many more issues concerned with first-hand reality ("Have *you* ever been tempted to break a law?" "How do you feel when people go out of their way to help you?").

Values clarification cannot utilize paper-and-pencil tests to measure student change nearly as well as can moral development. And values clarification has much less well-developed research findings to guide and support its work.

Yet values clarification and moral development are both growing bodies of knowledge. Both are open to change and elaboration, and neither claims to offer a complete values curriculum. They both reject the assumption that indoctrination is an effective way to improve moral behavior. They both aim at helping people think for themselves more effectively. Both employ a similar educational method: open-minded individual and group deliberations on complex life issues. And they both are concerned not only with reflection and discussion, but also with the experiences people have, the models they perceive, and the environments in which they live. Both approaches help groups and communities as well as individuals. Moral development is very concerned with issues of group life and justice, while values clarification can be used readily to assist a group to integrate its attitudes, activities, and beliefs better. Practitioners of both approaches seem personally to value the same kinds of things: democracy, truth, human dignity, and freedom, for example. For all those reasons, and because both approaches will continue to deal with people in the same world, we would expect the two approaches to become more rather than less complementary and compatible in the years ahead.

Values Clarification in
Operation:
Reports from the Field

From time to time, teachers who attend our courses or workshops or read our books later write reports about what happened when they tried to use values clarification in the classroom. We include four of those reports in this chapter, partly to help the reader put the ideas of the book into a reality perspective and partly to show how some teachers blend values clarification with other educational approaches. (All the names of the students in these reports have been changed.)

PRIMARY SCHOOL EXPERIENCES

I teach a first-grade class. Three things we did should give you the flavor of how I made use of values clarification. First our barometer.

A Feelings Barometer

Our "Feelings Barometer" grew out of the values continuum exercise. I realized that some kids were having feelings that the others simply were not aware of and I wanted to work toward making these feelings part of the awareness of all the kids.

At first we drew a happy face and a sad face symbols at our own desks. Anyone who happened to be near our desk might notice just how we were feeling that day. But many times the very person who was the cause of some of these feelings was not aware of what we were experiencing.

We talked about this and decided on a big wall mural where we could show the whole room at once just how we felt and then deal with those feelings right then and there, if we wanted to. We took over a bulletin board that is 16 feet long at little-people level. We made a line across the top and marked it off from zero to ten. At ten someone drew an enormous bright sun with a big smiling face in the brightest oranges and yellows and golds we could find. At zero someone drew a very sad face with blacks and purples and dark clouds and tears rolling down the sad cheek. In between we shaded from one set of colors to the next.

Then each of us had someone trace our heads on tagboard so that we could paint life-size pictures of our faces with a happy smile on one side and a terrible sad frown on the other. Then we stuck them up with a big pushpin wherever we fit on the continuum.

With the Feeling Barometer all done we talked once more about what we wanted it to do for us. We wanted people to know how we felt at any

Report submitted by Betty Van Aman. Used by permission.

particular time. We were free to move it at any time during the day, no matter what was going on in the room. When we actually got up and moved to the Barometer to change our faces, someone was bound to notice. Then whoever noticed would find out "Do you want to talk about it?" "Do you want to talk about it alone or with the group?" "Later maybe?" "Where do you want to go to talk?" If we got a "Leave me alone" answer, that's what we would do. But if we got a plea for recognition then we'd probably all go over to the rug for a few minutes and deal with what was happening.

We kept the Barometer up for the whole year once we got it working. It became the focal point for what was happening to us. It never became something old or uninteresting. Instead I saw steady growth in the kids in sensitivity and in sharing feelings openly with each other. For me it became more satisfying to see this kind of growth than to see the reading skills develop. And when I said good-bye to the kids I really prayed that their next teachers would be gentle when the kids brought their feelings out into the open in search for the response that they were used to by that time.

Our vocabulary for feelings really grew. We discovered exactly what embarrassment meant and how it felt, how many kinds of anger we could feel, how it felt to be on a happy high for several days in a row—or on a sad low. "Sympathetic," "understanding," "honest," "scared," "frightened," "hurt," and "jealous" were words that we had working for us. I knew our idea was a success when one day we found Debbie crying and she didn't know why or how we could help her. One of the girls suggested, "Let's pretend it's her birthday!" And that's exactly what we did.

Clarifying Opportunities Pop Up

> "Clarifying is an honest attempt to help a student look at his life and to encourage him to think about it in an atmosphere in which positive acceptance exists—an environment where searching is regarded as essential."

This quotation from your book [Harmin, Kirschenbaum, and Simon, 1973] helped me and guided me the most. In working deliberately to create this atmosphere in our first-grade room I have stumbled onto situations ideal for clarifying values more than I have instigated them. One situation comes to mind as being especially good in encouraging kids to state their values.

During the big Christmas rush a film, "The Littlest Angel," was rented for viewing by the primary grades. It is religious in theme, dealing with the humble gift the Littlest Angel presented to the newborn babe while all Heaven ran around creating superb gifts worthy of the king. It is an attractive film in its colors and animation and depicts the Littlest Angel as a blunder-prone kid. We took a vote and decided to go down and see it.

The class reacted immediately to the lonesomeness of the Littlest Angel and to the rough box in which he presented his gift. The rough box contained a butterfly, a robin's egg, a stone, and his faithful dog's collar. When we got back to the room we sat down on the rug and talked for a long time about how the little boy was feeling. Why was he making all those mistakes? What was he feeling? Have you ever felt that way? When? What did you do about it? What could he have done differently? What does it mean to be a misfit? How does it feel when you are doing things wrong? Or right? Why did he think another little boy would like the things in the rough box? Why did they mean so much to him? Do you have things that make you feel the same way?

After we talked about why the four items meant so much to the Littlest Angel, we talked about what we would put in a rough box if we were told to leave our home tonight and take only four small things in a little box. The idea seemed to appeal to everyone and we decided to go home and think about it and to look over the treasures that we would keep forever, to know why we made these choices. There was no hurry to make the decisions, but once they were made, we were to bring the boxes in and share the contents with the class. We decided to tape our sharing times and play the tape back at the end of the school year to see if we still felt the same way about our decisions.

Some kids came whooping in the next morning with their decisions all made; others took as much as a week to make up their minds. Even the choice of the box became important. As we all showed our boxes and their contents to the class and explained our reasons, I knew I was experiencing the most beautiful Christmas project I had ever seen. We had bypassed Santa Claus and gone into an incredible valuing process. We talked about the sadness of having to leave things behind that were loved but too big for the box. We dealt with loneliness and with trying to make happiness for ourselves and realized the importance of the loved ones in our lives. We felt great joy and satisfaction with choices thoughtfully made. We realized how much electricity and the power pack give us pleasure. We felt relief knowing that we would never really have to make a choice.

We kept the boxes in our rooms for a long time that year, and the kids played with them when they wanted to. And they would exchange boxes with a friend for a while. And finally they were taken home to be taken on trips, loaned to a sick friend, or stashed on a shelf.

I never did play the tape back for them at the end of the year. I don't remember why. Probably just got caught up in too much other stuff. But I still have the tape and I have listened to it many times. The students' choices and reasoning are still beautiful to me.

Getting to Subject Matter

After having studied your book *Clarifying Values Through Subject Matter* [Harmin, Kirschenbaum, and Simon, 1973], I decided to apply what I had learned to our own Thanksgiving Unit. We zeroed in on the Mayflower, its crew and passengers, and the length and rigors of the trip.

On the day before Thanksgiving, our class would culminate its studies by going out on the playground and outlining the exact dimensions of the Mayflower on the grass with popped popcorn. (Four of those big bags of that god-awful stuff from the drugstore will do it. Three for the Mayflower and one to eat.) After laying the popcorn down by the handful, we would invite enough fellow first and second graders from the building to join us until we had 133 kids standing within the amazingly small confines of that tiny ship. We'd mill around, try games, try marching, try being still, try jumping overboard, and try being sick overboard—just like the Pilgrims.

Then I decided to go for the values level. I worked closely with the two other first-grade teachers. We all agreed that the suburban child's understanding of Thanksgiving was turkey, overeating, relatives, and of course, the Indians. Everybody loves to be an Indian, suburban style. We decided to go for hardships, sacrifice, self-discipline, prejudice, and religious freedom.

It was our task to outline the Mayflower, but before we got to that point we spent a great deal of time in our classroom dealing with concepts and preparing for the voyage. We invited parents to join us on our voyage and each set of parents would be in charge of four or five kids. We prepared a small dittoed time schedule for these parents so that they could accomplish each of the simple tasks we decided were necessary. For instance, the list included "board the ship," "stay confined to Pilgrim areas only," "avoid the crew," "eat your lunch," "stand still for prayers and meditation" (regardless of what the crew was doing). Capt. Miles Standish would drill with the fathers (our principal was Capt. Standish), while kids and mothers stayed out of the way, got sick overboard if they wanted to, but no jumping overboard and no running or shouting were allowed. When land was sighted, the fathers and the captain would go ashore and return, mothers would go ashore and do the washing and return. Then we would all disembark and step off on the Plymouth Rock.

Parents agreed and we started the Pilgrim-hat-and-collar production line.

For food we cut up cheese and let it sit around the room for a few days, so that it lost its fresh taste. We broke up hardtack into small pieces. Then we took down the apples we had peeled in September and hung on strings to dry. With these ingredients, we packed a "Baggie" lunch for all the voyagers.

We called down to the high school drama department and asked for twenty-five or thirty cruel and drunken sailors. No problem. Costumes were easy since everybody had jeans and a knit hat of some sort. "Practice being abusive but remember these are little kids."

O.K. Everybody was all set. At 1:00 our room would go out to outline the ship and at 2:00 all the guests would arrive. At noon, it began to snow. I mean SNOW. It was a blizzard. We got the kids together and asked them how they thought we ought to handle this. It was decided that this certainly was a hardship but that the Pilgrims couldn't turn back and we wouldn't either. So out we went with the popcorn, which was quickly covered with snow. We decided to place chairs along the outline and march around the dimensions and stomp down a good path. And it worked. (Meanwhile back at the office the calls were coming in. Is the Mayflower going to sail? Isn't it snowing, you know?)

About 1:45 there was a roar in the hall. The high school boys had arrived singing and weaving and being abusive. The crew boarded the ship. The family units got together and we all went out in the blizzard to experience hardship, self-discipline, sacrifice, etc.

The crew was fantastic. Capt. Standish was great. The kids really got into it. The war veterans forgot to march, especially in such a small area. The lunches were awful and the kids loved them. The men went ashore and disappeared into the building. (I think to warm their feet.) They returned and the mothers lugged the laundry into the building. (I think to warm their feet.) And finally we all stepped off onto Plymouth Rock.

The guests who had to leave left, and the rest of us went back in to talk about what had just happened to us. What was difficult about that confinement? How did you feel when the crew was so mean to you? Has anyone ever treated you like that before? When? How do you think the Pilgrim kids were feeling? Did you have a hard time being quiet for prayers? Are there times when you have to be quiet like that now? What do you do then?

Did you stay in the right areas? Where would you have liked to be on the ship? Are there places today where you cannot go? Those sailors were pretty mean. How did you feel about that? Are people mean today? How long have you gone without hot water or hot food? How would you feel if your Dad had to carry a gun with him around town? Where do you want to be when you are sick?

Did you think of anything fun to do on the ship? What would you like to have had to make it all easier? When the Pilgrim kids finally got off the boat, what was waiting for them? How do you think they felt? What was waiting for us when we got off? What kinds of feelings were you having? How about tomorrow? What will you remember about today when you are celebrating at home tomorrow?

The discussion was full of new ideas about what the Pilgrims might have felt and we left with new feelings about our own Thanksgiving Day.

Many of the parents were moved by the whole thing and understood where we were going with it. Some were just downright cold. We all felt as if we had clarified some values that we had ignored for a long time.

REPORT FROM A
HIGH SCHOOL MATH TEACHER*

I am a second-year teacher at Northwest High School in House Springs, Missouri. The courses I teach are ninth-grade general math, algebra, and elementary algebra. The general math classes and elementary algebra classes have caused me a great deal of frustration and dissatisfaction. The students are turned off to math and to school. I have been very aware of the barrier existing between me as a teacher and them as students.

One source of my frustration stems from the fact that I worked in offices for three years after high school before going to college to become a teacher. Eight years elapsed from the time I graduated from high school until the time I entered the educational field as a teacher. I was unaware of how much students had changed. I had a very rigid, set view of how students should behave and relate to me as a teacher. Upon entering the classroom, I was shocked. I knew I could not survive in the new environment unless I changed my outlook and adapted. The students were not going to change to fit my views.

In my general math classes, the students are rewarded individually for their desirable behavior in class by being excused from the regular assignment on Friday. The first Friday after I learned about values clarification, I prepared voting questions, rank order questions, and a game similar to "Bombshelter." The students' responses amazed me. They really put themselves into the situations and used logical reasoning. This was the first time I realized they could think logically. Not only did this class session enable the students to look at their values and prejudices, but I was forced to examine mine more closely. I had prejudged these students as not being capable of logical thinking because I had never given them an opportunity to show me otherwise. The atmosphere of the class was changed and more relaxed after this session. I could feel the barrier between us become smaller. I was very pleased and excited with the results.

* Report submitted by Betty Vaughn. Used by permission.

The next Friday I tried the "Public Interview" in the classes. Again, I was pleased with the response I received from the students. I became more enthusiastic about using values clarification in my classroom. I was still at a loss, however, as to how I might incorporate values clarification in my other classes in which students were not excused on Friday. In fact, my first response to the program was, "That's fine for social studies or English, but how can I use this in a math class?"

It was at this point that I attended a value-clarifying workshop. I was beginning to use new methods and to implement new ideas but was very unsure of where I was going. Nevertheless, I was still seeking ways to improve myself and my classes. The workshop provided me an enjoyable and exciting experience. At the end of the two days, I was more in touch with myself. I found myself doing intensive inner searching, looking at my values, my past experiences, and how they had affected me, the person I was, the person I am, and the person I hope to be. I had a really good feeling inside about me and the people around me.

On Monday, I walked into my first class, which has been a difficult class to motivate, and saw 26 individuals rather than "a class" of 26 students. I felt honest and open, and I realized I really cared for each one as a person. This was a new and exciting experience for me in the classroom. I was so excited and feeling so open that I just had to share my experiences with my students.

That day I started each class by expressing my care and concern for them and their comfort. After several voting questions concerning their four-day weekend, I was asked in five out of six classes about my weekend. It was an unusual experience for them to be interested in me and if I enjoyed my weekend. I cared for them and they cared back. This gave me the opportunity I wanted to talk about my weekend. I then presented a very short lecture on values. I asked the students to write three or four "I learned . . . " statements about their weekend. Their involvement was astounding. I was prepared for disinterest. I really felt good when no disinterest was shown. The students were more attentive than ever.

We then did a few voting questions. I asked the students if this type of thing had anything to do with math or with algebra. After a short discussion, the students agreed that life involved looking at and solving problems, which is also what math is involved with. One student compared what we were doing with algebra by noting that in this case each person was the variable and subject to change. I really respected and admired her for that insight. Another student thought the "I learned . . . " statements helped raise his morale. He realized he was not as "dumb or stupid" as he thought, simply because he had difficulty working the word problems we were doing in algebra. I enjoyed their interest and their responses. I had gained a new respect for them and I think they had gained a new respect for me.

After this was done, I still had time for my planned lesson. I suddenly realized they were hearing what I was saying and not just staring at me. They were actually listening! For some of my classes, this was quite a change. They were interested in hearing what I had to say. I saw none of the usual bored looks, heard no talking, saw no one staring out the window. We were doing the math together. The students were involved in what I was saying and the problem I was working. They were asking questions and following the logic used. I feel they learned more math that day than any day prior to that time. The amount of time spent at the beginning of the period did not seem to affect the amount of math done that day.

Before attending the workshop, I was hesitant to use small groups. Since my attendance, I have formed support groups in my algebra classes. These groups are used for working problems and the opportunity to learn from each other as well as for values exercises.

On yet another occasion, upon handing back a quiz to my elementary algebra students, I had them do the following exercise.

1. Write down how you feel about your quiz grade.
2. Why do you think you did poorly/well?
3. How do you think you can improve your grade?
4. Make a commitment with yourself.

The students who cared to share their thoughts and commitments expressed the same ideas and feelings I would have expressed, but coming from the students they had more impact. If I had been expressing those same ideas, they would have turned me off and not listened. Periodically, they are asked to review and renew their commitments. This is totally private to the individual. I collect nothing. This is more in the realm of behavior management than values clarification. The workshop, however, gave me the courage to try something like this.

The workshop has helped me both as a person and as a teacher. I have become very enthusiastic about using values clarification in the classroom. I have found it can be and should be used in a math class. What better way to get a student to use his mind and think? I want my students to learn math in my class, but most of all I want them to learn to look at alternatives, weigh the consequences, and then to make a decision. If I can give them experience in this, then I feel I have fulfilled my responsibility as a teacher.

I am still a long way from where I want to be professionally, but I am coping much better since the workshop. It has given me a larger choice of alternatives in the classroom.

UNDERACHIEVING LITERATURE STUDENTS*

Having been a teacher of American literature for many years, I was delighted to find Robert Frost's poem "The Road Not Taken" in your book, *Clarifying Values Through Subject Matter.* I have always taught this poem as part of a poetry unit. This year as Director of the Alternative School (underachievers), I occasionally worked in tandem with the regular English teacher who was always grateful for assistance.

The juniors were a particularly difficult group. They were hard core toughies, mostly girls. There were only four boys in the group of 14. The boys mostly withdrew and grimly endured the antics that the girls could be depended upon to provide. Ann was the chief show-off, a cute sprightly girl until she decided to put on her scene, which included yelling obscenities, standing on the table, hugging the teacher, dancing around the room—all done with a smile on her face. This was a recurrent episode. When Ann started in, Dell joined in, competing for loudness and kookiness. The rest of the girls would chorus with catcalls and the boys would endure stolidly. That was the scene at the extreme. Some days they were very docile indeed; some days they just slept.

We decided to divide and conquer, so we split the group, carefully dividing the troublemakers as well as the silent boys. I ended up with Ann, but luckily it was one of her docile days. I decided I was going to teach them some Frost or die in the attempt. Their curriculum had been so barren of any real subject matter—mostly sand castles and rap sessions.

So I shepherded my group into a discussion corner of the room and handed out "The Road Not Taken." We began on the concept level. "What is the poet saying in stanza one?" (A typical teacher question.) Ann piped up that she thought the writer was trying to make a decision about which road to go down. "What was the difference in the roads?" (I kept it literal at first.) That raised some discussion and argument. "What made the author choose the road he did?" That caused some furrowed brows. Sam, the silent mechanic, said Frost chose it because it was not much "traveled." (It amazed me that he even spoke at all; his usual tack was to turn off and go to sleep.) That sparked the group and they went off on a discussion of why it was fun to go a different road than most people did. That took at least ten minutes and brought most everyone into the discussion with their own story of doing something different than the crowd, which included their misadventures with the law, their parents, and the Dean. I found this quite interesting in

* Report submitted by Eleanore Dedrick. Used by permission.

terms of what it said about each student. When they ran down, we turned to the last stanza.

"Why was the writer telling it with a sigh?" "Was there regret?" They couldn't decide. Finally Ann said yes, one always wonders what would have happened had one taken the other choice. I could have hugged her, except that I would have been covered with rouge and blue eye shadow.

"Give me an example of a choice when you later wondered what would have happened had you made a different choice?" No one responded, so of course the teacher had to explore her own experiences briefly; I had to keep it brief because that was all I could afford with this group at this time. They seemed interested and somewhat amazed that I would reveal myself to them. They hadn't had that much contact with me and didn't know what to expect. Then Ann began detailing her brush with the law last fall when she had been "busted" for smoking pot, how her folks reacted (it was all new to them), how she wished she had made a different choice that night, how that episode marked her as one of the "wild" girls of the school, and so on. She really got into her feelings about the whole thing—regret, anger at her folks for not understanding, anger at the police for their rough treatment, disappointment in herself—being arrested was the supreme disgrace, she felt. There were of course tears along the way in the telling.

We ended the class with this; we had gone on for 80 minutes! (In this class, luckily, we had blocks of time, so a class or a program could go on for whatever time was needed.) I refrained from talking about "assignments" at this time. Our journey into Ann's life was enough for that day. (It turned out, by the way, that few in the group knew about Ann's experience, whereas she thought "everyone in school" knew. Her reasoning was "As long as 'they' think I'm wild, I'll be wild!")

The next day we discussed what assignments would be worth doing in connection with this poem and they agreed on the following:

1. Extra credit: Write out answers to the questions on the Fact level, on the Concept level, and on the Values level. I reminded them that one of their resources was me. (They seemed to like specific assignments in which they could look up things and get specific answers. I suppose their lives contained *few* specific answers.)

2. Required: Write a short essay on this topic: "Are you at or are you coming to any new forks in the road? How do you think you will choose? What are the pros and cons of the alternatives?" They all agreed that if they couldn't hack that issue, they could do this one: "What was the most important choice you had to make in your life?"

The essays they wrote ranged from good to sketchy, but all were interesting and showed that they had wrestled with the ideas.

I felt the discussion was good considering this group. The power of classic literature captures the student, but a teacher needs worthy questions as a follow-up. The questions in your text were worthy, and they worked with this group. The other teacher reported that she liked the question sheet also, although her group responded much differently than mine. That this group focused seriously for 80 minutes on a piece of literature and that they involved themselves with their own experiences was a real step forward.

I feel this approach could be effective with any group, but its effectiveness with underachievers is the acid test!

A LEARNING DISABILITIES GROUP*

Eight young people were selected from a learning disabilities class at a junior high school in Elmhurst, Illinois, for the purpose of clarifying personal, social, and academic values for themselves. These particular youngsters were chosen because, in addition to evidencing disorders of thinking, they exhibited behavior which seemed to indicate deficient value processing.

I am acutely aware of the difficulty in modifying adverse behavior among so-called "disabled" students. When I was planning the project, the classroom teacher looked skeptical and commented, "After all, Marjorie, you've got to be realistic. You can't get blood out of a turnip!" Obviously, some educators hold to the conviction that valuing is an abstract concept which demands skills which are not available to special-education candidates. I am convinced that this tenet is unfounded and that, on the contrary, values-clarification techniques can be highly successful with this population.

As a matter of fact, a values format provides to me an unusually concrete presentation of heretofore vague, sophisticated approaches to the concepts of self-actualization. Value language is direct and experientially focused, and the activities provide an opportunity for involvement which is crucial for the learning of educationally handicapped children. Finally, the program can be carefully structured while at the same time allowing for creativity and flexibility.

Description of Group Members

For all practical purposes, Kate was a nonverbal quiet girl who typically sat with head and eyes lowered, her long hair shading her face. Rarely would a quick smile whip across her face, for usually she was silent and stoic. On occasion, she responded to another child in whispered, short phrases, though teachers had seldom heard her speak. Intelligence scores were low

* Report submitted by Marjorie Butterworth. Used by permission.

average and her written work was acceptable, though simplistically rendered. Her perceptual loss was minimal. (Confidential records indicated a childhood trauma but several attempts at psychotherapy had failed.)

Without intending to be callous, I would best describe Carl as a blob! The pudgy boy seemed unable to function unless he was spoon-fed and coddled. Any direction seemed to panic him and he repeatedly said, "I don't get it" or "I can't do it." Though his perceptual skills were weak in both visual and auditory areas, his verbal skills were average and his intelligence average. He sat holding his head—bored, uninvolved, and worried. Parental conferences revealed that the parents had little understanding of this personality problem. In their eyes, he was well-groomed, well-fed, and a doting mother drove him four blocks to school each day.

Mark was one of a large family whose parents had recently been divorced and he was becoming increasingly hostile and aggressive. Four other children in the family had severe learning problems, and the mother was herself an uncomplicated, simple person. She had a full-time job. At the time the boy came to my attention, he was experimenting with mild drugs. Of average intelligence, he was a severe underachiever.

Jane, too, was almost totally nonfunctioning in the academic environment and strongly disliked school and the teachers she had come to see as her enemies. Her peers were wary of her: One day she would be cute and friendly; and on the next, kicking, cursing, and spitting. Failure on the simplest level enraged her, though she adamantly refused to seek help or even listen to instructions. Her parents were nonplussed but had not sought the psychiatric help which had been recommended.

My peer model in the group was a delightful girl I will call Grace. She was a severe dyslexic and felt this disability acutely. She was often lethargic and moody, and it was to this problem I hoped to address myself throughout the workshop. I chose her as a model, nevertheless, for she was a straightforward, kind, and sensitive young girl whom her peers instinctively trusted. Sadly, she perceived the world grimly, saw herself as a potential failure, and feared all would be destroyed before she lived long enough to enjoy her two passions, nature and her friends.

Bob's behavior was similar to Kate's in that he rarely spoke. In addition, he exhibited ritualistic behaviors, such as hair stroking, pencil tapping, hand rubbing, paper shuffling, and chair rocking. He was expressionless and daydreamed. Unfortunately, Bob's parents perceived school personnel as a threat and refused to discuss the matter of Bob's school failure or social isolation. He related fairly well to a few boys in his class, but the quality of his friendships was markedly immature.

Dan was the class buffoon and appeared to feel comfortable only when he was imitating a television comic. He related to his peers by tripping, shoving, and teasing mercilessly. Unlike other group members, Dan was neither depressed nor anxious. But his bizarre, inappropriate, superficial responses resulted in academic failure and alienation. He seemed confused and unable to grasp what was required of him. His comedic talent was real, however, and I planned to try to help him channel this ability in a suitable fashion. Testing results indicated that he should have been an average student in all areas.

Nelly was an unpredictable girl. She had blond kinky hair styled in an afro, pale skin and dark eyes she enhanced with green eye shadow and black, smeared eye-liner! She wore what she considered sexy, grown-up clothes—high plastic boots and tight, short skirts. But on some days, she would drift slowly down the halls, wearing no make-up and dressed like a little girl in faded blue jeans and a pink blouse. She openly discussed her loneliness and attributed this to the fact that she was more mature than her classmates, and she had nothing in common with such babies! Nelly possessed an intriguing, innocent quality, and she was extremely loving and generous. She dreamed of being a school teacher! Her skills were very poor in all areas. She could neither read nor write and had trouble understanding any but the most concrete concepts. I worried about Nelly.

As the leader, I tried to impose upon myself the following guidelines:

- To structure each session to assure for each member a sense of belonging and an opportunity to become involved at whatever level he or she was capable:

- To direct activities ultimately to enhance self-awareness.

- To provide a vehicle through which the members could explore problems, alternatives, and constructive choices.

- To replace dogmatism with a spirit of inquiry and openness.

Physical Surroundings

The room in which the group was scheduled was pleasant, quiet, private, and sunny. In order to change the tenor of the room, I introduced the following changes:

1. Arranged chairs in a semicircle, with the leader's chair among them. Desks were pushed aside.

2. Made a tagboard chart of the seven questions which identify a position or stand on an issue. The list was titled "Where Do I Stand?"

3. Put up two posters that had been made for me earlier by two art students. They were graphic and colorful. One caption read, "The greatest kindness I have to offer you always: the truth," and the other read, "Whatever my secrets are, remember when I entrust them to you, they are part of me." Both posters were suggested by Powell's book, *Why Am I Afraid to Tell You Who I Am?* [1969].

4. A portable radio was playing, tuned in to a station playing rock music, low volume.

Time Schedule

The group was to be considered a pilot program and the administration allowed me two 20-minute periods a week for the sessions. Teachers were enthusiastic about the project and were cooperative about excusing the students from class.

Session 1. Six of the students reacted with varying degrees of surprise, distrust, and anxiety as they entered the unfamiliar environment. Only Bob and Kate behaved as if it were a routine occasion and sat down rigidly, silent. Though they knew who I was, some had not met me personally, so I introduced myself. "Hi," I said, "I'm Marjorie Butterworth." I knew they were all from the same classes, so I did not go through the formality of introductions.

Interestingly, the first reaction, enmasse, was the query, "Why did you pick *us?*" This was flung at me accusingly. Mark said, "Because we're dumb!" I answered as simply as possible, directly telling them what we were going to do and giving them an acceptable reason for why they had been chosen, without referring to them as a group with deficiencies.

The music was intriguing to them, so I immediately did a voting strategy:

1. How many of you like music?
2. How many of you want me to leave the music on?
3. How many of you *like* this music?
4. How many of you would like music on all the time in school?

A brief discussion of music likes and dislikes followed. I suggested that, since it had been agreed unanimously we all liked the radio on, we would take turns each session selecting the station. We agreed that sometimes it could get boring and we might want to turn it off.

Because of the nature of this group—the distrust, negativism towards school and teachers, as well as ingrown peer hostility—I decided to break the typical classroom mode as quickly and radically as possible and asked if they would like to play charades. I chose this game because of the physically freeing nature of it, the group spirit about it, and the structure that would allow the severly withdrawn members to be part of the action passively if they so desired. They were somewhat apathetic and still cautious about trusting this fun-type activity in school, but before the end of the session, Mark, Grace, Nelly, and Dan were playing well.

Session 2. This session was similar in structure to the first session, save that the voting procedure questions were geared toward how they felt at the moment—that is, tired, bored, hungry, and so on, and more pointedly, if they wanted to be in school. The latter question, of course, set off a barrage of vehemence from all save Grace, Bob, and Kate. Bob and Kate never responded verbally and only rarely revealed any reaction to the circumstances. (If any other behavior was evidenced from these two, I will note accordingly.)

After allowing the outpouring of anger and frustration, I first directed the discussion toward a *fact level.* Why are schools formed? What are the legal requirements? What are teachers supposed to do? What do students get from education? and so on. I knew the school issue was a basic one that was charged with much feeling and confusion, and I hoped to approach the school problem objectively at the outset.

In the school atmosphere most of them felt unsafe, unsure about why they were failures, defensive about academic demands, and powerless to control the feelings of frustrations and hopelessness. Grace and Nelly were the only group members who were relatively comfortable discussing conflicts and feelings, so I knew it would be necessary to approach this sensitive problem cautiously. My goals were modest. I had no delusions about actually changing feelings. I planned only to help them identify more specifically where the areas of conflict and anxiety were, what was in their power to change, and how they could use strengths more effectively. I trusted that by helping them to see the many facets in themselves and identify what was important to each of them, they would ultimately be able to handle the many obstacles and decisions with which they were faced daily.

As the leader, I tried very hard to avoid playing Almighty Wise One, instead functioning like an objective machine posing questions, allowing the group to try out alternative solutions. To maintain my humanity in their eyes, however, I joined many of the activities and answered questions from my own experience, rather than using that life experience to answer their questions.

With these goals in mind, I offered the following rules for their approval. The last rule was too sophisticated and philosophical in nature and confused them. The other rules were unanimously approved. They seemed intrigued with the idea that they would not be forced to answer questions and that the "teacher" would have to follow the same rules.

RULE 1   Group members may choose whether or not they wish to respond to questions. If they choose to remain silent, they may say "Pass." The leader of the group has the same rights.

RULE 2. Anyone coming into the group feeling the need to be alone may go to the music corner to read or relax. He or she may rejoin the group at any time.

RULE 3. Anyone who has something on his mind that he wants to talk about may indicate so at the beginning of each session.

RULE 4. Any subject may be discussed and all ideas considered.

RULE 5. We will try to avoid name calling and judging an idea as right or wrong. We will try to remember we are here to give each other new ideas, share feelings, and enjoy each other.

Session 3. Jane's turn to choose the music station. There was some flack about her choice of station, but eventually it was accepted.

Carl wanted to talk about something: "Why do we have to study government? It's dumb!" There followed five minutes of discussion which generalized to finding reasons for why we have to do or study anything we don't like. Grace: "Because when you grow up you're going to be voting and you have to know about government or we'll have terrible men in government, like we do now." Mark: "Yeah, they're stupid and so are teachers." Nelly: "But they're not *all* stupid." Jane: "Except Mrs. X - *everybody* thinks she stinks." Nelly: "I don't."

The strategy for the session was taken from "Twenty Things You Love To Do" (*Values Clarification,* Simon, Howe, Kirschenbaum, 1972). In order to focus their thinking on something specific, I suggested consideration of five areas: (1) what you like to *play,* (2) what *work* or chores you do well, (3) what *hobbies* you enjoy, (4) what you would like to *learn* more about, and (5) what you do with your *friends.*

Only Grace and Nelly had a genuine, personal list. Mark and Dan played clown because they could think of nothing to write. Mark scribbled across the paper, "Get grass!"

Session 4. Bob's turn to choose the music. He shrugged, sat down and didn't touch the radio.

The strategy for this session was a brief voting procedure. The most highly charged responses were to the following questions:

1. How many think most teachers are unfair?
2. How many think boys are smarter than girls?
3. How many don't like to show it when they're sad?

Next, using the values continuum strategy, each student was assigned a number for the sake of anonymity, colorful strips of paper with questions were spread on a large table, and corresponding continuum lines placed beneath the value query. The students were instructed to indicate by their code number where they stood on each continuum. The results are shown in Chart 1.

Chart 1   *Selected Values Continuum Questions*

1.   How do you feel about going steady?

It's great ____1____ 3 ___6___ 8 ___2___ 495 It's a dumb idea

2.   Should the sale of marijuana be legalized for sale to people over 18 years of age?

Yes ___91 4 5___ 7 2 _____ 8 ___3 6___ No

3.   Do you enjoy time with your family?

Have a super time ___6724___ 58 ___31_____ Very dull

4.   How do you like teachers to relate to you?

Be a
friend ___167___ 54 ___8_____ 3 ___Be strict and keep away

5.   As an adult do you think you will be happy and successful?

I expect to
get most of
what I
want ___438___ 7 ___65_____ 1 ___I don't expect to get much out of life

6.   How much of the time do you feel really great?

Almost all of
the time ___6 3 2 8___ 7 ___1_____ 45 Practically never

7.   Do you wish you could jump from a plane in a parachute?

Yes 9637 _____ 8 ___1___ 452 No

8.   How do you feel about school?

I think school
is great ___15___ 2 ___4_____ 8 ___36___ Ugh! I hate it!

Student	Code Number
Kate	5
Jane	6
Dan	3
Mark	9
Grace	1
Nelly	7
Bob	8
Carl	4
Miss B.	2

The students enjoyed this activity and were both secretive and nosy as they went about the task indicating their responses. The results were helpful to me. For example, Grace's response to question number five was significant, reinforced what I had already suspected to be a depressed area for her, and allowed me to store this piece of information in my memory in order to deal with it on a values level at a future date. Similarly, Kate's response to question number eight, which was totally incompatible with her behavior, gave me an insight into how she *felt* about school.

Session 5. Jane came in with something she wanted to discuss. Our district had just integrated the industrial arts and home arts programs, and both boys and girls were enrolled in these classes. Jane was offended by having to study what she referred to as "boys' junk." Mark, on the other hand, wanted to know why he had to take "that cooking garbage." A spirited but well thought-out discussion was generated concerning sex roles.

The strategy for the session was an either-or forced choice. On a simple form, the students were asked to rate themselves as leaders or followers and then to do the same for their best friends. A spontaneous dialogue ensued about how they viewed the popular kids in their class. Mark touched upon the use of power and the manner in which some people are controlled by others. In the time remaining, we completed rank order questions which had been written on the board before class.

Session 6. Kate came in early today and, instead of proceeding dumbly to her seat on the periphery of the group, stood at my desk. I asked her if she would like to help me by picking up Dan and Mark from class. This action would require that she *ask* for each boy from the classroom teacher. She went off spiritedly and returned with the boys! During the session she also contributed some brief but nonetheless verbal, logical responses. She continued to become more responsive and seemed to be operating on some level, albeit minimal.

The strategy for this session was the "values whip." Because of the nature of this group, I had to adapt and simplify this approach. There were two groups and each person had to turn quickly to a neighbor and give two statements: (1) something I like and (2) something I don't like. The response was structured, "That's very interesting." Bob, Jane, and Kate had trouble naming any values, but others in the group helped them define at least one statement. There were excellent group dynamics. Because I was in one group myself and there was much noise, I did not function at any time as a leader.

In the time left, each made a statement about what they had learned about someone else in the group. We repeated the exercise, this time using the response, "That's stupid!" A heated enthusiastic discussion followed as they discussed the feelings generated when they were called stupid.

Session 7. A public interview was the strategy for the entire session. This immediately led to a format I called "Taking a Position." The person being interviewed would close the interview by expressing a feeling or strong conviction. Then he or she would be asked to explain that position by responding to the following questions:

- Statement of belief.
- What happened to make me feel or believe this way?
- Am I proud of this position?
- Could anything make me change my mind?

Nelly's belief was, "I believe there is a God." Grace stated, "I believe that by the time I'm 30 years old, the earth will be destroyed by pollution."

Dan decided he wanted to take Nelly on and see if he could debate the belief with her. Carl wanted to tackle Grace's conviction. The counter-beliefs were stated well, without resorting to insulting, name-calling attacks. Bob spoke twice. A super session!

Sessions 8 and 9. I was to do some preparation for the "Who Are You?" strategy by focusing their thinking around several of the elements that make us who we are. Four general areas were defined: our *physical* selves, our *beliefs* and *feelings,* ourselves at *work* and *play,* and our *successes* and *failures.* Trust seemed to be building in each of them and I hoped this was an opportune time to introduce more direct self-exploration. I encouraged each person to make a statement that told us something about themselves in one of the above categories. I knew I had to move carefully as they sensed we were approaching personal material and they were very skeptical about "letting it all hang out." We started off with a simple physical description of ourselves and moved from there into more subjective observations. By the end of the session they had evidenced their ability to handle the strategy, and Nelly, Grace, Mark, Dan, Carl all warmed up to the challenge. Jane, Bob and Kate were reticent but did contribute.

Session 10. We opened the session with "What's in Your Wallet?" [from Simon, Howe, & Kirschenbaum, *Values Clarification,* 1972, p. 32], which brought laughter and shared fun. The tenor of the group was subtly changing from one of defensive criticism to gentle bantering. We continued the public interview strategy and ended with an adaptation of "The Fall-Out Shelter Problem" [from Simon, Howe, & Kirschenbaum, 1972, p. 23]. I had brought some snacks and the feeling in the group was relaxed and trusting.

Session 11. Carl came barreling into the room angry and upset. Jane was sulky. Grace had just made the Honor Role and was ecstatic. Bob had reverted to his zombie-like stance. I decided to discuss ways of feeling, using for a guide the suggestions from *Reality Games* (1972, p. 185), by Sax and Hollander. We talked about the circumstances that led each of them to feeling the way they did and possible things to be considered that might make them feel more put-together. I was careful not to encourage them to find easy answers to merely escape from unpleasant feelings but to try to look at the series of events that had brought about their respective feelings. The session ended and I felt that we had only touched the tip of the iceberg.

Thus Far

I am pleased with the way values-clarification strategies are leading this particular group of youngsters. As always, I seem to run short of time and am frustrated by unfulfilled objectives. However, I can see the positive changes that were brought about, and I am enthusiastic about adapting the techniques to other groups of children with special learning problems.

TEACHER REPORT ON A
TEACHER IN THE FIELD

In this chapter, we have examined reports made by teachers in their own writing style, largely about the children they were teaching. We have said little in the book about the changes that take place in teachers as they begin to master the techniques of using clarifying questions and interacting with students nonjudgmentally. A rather dramatic illustration of what can happen is contained in the following report. Before you read it, you should know that many teachers have reported changes in themselves, changes that were very satisfying to them and changes that in many cases persevered long after the course or the workshop was over.

One autumn, in Chappaqua, New York, the School of Education of New York University was conducting a value-clarifying workshop with approximately 45 teachers who represented all of the grades from kindergarten through grade 12.

It had been the practice for a number of years in conducting these workshops that teachers would choose one or two students in their classes and would concentrate upon using the clarifying processes with these selected students. Each week the teachers in the workshop were expected to make a report on some transaction they had had with their student or students, reporting in detail what the students had said and what the teacher had said. Typically the workshop lasted for 15 or 16 weeks, and the two sessions before the close of the workshop were given over to a different kind of reporting. At this time, each teacher was asked to give a public report on any changes or absence of changes that would characterize the students she or he had been working with during the semester. Ordinarily, these reports were very brief and to the point, and there were reports of failure here and there amongst a very large number of successes.

On the final night of the workshop, a man was asked to start the session off with a brief description of the results that he had achieved with his two students. Instead of beginning in this vein, the man started to talk about his early childhood—where he was born, his parents, and so on—and the director of the workshop intervened, stating that the session called for a report on the changes in his students and he was not exactly following the agenda! The man said that he thought that the whole group would be very much interested in hearing what he had to say and he would like permission to continue. Rather reluctantly, the director of the workshop said in this one instance it would be approved and suggested that the man go ahead with his story. And, what a surprise that story turned out to be!

He said that as a child he had been a *double* prodigy in the field of music. He had an extraordinary voice and he was most outstanding in playing the violin. By the time he was in his early teens, he had played in all the major cities of the United States and had sung also in these cities. As a teenager he began to be invited abroad and over a period of four or five years had displayed his vocal and violin talents in all of the major cities of Europe. Life was one success after another for him, and when he would return home to the United States, he would receive the congratulations and the plaudits of his countrymen.

Something happened to all of this, and the man said he could not explain it, but there came a time in his life when he put his violin away in the attic and he resigned from the church choir. In his everyday life, day in and day out, he neither sang nor played the violin.

Years passed, he married and had children, and he had been teaching in Chappaqua for some time when he registered for the present workshop. The workshop required that he try to clarify the purposes and aspirations of two students, the attitudes and interests of these same two students, the beliefs and the thinking of these same two students, the activities of these students in relation to everything else. The man continued with his talk and said that as he raised these questions over and over again with the students, he began to relate the questions to his own life and to his own activities and to his past and to his future. He said that he seemed to be getting a very serious kind of education for himself, when all that was promised was some help in working with his students. This preoccupation with his own life continued, and one day when he returned home from school, he went to the attic and took the violin downstairs. After tuning it as best he could, he began to play. His wife, of course, was astounded and his children were surprised and pleased. Shortly after, he applied to the church choir to see if he might try out for an opening; he was accepted and was now singing in the choir.

At this moment in his report, he paused and said that he thought that what had happened to him might in some way have also happened to other people who did not wish to talk about themselves, and that his first reaction was to say nothing about it. He overcame this internal resistance, he said, and he wondered aloud if his report about himself wasn't every bit as significant as the report he might have made about the two students with whom he had been working.

A CONCLUDING STATEMENT

Something has been said about the changes which seem to have taken place in children whose teachers carried on clarifying processes. Something also was said about a dramatic instance in which a teacher seems to have changed remarkably as he practiced the clarifying responses with his students. But we have said practically nothing about changes in society. Values clarification can change society by changing individual people—especially teachers and their students. It is part and parcel of what we have said throughout this book.

Clearly we do not want you to choose an "either/or," to feel that teacher education should be concerned either (1) with what you do or (2) with what you are as a person. We have tried to make it very clear that both are needed in education. One should continually be related to the other, and our criteria for a value are consistent with this view. Teacher education should emphasize cognition, and reflective thinking. And the affective side—the side of feelings, attitudes, interests, hopes and purposes and aspirations and other things like these—should be emphasized, as well.

We have also stressed our conviction that the development of values comes from the experiences we have and our reflections on these experiences. As we've seen, both Dewey and Whitehead said that the connections we can make from each new experience to what we have experienced in the past is the primary channel we have for enrichment of the quality of our experiences. Nearly all of the examples given in this book can provide students and teachers with this opportunity to think, and to relate their thinking to probable consequences and to probable past valuations. We place a great deal of emphasis upon opportunities to choose freely, which must be accompanied by reflection before definite choices are made. This, too, can contribute to the enrichment of an experience.

Still another criterion of a value deals with its penetration into our ongoing life, with the ways we share our ideas with other people. As we share, we see the reactions of other people to what we are saying or to what we are doing, and in this transaction we learn something about what other people think of us. This constitutes another alternative for us to reflect upon. It does not follow, of course, that we would immediately want to change what we have said so that others will be pleased; or if we see signs of pleasure, that we would not immediately wish to change what we had said to challenge the listeners.

The object here is the sharing. As Julian Huxley said, "I would go so far as to say that the lack of a common frame of reference, the absence of any unifying set of concepts and principles, is now, if not the world's major disease, at least its most serious symptom" (1960, p. 88). Although this statement was written more than 20 years ago, we see it as generally true in today's world. We believe that our book can help alleviate this situation. We believe that boys and girls and young men and young women who have frequent opportunity to make choices, who have frequent opportunity to defend those choices, who have frequent opportunity to share their thinking and valuing with their peers and with their elders, are actually learning how to develop a unifying set of concepts and principles. Without the freedom to explore new frontiers of knowledge, without the freedom to share these explorations, we do not see how much can be accomplished in integrating our world.

In our criteria for a value, we also stressed prizing and cherishing as very important components. This suggests joy and zest in life; it suggests a motivation for achievement. It implies also that values *lead* us into action; they do not coerce us. That is to say, we cherish them and they inspire us and lead us; they do not pursue us as does conscience at times.

In some alternative programs of value education that have been proposed recently, there is no mention at all of this matter of prizing and cherishing and holding dear those things that we value. The more or less complete absence of any consideration of this point suggests to us that this quality of a value is not given much importance. In fact, one program of value education suggests a series of stages through which each person passes. We believe that if these are seriously and carefully examined, they bear a stronger relationship to a concept of *power* than they do to a concept of values. The first stage involves an almost total reliance on the superior power of the human beings around us when we are in our infancy; a second stage suggests that when we have learned that persistent crying or demanding will help us to have our desires met, this feeling of power transcends the feeling of fear. It is a stage of self-centeredness. This, in turn, is followed by "the good girl" or "good boy" stage, in which our actions are determined largely in terms of pleasing those who are in power. We are good girls or good boys in their presence and perhaps on a number of occasions when they are not present. But looking underneath there is again the idea that this will make of us more powerful people. The fourth stage is one where we use the opinions of our peers as the authority for what we do and what we say. There is little doubt that at around the age of 10, children begin to be very much interested in gangs and clubs, and friendships that include and exclude others. This matter of obeisance to the peer group is another aspect of power theory: we have reached the stage where the groups with which we associate dominate our choices. Again, the domination of choice making is an expression of power. This fourth stage then develops into a stage where we come to see that law and social requirements constitute the basis for morality, and we begin to respond to moral situations within this framework. Stage six is a level that is rarely reached by growing boys and girls, and is not even reached by many adults. This sixth stage, the highest stage, is related to conscience as the determiner of what to do in situations of moral conflict. The definition of conscience is not clearly given, because with our different backgrounds and our different experiences it may indeed be true that each of us has a conscience which is uniquely our own. Hence the probability of building "a unifying set of concepts and principles" is an almost impossible task.

Examining very closely this concept of value development, we find there is something authoritative about the entire list. In another sense, there is something almost puritanical about the presentation of stages. The absence of any allowance for the feeling of joy you get from prizing or cherishing heightens this atmosphere of puritanism.

One more feature of our theory deserves discussion. We have placed a great deal of emphasis upon the thinking of children, the experiences of children, the sharing of these experiences, and the activities that follow from choice making. If children experience these activities, they are almost sure to learn that a number of their decisions do not result in the predicted or anticipated consequences. In other words, "to err is human." Before too long, young people began to see that the possibility of failing, or the possibility of not realizing their ultimate purposes, constitutes another alternative! In other words, instead of the world being altogether rosy and self-rewarding, we, along with our students, share in a number of lost hopes. Our thinking and our feelings and our actions fail to bring the results we want. This is tremendously important for everyone to learn.

The earth shakes a little bit when we first learn that *certainty* is not often found. It takes quite some time for us to think in terms of probabilities. As Huxley says,

> Tactically, science proceeds by means of working hypotheses, which are later tested out by checking against factual observation. The campaign for certitude then proceeds to organize prediction by formulating observed regularities in the form of scientific laws, and to organize comprehension by formulating our ideas in the form of scientific theories.
>
> Scientific laws, let us remind ourselves, are never more than an approximation to the truth, though the approximation may be an extremely close one; and scientific theories never have more than a limited comprehensiveness. (1960, p. 249).

It takes us back to a point of view that says that no matter how sure we are of a predicted outcome, our thinking should provide for some small hole in the structure, that would suggest something short of certainty; it would also suggest at least a possibility that we might be wrong and that we might have to reconstruct the situation again and again. There was a time, not so very long ago, when scholars in particular seemed to feel an obligation to state their beliefs in more or less absolute terms. They were sure of themselves, as the following examples suggests:

> The scholars of Cambridge were not disturbed at all when, in the seventeenth century their vice-chancellor, Dr. John Lightfoot capped years of study by announcing that "heaven and earth, centre and circumference, were created all together, in the same instant, and clouds full of water," and that "this work took place and man was created by the Trinity on October 23, 4004 B.C., at nine o'clock in the morning." Lightfoot did not know, but other scholars later showed, that at the very hour he so meticulously specified, a very cultivated people, and one well equipped to savor the achievements of a great civilization, were swarming in the great cities of Egypt, all unaware that they had jumped creation's gun (Schneider, 19XX, p. 110).

Many teachers have corresponded with us about the first edition of this volume, and we seriously invite you to continue. Unlike the Vice-Chancellor of Cambridge of long ago, we cannot be sure that we will be helpful in our every response, but we will do our very best. And we hope that many of you will do what you did in previous years: you will send to us suggestions that will help to clarify what we are all trying to do in this great venture.

Appendix A
Questions for Incomplete Value Sheets

1. "Merry-Go-Round."
    a. When was the last time you were on a merry-go-round?
    b. If you happened to be in line and overheard the incident which takes place in the poem, is there anything *you* might have said to that little boy?
    c. Have you ever experienced anything similar to that boy's feelings?
    d. What prejudice, subtle or otherwise, have you ever personally faced?
    e. If you wanted to do something about the problem of "civil rights," what are some things you could do?
        (1) Right in this school, through some school group.
        (2) In your town, with some community organization.
        (3) On the national level.
    f. Perhaps you believe that nothing needs to be done about this problem. If so, state that position clearly and forcefully.

2. Questions for "The Human Being Is Made up of Oxygen, etc."
    a. What is the point of this statement?
    b. Are you serious in believing that you are worth more than $1.00? Explain.
    c. What are some ways we measure the worth of human beings?
    d. Can you list some things you have done which show what you think human beings are worth?

3. Some questions for "Louis Armstrong on His Art."
    a. Underline the places where Louis Armstrong tells you what he feels about art.
    b. Circle the statements which he uses to describe "other" artists.
    c. Is there anything you do which you are as dedicated to as Mr. Armstrong is about his trumpet playing?
    d. How does one go about beginning to care that deeply?

4. Questions for "Shuttlesworth's civil-rights biography."
    a. Why do you suppose Mr. Shuttlesworth would take all of that?
    b. Maybe it is all right for him to feel that strongly, but what right does he have to involve his children in his problems? Comment.
    c. Could Mr. Shuttlesworth move into your neighborhood? Would you want him to?
    d. If you believe in his cause, are there any things you could do to help it?

5. Some questions for "In Germany they first came for the Communists, etc."

    a. In a few words, what is the central meaning of this statement?

    b. What is the Pastor *for* and what is he *against?*

    c. Which category are *you* in? When would they have come for you?

    d. List some things going on in our world right now about which you might need to speak up.

    e. How do you think one goes about speaking up? How do you do it? What are the ways?

    f. Could you pick something you listed in **d** above and work out a strategy by which you could, indeed, speak up for it?

    g. Is there something in your school, some "injustice," about which you could well speak up?

    h. If you are not to speak up, who should do it?

    i. Why stick your neck out? Why not?

    j. We need to *value* what we do and to *do* something about what we value. Do you agree? If so, when was the last time you acted upon one of your values?

Appendix B
Evaluating Value Sheets

Part 1
Scheme for Evaluating Lesson Plans

Here are five basic areas you can use to evaluate your value sheets. Note that there are three positions on the continuum. *Position 1* is considered higher than *position 3*. As you reread your plans and come to understand the coding, we hope you will constantly be thinking of ways to lift your ideas increasingly towards the "1" end of the continuum.

T. Topic

1. A real live topic and a problem that students are aware of or may easily be made aware of. The topic is likely to touch many students deeply.

2. A mildly live topic, probably of some concern to some students.

3. A topic that may provide some intellectual exercise, but that probably will not penetrate the lives of most students very much.

Th. Thinking

1. Excellent thinking is stimulated here. Plenty of opportunity for reflection is included.

2. Some thinking, but could use more.

3. Routine, rote, or simple responses from students are likely. No real mental exertion demanded.

Alt. Alternatives

1. You have made provisions, broadly, for a consideration of alternatives. Students value indicators have been elicited consistently.

2. Some consideration of alternatives has been indicated, but student opportunity to examine a wide range of alternatives needs to be increased.

3. This sheet does not adequately involve students in a broad enough consideration of the alternatives available for action or valuing.

A. Action

1. This sheet hits squarely at some present (or near future) implication. Student behavior will probably change as a result of lesson. It seems destined to make a real difference in their lives.

2.   Some relevance to action here, but the students need to be more conscious of the behavioral consequences of the lesson, sensitive to what they can do about it.

3.   This sheet may provide intellectual, exercise, but it probably make little difference in the students' lives. Frankly, you are probably wasting your time and theirs.

B.   Penetration

1.   This topic is handled so that it really penetrates deeply. It touches the emotions, the hidden parts of us, perhaps painfully, but productively.

2.   Some penetration, but could be sharper and stronger.

3.   Bland, conventional, ambivalent, superficial treatment. Can easily be handled off the top-of-the-head, whereas values cannot be.

PART 2
LOOKING AT SPECIFIC QUESTIONS

As you begin using some of the value sheets in this book, we hope you will begin to consider making your own. Drawing up the questions will become easier if you view your questions within the framework of the statements below. Code a few of our sheets, with the letter codes in the left-hand margin. It is good practice for making up your own sheets.

Q   *Question narrow*   This is a question for which there is only one answer.

Th   *Thinking*   This should stimulate real thinking.

Pr   *Problem*   You have identified a real problem here. Good.

M   *Moralizing*   Watch it. Moralizing can too easily fall low. It puts forth your values and tends to encourage dependency.

CT   *Changed topic*   Here you are going off in a new direction before adequately developing the previous emphasis.

Int   *Intellectuality*   Provides good intellectual exercise, but probably no real penetration into students' lives. You need to lift this toward reality and toward action.

E   *Enough is enough*   You are probably overdoing this point. Pushing too hard may just build up more resistance.

Cr   *Criticism*   Either direct or implied, criticism rides the rails of this question or statement. Is there another way of getting at your point?

V-C   *Values clarification*   This will most likely advance the process of clarifying values.

A   *Action*   This makes a significant bid for some action to grow out of the lesson.

SW   *So what?*   I'm afraid that this produces a "so what" in the reader of your plan and may well do the same with a class. It just doesn't seem to matter.

Appendix C
Additional Value Sheets

PETS AND YOU

Dog owners spent $530 million on dog food last year, reports the Wall Street Journal, which adds that this is about 50 percent more than Americans spend on baby food!

Americans will spend $1.5 billion to acquire pets this year and in addition to the initial investment and the food bill, about $800 million will be spent this year on nonfood items for pets. (For dogs: pajamas, cashmere sweaters, mink collars, Halloween costumes and Santa Claus suits, and cosmetics—color shampoo, creme rinses and hair dressing, perfumes, 11 shades of nail polish including lavender and green, a spray dentifrice, tranquilizers, etc.) Not to mention the millions spent on veterinarian fees and boarding kennels. Pets are big business.*

To think on and to write on:

1. If you have a dog, should you feel badly about the above? Why? Why not?

2. If you don't have a dog, do you spend your money on something that might be written up to sound as ridiculous? Explain.

3. A person who teased a dog owner with the quotation above was found to drive a convertible car with automatic transmission, automatic window lifters, power brakes, power steering, and an automatic headlight dimmer. Comment.

4. Should I come close to starving myself so that others can eat? Discuss.

5. Where do you stand on this issue: "What we spend our money on tells everyone what we value, respect, hold dear, cherish, etc.?"

*From Charles A. Wells, "Between the Lines, the Wells Newsletter," September 15, 1964.

TV, COMICS AND VIOLENCE

On the television screen, about 50 actors and actresses (by latest count) keel over gloriously every week. In comic strips, characters are being punched, stabbed, choked, and shot to death with approximately the same consistency. In fact, murder and mayhem have become an integral part of entertainment in this country, that viewers of all ages tend to think of violence as part of wholesome living, like having picnics on Sunday . . .

It is time we stopped recommending brutality as a way of having fun. It takes no particular strength or courage to hit somebody in the mouth, kick him in the stomach, break a piece of furniture over his head. And even a child's forefinger can pull a trigger.*

To think on and to write on:
   1.   Really, now, what's all the fuss about?
   2.   You've watched TV and read comic books, and you're not violent. Comment.
   3.   What policy will you take to your own children about TV and comics?
   4.   Do you do anything to affirm that life is valuable?
   5.   Does a tabloid like the *New York Daily News* make life seem less valuable? Do you advocate censorship? What can be done?
   6.   Do your TV and reading habits contribute to your immaturity? What IS the impact of your TV and reading time? Explain.

*From Stephen Baker, "T.V., Comics and Violence," *Today's Child News* magazine, June, 1964, *12.*

THE ABRASIVE MAN

   I.   We have a shortage in teaching of what I shall call the "abrasive man." He is obviously a controversial figure. He disturbs the peace of the affluent suburb and the apathetic city. He doesn't fit in. He creates ripples when we prefer calm water. Once the well-rounded man was the well-educated man. Now we are likely to think of him as a smooth, unabrasive fellow, a nice guy. He revolves in a nice little circle, in a nice suburb where nice people live, "our kind of people," you know. It's a good life with one fatal weakness. It often puts these nice people out of touch with the disturbing problems of the city and the rest of the world. To communicate is to share ideas and feelings in a mood of mutuality. We cannot escape the moral and social consequences of noncommunication, of self-isolation from the troubles of the world. In the long run, walling one's self off from our fellow man deadens the personality, makes it insensitive to the aspirations, the pain, the rich pleasure of other people.

†From Edgar Dale, "Journalism! A New Dimension," *The News Letter* of The Ohio State University, February, 1965, *30,* p 4.

EDUCATION FOR CREATIVITY

   II.   To be creative is to be thoughtfully involved, a concerned and active participant, not a disengaged spectator. Creativity is an experience in depth which transforms pleasure into joy, entertainment into delight, listless apathy into dynamic living. The great tragedy in life is not death but never having lived. The creative person, on reviewing his life, can say with Virgil's Aeneas: "Many of these things I saw, And some of them I was."*

To think on and to write on:
1. Which of the above quotations seems to say more to YOU? Why?
2. Are you unabrasive?
3. Does Dale want us to be hostile, aggressive, ornery? Explain.
4. In what events of our time have you participated?
5. List as many ways as possible to avoid ending up life with a large component of mediocrity?
6. Which of the items you listed for #5 are you doing now? When do you start?

*From Edgar Dale, "Education for Creativity," *The News Letter* of The Ohio State University, December, 1964, *30,* p. 4.

UNDER THE SWAY OF THE GREAT APES

Edwin P. Young, an uncelebrated philosopher, once observed of football, "After all, it's only a game that kids can play." This is no longer strictly true. If it were, the networks would not have bought it up as a vehicle to sell cigarettes, cars and beer.

The evidence suggests that it satisfies some inner need of the spectator so completely that it can rivet him to his chair through a holiday in disregard of family life or bring him to his feet howling for [Allie] Sherman's head when the outcome fails to gratify.

If sports have ceased to be only games that kids can play and become psychotherapy for the mob, it is too bad, especially for kids who will grow up hating them or busting gussets to achieve therapeutic professional excellence.

What is worse, though, is the distortion of values that radiates throughout the society. For thirty minutes of farce, Liston and Clay can earn more than the entire faculty of a public school can make in a decade†

To think on and to write on:
1. Did you watch football on New Years Day?
2. Is it a pattern of yours? Is it something about which you are proud?
3. How would you answer Mr. Baker?
4. Do you think the publishers of *Harpers* or *Atlantic* could benefit from taking ads during the televising of a football game? Comment.
5. Does this sheet make you want to do anything different in your life?

†From Russell E. Baker, "Under the Sway of the Great Apes," *The New York Times,* January 5, 1965. © 1965 by The New York Times Company. Reprinted by permission.

A STUDENT'S REPORT OF A CAMPUS INCIDENT

Someone was caught cheating on an exam in an advanced biology class. The teacher tried to take the paper away, but the boy held on to it. When the teacher finally got hold of the test, several index cards fell out from between the pages. The boy screamed that they were not his. To make a long story short, the teacher informed the student that this would have to be reported to the authorities. The boy threatened to kill the teacher, and they scuffled until other teachers came to get the boy away. The boy had been accepted by a medical school, and this incident meant no med school for him. His actions were explained by a weak personality cracking under the system. But what amazed me was the reactions of other pre med students. Their near joy was hard to hide. How awfully sadistic. Or was their joy a sign of relief for not having been caught themselves?

To think on:
   1. What is your first, most immediate reaction? (Use free association. Don't write sentences; just put down words.)
   2. In what ways do you identify with the boy?
   3. In what ways do you identify with the teacher?
   4. The author of the incident raises a point about the other students in the class. Comment on that.
   5. To cheat or not to cheat? What is the rationalization for each position?
   6. What alternatives were open to the student? To the teacher? To the other students?

A VALUES SHEET FOR HIGH SCHOOL STUDENTS

Divorce

Divorce was one way out and so they took it—
   escaped from their prison marriage to unbarred air.
Crazy with freedom, two so long cramped and crooked,
   they danced different ways and began to lose that pallor,
   laughing along at last where the wind has no door.

They were like school bent children released into summer
   as if after June there were nothing further to learn—
   chewed candies of whim and swam when the days turned warm
   from their lives in the leaves no one could call them home.

Wintered again, they look back at that green illusion,
   pick at their locks and their partners, dreaming a plan
   to tunnel a way through the walls of their own confusion

and find outside, the woman, the ideal man—
the god they needn't love, who will worship them.*

To think on and to write on:
1. How are you going about finding someone to marry? Describe your approach.
2. What is *your* understanding of the last two lines of the poem?
3. What are some of the pitfalls of this marriage game? List them.
4. What are you going to do about finding a marriage partner?

*Harold Witt, "Divorce," *Saturday Review,* October 3, 1964.

GRADUATION DAY

Jan Jordan attended Americus, Georgia High School for four years. Her graduation day was in June, 1964. Like other seniors, she invited her friends to the graduation. Unlike other seniors, some of her friends were Negroes.

When they arrived at the gate of the stadium, where the exercises were to be held, they were turned away by police and school authorities. After some efforts to negotiate, Jan, who was then in her cap and gown waiting for the procession to begin, was informed that her friends were not being admitted.

She then stepped out of line, walked to the head of it and said to the faculty member in charge: "I think my friends have as much right to come to my graduation as anyone else's friends do."

With this, she started walking towards the stands, where several thousand people were expectantly waiting for the procession to begin. They watched in amazement as this lone senior, followed by her father and kid brother (her mother stayed at the gate with those who had been barred), walked steadily toward them, slowly climbed to the top of the stands, and sat down. Then the other seniors marched out on the field and seated themselves on the platform facing the stands, and facing Jan and her father and brother.

After speeches by honor students on "Moral Responsibility" and "Reverence," each graduate was called to the rostrum and given a diploma. Jan's name was not called.*

To think on and to write on:
1. What do you think about what Jan Jordan did? Would you do it? Why? Why not?
2. What did she hope to accomplish? Was this a way to do it? What else might she have done?
3. Is there anything you want as badly as she wanted this? Would you be willing to risk your diploma for it? Explain.

*From J. L. Jordan, the *Koinonia Newsletter,* #29, September 15, 1964, of the Koinonia Farm, Americus, Georgia.

4. There is more to the story: "Next day, because she felt that some might not have understood her strange action the night before, Jan placed an ad in the Americus paper. It was headed: "Why I Did Not Graduate with My Class at Americus High," and stated simply that because her friends were not admitted on the same basis as other's, she felt unable to participate."

5. Does this story have *any* implications for your own life?

Note: As of September, 1964, the Americus Schools were integrated.

AN OPEN-ENDED LIST OF ALTERNATIVES FOR A WINTER VACATION

Directions: Below are some activities various people were involved in during winter vacation. We need some other ideas from *you*. When the list is long enough, we would like to ask each of you to categorize the items in the following ways:

X—This is definitely not for me.

U—Unlikely that I would do it.

N—Neutral or u..sure.

P—Possibly I would do this in the future.

A—I affirm this; I will definitely try to build it into my life, if I have not already done so.

1. Worked up a show and performed it in a hospital ward.

2. Made up a basket of food and delivered it to some needy family.

3. Organized a group to go caroling in the neighborhood.

4. Invited some children from an underprivileged neighborhood to spend a day with me and returned the visit.

5. Wrote many letters to go out with Seasons Greetings cards to friends in many different parts of the country and world.

6. Organized a block party for New Year's Eve where everyone brought some specialty of the house to share with neighbors.

7. Enjoyed it with just my family.

8. Made the decorations for our tree.

9. Repaired some broken toys to be distributed to children in an orphanage.

10. Solicited friends, relatives, and neighbors for old clothes to send to needy children in a migrant worker camp.

11. Contributed substantially to a dozen different organizations which appealed for funds.

12. Devoted a whole day to helping some other student complete a term paper, *not* doing it for him.

13. At the year's end, evaluated how the year had gone and made plans to make it more significant the next year.

14. Made with my own hands almost all the presents I gave.

15. Sat down and wrote some letters to public figures affirming some position they had recently taken or acknowledged some beautiful act of some other person.

16. Bought a ticket to a play for a child who had never seen one.

17. Attempted, without moralizing, to pose alternatives on some basic issues of our time peace–war, race, economics, etc.) to friends and relatives.

18. Tried to lift the usual level of family relations to a higher plane in keeping with the season.

19. Avoided taking the paths of least resistance in present giving, and really tried to find out what the various receivers really would enjoy.

20. Went out of my way to help children in the neighborhood capture a less materialistic and more spiritual significance to the holiday season.

Appendix D
Practice Activities for the Clarifying Response

Here are several suggestions for those who wish to practice the clarifying response. In general, the beginning activities are easier than the later ones. Some require the use of tapes (audio or video) or the cooperation of other people.

If you want to use these activities to assess your own competency, here are some criteria for excellence for clarifying responses you can use.

CRITERIA FOR EXCELLENCE
FOR THE CLARIFYING RESPONSE

1. *Did the clarifyer try to promote his own values?* Was praise, criticism, or moralizing used to guide the student's thinking? (Although sometimes an adult may want to guide a student's thinking, it is unappropriate when you are trying to encourage the student to use the clarifying process. That process, of course, puts the responsibility on the student to look at his ideas or his behavior and to think and decide for himself what it is he wants.)

2. *Was the emotional climate conducive to thoughtfulness?* A respectful, accepting adult attitude is usually best. Fear, guilt, embarrassment, or other forms of emotional distress clog clear thinking.

3. *Was the clarifying response gentle enough?* It should be stimulating but not insistent. A student should be able comfortably to decide not to think about the issue.

4. *Was the interaction brief enough?* Too many adult comments and the student has so much to think about that she may dismiss the whole mess. A clarifying response does not try to do big things with brief exchanges. It sets a mood of thoughtfulness. The effect is cumulative.

5. *Did the exchange end gracefully?* Usually after one or two rounds, it is best for the adult to offer to break off the dialogue with some noncommittal but honest phrase such as "Nice talking to you," "I see better what you mean," "Thanks for chatting," "Got to get back to my work, thanks," or "Very interesting. Let's talk about this again sometime."

6. *Were the responses more to obtain data than to stimulate thinking?* Clarifying responses are not intended for interview purposes. You listen carefully not primarily for information but for possible gaps in the clarifying process.

7. *Was the clarifying response used on an appropriate topic?* It is best for attitudes, feelings, beliefs, purposes. It is not for facts. It is not appropriate when you have in mind a correct answer for the student to give. The clarifying response is not for drawing a student toward a predetermined answer.

338

8. *Was the response used on persons who seemed to need it most?* Many students learn how to think through value issues from parents or others. Other students have a harder time of it. Clarifying responses are especially useful for students who show by extreme apathy, conformity, or flightiness that they may not have learned how to guide their own lives.

9. *Was the response used sensitively and creatively?* Clarifying responses are not mechanical; they do not follow a formula. They must be used creatively, to fit yourself and your situation.

Activity 1   *Self-Survey of Current Behavior*

This activity helps you see how frequently and easily you now use clarifying responses. It also provides a check of how wide your repertoire of responses is.

What you do is familiarize yourself with our definition of a "clarifying response" (see chapter 5). Keep that definition in mind during five to ten hours of your teaching, counseling, or supervising work. (If you don't have a job, you may substitute laboratory teaching and informal relating with friends and colleagues). Make notes of instances in which you think you acted in a way that was more or less in the clarifying style.

These need not be consecutive hours of work. You may keep in mind the task of identifying clarifying incidents for one hour a day for several days, you may keep the task in mind during the mornings, etc.

However, try to distribute the time over different kinds of activities. Do not restrict your self-observation to reading lessons only, for example. Especially try to include both your interaction with groups and with individuals.

Jot down notes as soon as convenient after you think you have performed in the clarifying mode and then elaborate later, during free time. This may require some interruption in your work, of course, but it may make it much easier for you to recall incidents.

Your elaborations need not be prepared in any formal way. Merely identify what the situation was and what you did or said. It would be helpful if your incidents were typed, however. Note also the total number of hours you observed yourself for this activity.

Bring the incidents that you identify as possibly being in this clarifying style (and any questions you have) to an aide for reaction and advice.

In general, there are three questions this assessment procedure can help answer: How frequently do you use clarifying responses? How appropriately and easily do you use them? How many of the 30 response types listed in chapter 5 do you use?

Activity 2   *Observation of Others*

This activity familiarizes you with how others use clarifying responses and gives you practice in listening for them and distinguishing them from other responses.

This is similar to Activity 1 except that you observe and make notes of 30 minutes or more of another person's professional behavior, listing examples of responses that you judge would either encourage and discourage students from further thinking about their values.

Bring reactions and questions to a discussion group or an aide, if you like.

Activity 3   *Test of Identifying Clarifying Responses—A*

Below are some remarks that teachers have made. Which seem to you to be in the clarifying style, as we define it? Mark those C. Use an NC to mark those that seem to be essentially nonclarifying. Use a ? for those about which you are unsure. Our judgments appear below. Of course, discuss any questions you have with a colleague, an aide, or a discussion group.

1.   T says: Think about your position on war and peace.

2.   (To nonattentive student): Do you want to grow up to be a dumbell?

3.   Each person in the second row think of something that you did last weekend of which you were proud. You may stand and tell the class what that was if you would like to do so, after we give everyone a moment of thinking.

4.   What do you think Whitman was trying to say in the poem?

5.   What is Paul Revere famous for?

6.   You talk about the dangers of centralized government. I wonder if you have *done* some things to help prevent that from coming about?

7.   Why did you just hit Sammy like that?

8.   Do you agree with the author?

9.   How would you like to explore as Magellan did?

10.   Have you had those ideas for a long time?

11.   I understand how upset you must feel, Nellie.

12.   What's so bad about stealing?

13.   Don't you want to be liked by other people, John?

Answers for Activity 3

1.   This teacher comment would probably have the effect upon a student of stimulating his thought about war. There is no single "right answer" the teacher seems to be leading to. We would call this more C than NC.

2.   This is probably more a statement (saying "I think you're stupid") than a question and is probably not going to stimulate the student to think much on the issue. In most cases this comment deserves an NC.

3. Most students do not think about pride in any deliberate way. This is likely to be clarifying (C).

4. Usually this is NC, leading the students to discover a meaning the teacher has in mind, as opposed to finding their own meanings. Contrast this with, "What does that poem mean to you?"

5. NC; a simple memory question. Clarification is seldom a consequence of such questions.

6. An excellent example of C. Such responses help people see that they should integrate ideas into actual behavior.

7. NC. Seldom does the teacher speaking that way expect a student to stop and think the issue through. And the student seldom does more than give some answer to defend himself.

8. C.

9. C.

10. C. A useful question for encouraging a student to examine the origin and background of ideas: Are they really his: Did he absorb them unthinkingly? Has he just now come onto the ideas without much thought?

11. NC. This explains to Nellie that the teacher understands and accepts her feelings. It is a very useful teacher act, but not clarifying as we defined it.

12. C. (NC if a judgmental tone was conveyed with the question.)

13. Probably the teacher is *telling* the student something and therefore this would be an NC. If increased clarity for the student did result, it would be a C, of course.

Activity 4   *Test of Identifying Clarifying Responses—B*

Which of the following teacher responses seem to be clarifying (mark them C)? Which seem essentially nonclarifying (mark them NC). Our judgments appear below each group of questions.

A student says, "We have a brand new puppy at home."

Teacher responses:

1. Isn't that nice. Have you named it yet?
2. Did you want a puppy for a long time?
3. What kind? Can you tell us something about it?
4. You sound happy about that. What's good about having a new puppy?
5. Were you in on the decision and plans to get the puppy?

Answers

Responses 1 and 3 sound psychologically accepting, but probably have little clarifying impact. Responses 2, 4, and 5 are more like the 30 clarifying responses in chapter 5; they are more likely to stimulate thinking on choices, prizings, and behavior.

A student says, "I'm gonna quit school when I'm old enough."

Teacher responses:

6. Many students who have done that find it hard getting a decent job, you know.

7. You might as well quit. School doesn't seem to have helped you much, has it?

8. Before you decide, let's go over the want ad pages together and see what kinds of jobs might be available for you were you to drop school.

9. How does it feel to have plans like that?

10. Have you thought about *why* you plan to quit?

11. Let's list the pros and cons of staying and dropping.

12. Is there anything I can do to help you get what you want?

13. Dropping out is one alternative. Here are several others: changing schools, working part-time, trying to change this school to make it better for you. Have you considered these? Are there other alternatives?

14. Do you think that you will *ever* want to get a diploma?

Answers

All seem to have substantial clarifying potential, *except* for the first three (6, 7, and 8). Note that 6 and 8 carry essentially the same teacher message, one directly and one through a discovery approach.

Activity 5   *Written Practice in Clarifying—A*

Below are listed ten things different students might say. After each statement, write *two* different things that a teacher might say that would help the youngster clarify her values. Do not worry that you know nothing about the students. Just write any responses that might conceivably be appropriate (as long as they have value-clarifying intent.)

After you have written the best responses you can think of, check the criteria for excellence on which to judge your responses. Also check chapter 5 for other ideas for responses. Or have a colleague, an aide, or a discussion group check to see if your written responses tend to clarify values.

1. Arithmetic is my favorite subject.

2. I'm one of the strongest boys in the group. I can lift very heavy things. Want to see?

3. One of the most important things is to treat others the way you want to be treated.

4. I'd like to be a doctor some day.

5. I'm mostly interested in parties and school work.

6. I intend to get me a job this summer and earn some money for college.

7. You can't never expect boys to like dancing; that's girl stuff.
8. I just don't know what to do this weekend.
9. Do you think the boys who want to wear their hair long should be made to get haircuts?
10. I wish there were no more wars.

Activity 6   *Written Practice in Clarifying—B*

Below are ten things students have said and then ten actions a teacher might observe. For each item, write as spontaneously as you can, a response a teacher could make that might have a values clarification effect. You may write more than one response, if you like, or you may ask a partner to role-play brief exchanges with you. (Have the partner begin by saying one of the statements below. You then are to give an appropriate response).

For checking written responses, see the suggestions in activity 5. You may use those same methods for checking oral responses (if you use the role-playing method), or you may want to have your partner help you evaluate your responses. You may also find it useful to tape and listen to yourself in such a role playing situation.

Note especially if you are able to use a variety of clarifying responses, or if you tend to use five or six common responses repeatedly. It is often useful to see how many of our 30 responses you have used.

1. I'm afraid of snakes.
2. I'd like to marry and raise a family some day.
3. I intend to go sailing during the vacation.
4. Can poverty be eliminated?
5. Niggers who are too lazy to get off relief deserve to live in the slums.
6. Honesty is the best policy.
7. Why can't girls play professional football?
8. I have nothing to do. What is there to do?
9. I love chocolate ice cream sodas.
10. I often feel lonely when I get tired. Why is that?

11. A boy picks up a pencil that rolled off a friend's desk.
12. A student stands by himself when others are playing in the playground.
13. A student wins a race.
14. A boy came in late to class for the tenth time.
15. A boy turns out to be the tallest in the class.
16. A girl blushes when she is chosen as the prettiest in the group.
17. A boy cries during a sad movie.
18. The dull boy in the class looks out the window all day long.
19. Johnny teases Sally.
20. Sally flirts with Johnny.

Activity 7. *Judging the Appropriateness of Responses*

Below are student-teacher exchanges. They cannot easily be evaluated without more data, but which *seem* to be poor examples of teaching, especially from the value-clarifying perspective? Can you say why some strike you as being poor? How would you improve those you judge as being poor? Our judgments appear below each exchange.

1. *T:* Let's stand and salute the flag.

   S: Why do we have to do that?

   T: Why do you *think* we have to do that?

Answer

We would say that that teacher response is relatively poor in terms of value clarifying, not as good as something like, "There is a school rule saying all classes should begin with a flag salute. Is that something that bothers you?" or "You seem not to like saluting the flag. If that is so, I wonder if you have reasons you would be willing to share with us."

2. *S:* What time is the assembly today, Miss Jones?

   T: What time would you *like* it to be?

Answer

Probably an inappropriate use of the clarifying strategy. A simple question usually deserves a simple, straightforward answer. One cannot use *everything* for value-clarifying purposes.

3. *S:* How old are you, Miss Smith?

   T: How old do I look?

   S: I'd say about 40 or 50.

   T: Well, I'm old enough to believe that's a compliment, so don't worry about the details. Pretend I'm as old or as young as you would like me to be.

Answer

This teacher avoided the issue nicely enough, we'd say, and was wise not to try to make a value issue out of a simple question of fact. The flip line probably communicated to the students that she was not about to reveal her age, although it would be good if someone would find an appropriate way to say that more straightforwardly.

4. *S:* Can I borrow your book, Mr. Williams?

T: Will you promise to bring it back?

S: Yes. I just want to check the spelling of a name.

T: Do you usually return things you borrow?

S: Yes, surely.

T: Have people not returned borrowed things to you?

S: Well, sometimes. Yes.

T: Can you see why people often hesitate to lend things to others?

S: Never mind, Mr. Williams. I'll get the book someplace else.

Answer

Color this exchange double poor. There is enough clarifying to sink the most conscientious student, and all teacher responses except (perhaps) the first are too strained from the original issue to be real. Clarifying exchanges are best restricted to *brief* exchanges; just enough to stimulate thinking, not so much that the student is left bewildered.

5. *S:* I'm joining the Boy Scouts today.

T: Are you glad you're joining?

S: Yes. It's fun at the meetings.

T: Did you consider other groups or organizations that you might have joined in addition to or instead of the Boy Scouts?

S: No. Not really.

T: O.K., I was just wondering.

Answer

A fine example of clarifying, we would say.

6. *S:* Are you religious, Mr. James?

T: Sometimes. Why do you ask?

S: Just wondering.

T: Fine.

Answer

Good example of a teacher not making too much out of a student initiative. If there is enough interest, there will be another time and another way to get to the issue again.

7. *S:* (Slams into a girl as he rushes out of the room).

    T: Billy, come back here. Can you think of what would happen if everyone pushed like that?

    S: I suppose so.

    T: Are you proud of that kind of behavior?

    S: No.

    T: Well go along now, and think about this.

Answer

This is a tricky accident. It usually turns out to be "poor" in terms of value clarification, mainly because the student usually considers the incident as being a rebuke to his behavior. That is, students often see teacher talk such as that as indirect criticism. If, however, the student did end up reflecting on his behavior, alternatives, consequences, his feelings about it, and so on, it *would* be good clarifying. Here the tone and the specific details are important.

8. *S:* My mother is pregnant, Mr. Burns.

    T: Well, don't blame me!

Answer

No comment, except that the alternative teacher response, "Would *you* like to be pregnant some day?" is probably not as good as "How do you feel about your mother being pregnant?"

Activity 8   *Role Playing With a Group of Three–A*

Form a group of three by finding two others who wish to practice clarifying responses. Person Number 1 (the talker) begins by saying something about a goal, aspiration, attitude, interest, feeling, belief, activity, or problem. He may pick something from chapter 5, or he may make up his own statement or question.

Person Number 2 then acts as the responder and makes a response. The exchange continues until the responder (Person Number 2) breaks off the conversation.

Person Number 3 acts as an observer and reports to the talker and the responder what he heard and how he judges the exchange. Then the three discuss the exchange, shift roles, and try another exchange. This may be continued for as many rounds as the group desires.

Use the criteria for excellence to evaluate exchanges.

Activity 9   *Role Playing With a Group of Three–B*

This activity is the same as activity 8 except that Person Number 1 begins by saying something a student might well say about one of the following value-rich areas:

money

friendship

love and sex

religion and morals

use of leisure time

politics and government

work, occupations

family

maturity

character traits

Discuss and evaluate as in activity 8.

Activity 10   *Practice with an Aide*

Ask an aide to role-play a student while you practice clarifying responses.

Activity 11   *Field Practice*

Try making clarifying responses in a real situation or a microteaching situation. Have the session recorded, or have someone observe your work to assess your ability to recognize opportunities suitable for clarifying responses and use clarifying responses effectively.

Bibliography

Allport, Gordon. *Becoming: Basic Considerations for a Psychology of Personality.* New Haven: Yale University Press, 1955.

Arno, David H., and Richard L. Gorsuch. *Values and Value Changes As They Relate To The Use of Alcohol By Children and Adolescents.* Institute of Behavioral Research, Texas Christian University, March, 1974.

Asch, Solomon E. *Social Psychology.* New York: Prentice-Hall, 1952.

Bachelder, Richard L. (Ed.) *Evaluating Values Development Materials and Programs* (A Working Draft). Research and Development Division, National Board of YMCA's, October 1973.

Barman, Charles R. *The influence of values clarification techniques on achievement, attitudes and affective behavior in high school biology.* Unpublished doctoral dissertation, University of Northern Colorado, 1974.

Barman, Charles R. "Value Clarification and Biology," *The American Biology Teacher,* April, 1974, *36* (4), 241—42.

Betof, Edward. *The degree of implementation of values clarification by classroom teachers following an intensive thirty-six hour workshop.* Unpublished doctoral dissertation, Temple University, 1976.

Brown, Georgia J. "An investigation of a methodology for valu e clarification: Its development, demonstration, and application for teachers of the Elementary School." Unpublished report.

Clarke, Jay, *et al. Operation Future: Third Annual Report.* San Diego: Pennant Educational Materials, 1974.

Clarke, Jay. *Beginning Values Clarification.* Pennant Press, 1975.

Cochrane, Don. "Moral Education—A Prolegomenon," *Theory into Practice,* October 1975, *14,* 236—46.

Covault, T. *The application of value clarification teaching strategies with fifth grade students to investigate their influence on students' self-concept and related classroom coping and interacting behaviors.* Unpublished doctoral dissertation, Ohio State University, 1973.

Curwin, Richard. *The effects of training in values upon 28 student-teachers and pre-service teachers of English.* Unpublished doctoral dissertation, University of Massachusetts, 1972.

Cutick, R. A. *Self-evaluation of capacities as a function of self-esteem and the characteristics of a model.* Unpublished doctoral dissertation, University of Pennsylvania, 1962.

Dewey, John. *Moral Principles in Education.* Boston: Houghton Mifflin, 1909.

349

Dewey, John. *Human Nature and Conduct.* New York: Holt, 1922.

Dewey, John. *Art as Experience.* New York: Minton, Balch, 1934.

Dewey, John. *Theory of Valuation.* Chicago: University of Chicago Press, 1939.

Fraenkel, Jack R. "Teaching About Values." In *Values of the American Heritage: Challenges Case Studies, and Teaching Strategies.* Yearbook of the National Council for the Social Studies, 1976.

Friedenberg, Edgar Z. *The Vanishing Adolescent.* Boston: Beacon Press, 1959.

Gardner, John W. *Self-Renewal.* New York: Harper and Row, 1964.

Gordon, John E. *An abstract of the effects on white student teachers of value clarification interviews with negro pupils.* Unpublished doctoral dissertation, New York University, 1965.

Gordon, John E. *The effects on white student teachers of value clarification interviews with negro pupils.* Unpublished doctoral study, New York University, 1965.

Gorsuch, Richard L., David Arno, and Richard L. Bachelder. *Summary of research and evaluation of the Youth Values Project, 1973—1976.* Mimeographed paper, Akron, Ohio: YMCA and National Board of YMCA's, 1976.

Gray, R. D. III. *The influence of values clarification strategies on student self-concept and sociometric structures in selected elementary school classrooms.* Unpublished doctoral dissertation, University of California, 1975.

Guziak, S. J. *The use of values clarification strategies with fifth grade students to investigate influence on self-concept and values.* Unpublished doctoral dissertation, Ohio State University, 1974.

Harmin, M., H. Kirschenbaum, and S. B. Simon. *Clarifying Values Through Subject Matter.* Minneapolis: Winston Press, 1973.

Huxley, J. *Knowledge, Morality, and Destiny.* New York: The New American Library, 1960.

Hopp, J. W. *The applicability of value clarifying strategies in health education at the sixth grade level.* Unpublished doctoral dissertation, University of Southern California, 1974.

Jonas, Arthur H. *A study of the relationship of certain behaviors of children to emotional needs, values and thinking.* Unpublished doctoral dissertation, New York University, 1960.

Josephson, Barnet L. *A study of the effects of a value clarification technique on junior high schools students' work attitudes and self-awareness.* Unpublished masters thesis, George Peabody College, 1970.

Kelley, F. W. *Selected values clarification strategies and elementary school pupils' self-concept, school sentiment and reading achievement.* Unpublished doctoral dissertation, Fordham University, 1976.

Kirschenbaum, Howard. *Values Clarification: An Advanced Handbook for Trainers and Teachers.* La Jolla, Calif.: University Associates Press, 1977.

Klevan, Albert. *An investigation of a methodology for value clarification: Its relationship to consistency in thinking, purposefulness and human relations.* Unpublished doctoral dissertation, New York University, 1957.

Kohlberg, Lawrence. "The Cognitive-Developmental Approach to Moral Education" *Phi Delta Kappan,* June 1975, *56* (10), 670—77.

Kohlberg, Lawrence. "Moral Education for a Society in Moral Transition," *Educational Leadership,* October, 1975, *33* 46—54.

Kohlberg, Lawrence. "The Relationship of Moral Education to the Broader Field of Values Education." In J. Meyer, B. Burnham, & J. Cholvat (Eds.), *Values Education: Theory, Practice, Problems and Prospects.* Waterloo, Ontario: Wilfred Laurier University Press, 1975.

Lang, Melvin. *An investigation of the relationship of value clarification to underachievement and certain other behavioral characteristics of selected college students.* Unpublished doctoral dissertation, New York University, 1961.

Little, R. J. *A comparative study of the lecture approach and a values clarification approach to the teaching of driver education.* Brandt County, Ontario: Board of Education, 1975.

Lockwood, Alan L. "A Critical View of Values Clarification," *Teachers College Record,* September, 1975, *77,* 35—50.

Loggins, Dennis. "Clarifying What and How Well?" *Health Education,* March/April 1976.

Machnits, Ernest. *A study of the relationship of certain behaviors of children to emotional needs, values and thinking.* Unpublished doctoral dissertation, New York University, 1960.

Macmillan, C. J. B., and George F. Kneller. "Philosophy of Education", *Review of Educational Research,* February, 1964, *34* (1), 22—43.

Martin, Donald. *A study of the relationship of certain behaviors of children to emotional needs, values, and thinking.* Unpublished doctoral dissertation, New York University, 1960.

Massialas, Byron G. and Nancy F. Sprague. "Teaching Social Issues as Inquiry: A Clarification," *Social Education,* January, 1974, 10—35.

Metcalf, Lawrence E., ed. *Values Education: Rationale, Strategies, and Procedures.* Washington, D.C., National Council for the Social Studies, 1971. Pp. 1—28.

Murphy, Gardner, *Human Potentialities.* New York: Basic Books, 1958.

Nowicki, S., and B. R. Strickland. "A Locus of Control Scale for Children," *Journal of Consulting and Clinical Psychology,* 1973, *40,* 148—54.

Ojemann, R. H. *The meaning of causal orientation.* Preventive Psychiatry Research Program, State University of Iowa, 1961.

Olmstead, Richard. "Holes in Their Socks: A Critical Analysis of the Theory and Practice of Values Clarification." In J. J. Jelinek (Ed.), *The Training of Values: The Third Yearbook of the Arizona Association for Supervision and Curriculum Development.* Tempe, Ariz.: Arizona Association for Supervision and Curriculum Development, 1975. Pp. 171—85.

Osman, J. "The Use of Selected Value Clarifying Strategies in Health Education," *Journal of School Health,* 1974, *43* (10), 621—23.

Peck, Robert F. and Robert J. Havighurst. *The Psychology of Character Development.* New York: John Wiley & Sons, 1960.

Piers, E. V. and D. B. Harris. *Manual for Piers-Harris Children's Self-Concept Scale.* Nashville Counselor Recordings and Tests, 1969.

Powell, J. *Why Am I Afraid to Tell You Who I Am?* Niles, Ill.: Argus Communications, 1969.

Pracejus, E. *The effect of values clarification on reading comprehension.* Unpublished doctoral dissertation, University of Pittsburgh, 1975.

Raduns, L. *The development of an instrument to measure value clarification in the area of ecology.* Unpublished master's thesis, University of Florida, 1973.

Raths, James. "Clarifying Children's Values," *The National Elementary Principal,* November, 1962, *42* (2), 35—39. a

Raths, James. "Clarifying Children's Values," *Childhood Education,* November, 1962, *42* (2), 38. b

Raths, Louis E. and Selma Wassermann. *Thinking Box #1. Westchester, Ill.: Benefic Press, 1971.*

Raths, Louis E. and Selma Wassermann. Thinking Box #2. Westchester, Ill.: Benefic Press, 1971.

Raths, Louis E., Selma Wassermann, Arthur Jonas, and Arnold M. Rothstein. *Teaching for Thinking: Theory and Application.* Columbus, Ohio: Charles E. Merrill, 1967.

Rogers, Carl R. *On Becoming a Person,* Boston: Houghton Mifflin, 1961.

Rokeach, Milton. "Toward a Philosophy of Value Education." In J. Meyer, B. Burnham, & J. Cholvat (Eds.), *Values Education: Theory, Practice, Problems, and Prospects.* Waterloo, Ontario: Wilfred Laurier University Press, 1975.

Rutkowski, D. M. *The use of values-clarification strategies in chemistry classes to develop positive attitudes toward science.* Unpublished master's thesis, State University College of New York at Oswego, 1975.

Sax, Saville and Sandra Hollander. *Reality Games.* New York: Popular Library, 1972.

Sears, P. S. and V. S. Sherman. *In Pursuit of Self-Esteem.* Belmont, Calif.: Wadsworth Publishing, 1964.

Simon, Sidney B. *Value clarification: Methodology and tests of an hypothesis in an in-service program relating to behavioral changes in secondary school students.* Unpublished doctoral dissertation, New York University, 1958.

Simon, Sidney B., Leland W., Howe, and Howard Kirschenbaum. *Values Clarification: A Handbook of Practical Strategies for Teachers and Students.* New York: Hart Publishing, 1972.

Sklare, Gerald B. *The effects of the values clarification process upon the values, clarity of values and dogmatism of high school juniors and seniors.* Unpublished doctoral dissertation, Wayne State University, 1974.

Smith, B. C. "Values Clarification in Drug Education: A Comparative Study," *Journal of Drug Education,* 1973, *3* (4), 369—76.

Smith, John E. *Value Convictions and Higher Education.* New Haven: The Edward W. Hazen Foundation, 1958.

Stewart, John S. "Clarifying Values Clarification," *Phi Delta Kappan,* June, 1975, *51* (10), 684—94.

Superka, Douglas P., Christine Ahrens, Judith E. Hedstrom, with Luther J. Ford and Patricia L. Johnson. *Values Education Sourcebook.* Boulder, Colo.: Social Science Education Consortium, 1976.

Swift, M., and G. Spivack. *Devereux Elementary School Behavior Rating Scale. Rev. ed.* Devon, Pa.: Devereux Foundation, 1974.

Wenker-Konner, R., E., Hammond, and A. Egner. *A functional analysis of values clarification strategies on the participation rate of ten fifth graders.* Department of Special Education, University of Vermont, Burlington, 1973.

Whitehead, Alfred North. *The Function of Reason.* Boston: Beacon Press, 1958.

Wilgoren, R. A. *The relationship between the self-concept of pre-service teachers and two methods of teaching value clarification.* Unpublished doctoral dissertation, University of Massachusetts, 1973.

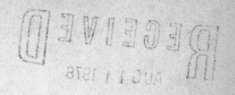

RECEIVED

AUG 1 1 1978

MISSION COLLEGE
LEARNING RESOURCE SERVICES

AUG 1 4 1978

MISSION COLLEGE
LEARNING RESOURCE SERVICES